East Asia's
Changing Urban Landscape

Urban Development Series

The Urban Development Series discusses the challenge of urbanization and what it will mean for developing countries in the decades ahead. The series aims to delve substantively into a range of core issues related to urban development that policy makers and practitioners must address.

Cities and Climate Change: Responding to an Urgent Agenda

Climate Change, Disaster Risk, and the Urban Poor: Cities Building Resilience for a Changing World

East Asia's Changing Urban Landscape: Measuring a Decade of Spatial Growth

The Economics of Uniqueness: Investing in Historic City Cores and Cultural Heritage Assets for Sustainable Development

Financing Transit-Oriented Development with Land Values: Adapting Land Value Capture in Developing Countries

Transforming Cities with Transit: Transit and Land-Use Integration for Sustainable Urban Development

Urban Risk Assessments: An Approach for Understanding Disaster and Climate Risk in Cities

All books in the Urban Development Series are available for free at
https://openknowledge.worldbank.org/handle/10986/2174

East Asia's
Changing Urban Landscape
Measuring a Decade of Spatial Growth

WORLD BANK GROUP

ISBN (paper): 978-1-4648-0363-5
ISBN (electronic): 978-1-4648-0364-2
DOI: 10.1596/978-1-4648-0363-5

Cover photo: © Jakub Halun/Wikimedia Commons, "Huangpu River in Shanghai, view from the Oriental Pearl Tower." Used via a Creative Commons license, creativecommons.org/licenses/by-sa/3.0/.

Cover design: Critical Stages

Library of Congress Cataloging-in-Publication Data has been applied for

Contents

Boxes

Figures

Maps

Tables

Acknowledgments

This report was prepared by a World Bank team comprising Chandan Deuskar, Judy Baker (Task Team Leader), and David Mason. It is based on a work program that was developed by Victor Vergara, Arish Dastur, and Chandan Deuskar. The analysis and interpretation of geospatial data—including all satellite data processing to map urban expansion as well as the calculation of urban metrics—were developed and led by Professor Annemarie Schneider (University of Wisconsin-Madison) with assistance from Carly Mertes and a technical team including Sarah Graves, Jo Horton, Ian Schelly, James Rollo, and Clint Gilman. Somik Lall and Tuo Shi contributed to the report. Additional graphics were prepared by Stephen Kennedy. The study team cited as the source of maps, figures, and tables in this book includes the contributors listed above.

Population distribution data were produced by the WorldPop project, led by Dr. Andrew Tatem (University of Southampton), with mapping carried out by Nirav Patel (George Mason University), and supported by Forrest Stevens and Andrea Gaughan (University of Louisville). Population data for China were from the China Data Center at the University of Michigan. The software used to display the data online, the Platform for Urban Management and Analysis (PUMA), was developed by GISAT as a related activity.

Peer reviewers of the concept note and the draft report included Om Prakash Agarwal, Keith Bell, Arturo Ardila Gomez, Nancy Lozano Gracia, Ellen Hamilton, Alexandra Ortiz, Robin Rajack, Mark Roberts, Friedemann Roy, and Harris Selod. Shlomo Angel, Abigail Baca, and Alain Bertaud also provided guidance to the team.

Deborah Appel-Barker, Susan Graham, and Patricia Katayama, from the Publishing and Knowledge Division of the World Bank Group, coordinated the production and online distribution of the book. Communications Development Incorporated helped draft the separate overview, which was designed by Allied Design and Urbanism. Dissemination of the work was coordinated by Chisako Fukuda.

The work was carried out under the guidance of Abhas Jha (Practice Manager, Global Practice for Social, Urban, Rural and Resilience [GPSURR], East Asia and Pacific [EAP]); Marisela Montoliu Munoz (Director, Urban and Disaster Risk Management, GPSURR); and Ede Jorge Ijjasz-Vasquez (Senior Director, GPSURR). Guidance was also provided by John Roome (previous Sector Director of Sustainable Development for the EAP Region of the World Bank) and Vijay Jagannathan (previous Sector Manager of Infrastructure for the EAP Region of the World Bank).

This activity was made possible through the generous support of Australian Aid.

Foreword

The shift from rural to urban societies is having a massive impact on the economic, social, political, and environmental landscape of countries across the globe. While this transformation is going on, there is still an opportunity to set the course of urbanization on a more sustainable and equitable path. Within a few decades, this window of opportunity will close, and future generations will be left to deal with the consequences of how we urbanize today.

Urbanization that took place over a period of several decades in Europe and North America is happening in just a few years in East Asia, as shown by the emergence of megacities and hundreds of small and medium urban settlements. The region will continue to urbanize rapidly as economies shift from agriculture to manufacturing and services, with several hundred million people migrating to cities over the next two decades.

While there is a growing recognition of the importance of urbanization in East Asia and elsewhere, there is little systematic data on the scale and form of urban expansion. Comparisons between countries are complicated by inconsistent definitions and approaches to measuring urban area and population. National governments and international institutions are trying to form coherent strategies to prepare for urban growth, but they often lack answers to basic questions on the location and rate of urban growth, the impact of population growth on spatial growth, and differences in urbanization trends across countries.

East Asia's Changing Urban Landscape: Measuring a Decade of Urban Expansion presents the findings of a study, conducted with support from Australian Aid, which attempts to fill some of these information gaps through empirical observation. The study analyzed the built-up areas throughout the region in 2000 and in 2010 using satellite imagery. The data produced as part of this research allows deeper exploration of issues involving urban expansion, urban population change, and urban density. In addition to this publication, a large new dataset based on the research has been released. No such dataset existed previously, and it is provided so that other institutions and researchers can utilize the data to perform analyses on a range of related subjects. We hope that this book and the accompanying data will be valuable contributions to our understanding of urbanization in the region and a step forward in proactively advancing toward a more sustainable and equitable urban future.

Antonella Bassani
Director, Strategy and Operations
East Asia and Pacific Region
The World Bank Group

Ede Jorge Ijjasz-Vasquez
Senior Director
Social, Urban, Rural and
    Resilience Global Practice
The World Bank Group

Abbreviations

EAP	East Asia and Pacific
EVI	enhanced vegetation index
GDP	gross domestic product
GIS	geographic information system
Lao PDR	Lao People's Democratic Republic
LP/R	land pooling/readjustment
m	meter
MODIS	Moderate Resolution Imaging Spectroradiometer
PPP	purchasing power parity
PUMA	Platform for Urban Management and Analysis
SAR	Special Administrative Region
sq. km	square kilometer
sq. m	square meter
UN	United Nations

Executive Summary

Urbanization in East Asia is a transformational phenomenon that can help improve the lives of hundreds of millions of people during the coming decades. Urban policy makers and planners have an important role to play in ensuring that urban expansion, and the economic growth it brings, is efficient and inclusive. Once cities are built, their urban form and land use patterns are locked in for generations, making it critical for cities to get their urban form right today, or spend decades and large sums of money trying to undo their mistakes.

Urbanization is a key process in ending extreme poverty and boosting shared prosperity. In the coming decades, urban areas will be where millions of East Asians will have the chance to leave extreme poverty behind and to prosper. The findings in this study reinforce the connection between economic growth and urbanization. However, although the growth of urban areas provides opportunities for the poor, urban expansion, if not well planned, can also exacerbate inequality in access to services, employment, and housing.

This study uses a consistent approach to measuring urbanization across East Asia. Urban leaders, policy makers, and researchers trying to understand or respond to urbanization have been hampered by the lack of internationally comparable data, given that each country defines urban areas and populations differently. This study uses satellite imagery and other data to expand the knowledge of urbanization by defining and measuring the physical extent of urban areas and their populations in a consistent manner, across East Asia, for 2000 and 2010.

The EAP region underwent rapid urban expansion and urban population growth between 2000 and 2010. East Asia had 869 urban areas with more than 100,000 people in 2010; 600 of these urban areas were in China. Although new urban expansion was remarkable (spanning more than 28,000 square kilometers), urban populations grew even faster than urban land. If the region's new urban population from 2000 to 2010, nearly 200 million people, were a country unto itself, it would be the world's sixth largest. However, despite the region's large urban population, only 36 percent of its total population lives in urban areas, suggesting more decades of urban growth to come. Lower-middle-income countries had the fastest urban population growth, whereas upper-middle-income countries had the fastest spatial growth. Despite the visibility of "megacities," there was more urban land and population, as well as more growth, in small and medium-sized urban areas.

Urban population densities in the region were high, on average, and are increasing. Despite appearances, urban expansion in EAP has been relatively spatially efficient. Most urban areas outside China became denser. Although many Chinese urban areas declined in population density, the country's overall average urban population density remained stable.

Hundreds of urban areas in the region now cross local administrative boundaries. About 350 urban areas in East Asia spill over local administrative boundaries. In 135 of these urban areas, no single jurisdiction encompasses even half of the total urban area.

Policy makers at the national and municipal levels have important roles to play in ensuring that urbanization proceeds in an economically efficient, sustainable, and inclusive manner. Governments, particularly in lower-middle-income countries with rapid urban population growth, can prepare for future spatial expansion by facilitating the supply of urban land. National governments can help foster the economic benefits of urbanization through national urbanization strategies and by supporting investment in small and medium-sized cities, where the largest amount of urban growth is occurring.

Spatial planning can help reduce inequality in access to urban opportunities and amenities. The pattern of urban form is one of many factors that affect the ability of the urban poor to access economic opportunities in their cities. Ensuring a spatial match between jobs, affordable retail, public transportation, health and education services, recreational areas, and affordable housing is one of the means of fostering such access. Land acquisition for urban expansion can be disruptive, but it can also help bring opportunities to peri-urban residents and allow them to benefit from urban growth. Addressing the vulnerabilities of recent rural-to-urban migrants can also help ensure that the advantages of rapid urbanization are inclusive.

The environmental benefits of high urban population densities can be boosted by ensuring that density is well coordinated, located, and designed. Sufficiently high urban densities can contribute to sustainability. The benefits of East Asia's already high urban densities can be maximized if density is allowed to locate where there is demand for it; if it is supported by the coordinated location of jobs, services, and public transportation; and if it is designed so that it produces a walkable, livable urban environment.

Risk-sensitive land use planning can ensure that urban growth does not expose the urban poor to natural disasters.

The future prosperity of East Asia's urban areas will depend in large measure on tackling the challenge of governing multijurisdictional urban regions effectively. Many of the region's urban areas cannot be effectively served by local governments acting independently. International experience suggests that regional government authorities and other mechanisms can help coordinate urban service provision across municipal boundaries. Overcoming issues related to metropolitan fragmentation requires considering tradeoffs between localized and centralized administrative authority.

The data produced as part of this study can benefit future research. A wealth of spatial and other data generated by this study is being released publicly online, along with interactive online maps. Combined with other sources of data at various scales, such data can help further the understanding of urbanization in East Asia.

For more information and to access the data set, please go to

www.worldbank.org/eap/MeasuringUrbanExpansion

CHAPTER 1

Introduction

Why Urban Expansion Matters

As urbanization rapidly transforms the face of the East Asia and Pacific region and the lives of its citizens, urban policy makers and planners have an important role to play in ensuring that urban expansion, and the economic growth it brings, is efficient and inclusive, allowing all residents a chance to benefit from the prosperity that cities offer. In this time of change, the form that urbanization takes will have long-lasting effects on the lives of hundreds of millions of urban residents and those of the many more to come.

Much of the urban infrastructure that will be built in East Asian cities is being built today, or will be built in the next 20 to 30 years. It took Europe more than 50 years to urbanize the equivalent number of people that have moved to urban areas in East Asia in just the past 10 years. Once cities are built, their urban form and land use patterns are locked in for generations, making it critical for cities to get their urban form right today, or spend decades and large sums of money trying to undo their mistakes.

Urbanization is key to providing economic opportunity. In the coming decades, urban areas can be the places where millions of East Asians will have the chance to leave extreme poverty behind and to prosper. The agglomeration effects of cities—reducing the cost of service provision and the transport of goods, allowing specialization, enabling the flow of ideas and spillovers of knowledge between firms, nurturing entrepreneurship, and others—mean that urbanization results in a boost to productivity and economic growth. Few countries have transitioned from poverty to prosperity without urbanizing (Ciccone and Hall 1996; Glaeser and Joshi-Ghani 2013; Glaeser and Maré 2011). Compared with other developing regions, East Asia is urbanizing at higher incomes, providing its cities with

Urbanization is key to providing economic opportunity.

the opportunity to finance the housing and infrastructure needed to support the growing concentration of people in its cities.[1]

However, to end extreme poverty and boost shared prosperity, urbanization must be inclusive. The findings in this study reinforce the connection between economic growth and urbanization (figure 1.1). However, even as urban growth provides opportunities for the poor, it can also aggravate existing inequalities in access to services, employment, and housing. The spatial expansion of a city directly affects the poor in its path. Land is often taken or bought cheaply from poor rural landowners on the urban fringe. Displaced from their homes and livelihoods, these people often do not benefit from the rising value of their former land. In other cases, urbanization simply engulfs rural settlements, creating urban villages that are excluded from urban services and land rights, and that gradually become slum-like areas of concentrated poverty. Large cities without affordable housing and efficient public transportation can force the poor to live far from work, schools, clinics, markets, and other amenities. They are then required to either endure long, expensive commutes, or resort to informal housing closer to the city center without land rights or services. Getting urban form, density, and administrative coordination right will be essential to ensuring that urbanization helps achieve the World Bank's twin goals of ending extreme poverty and boosting shared prosperity.

Figure 1.1   Changes in proportion of urban population (urbanization rate) and GDP per capita, 2000–10

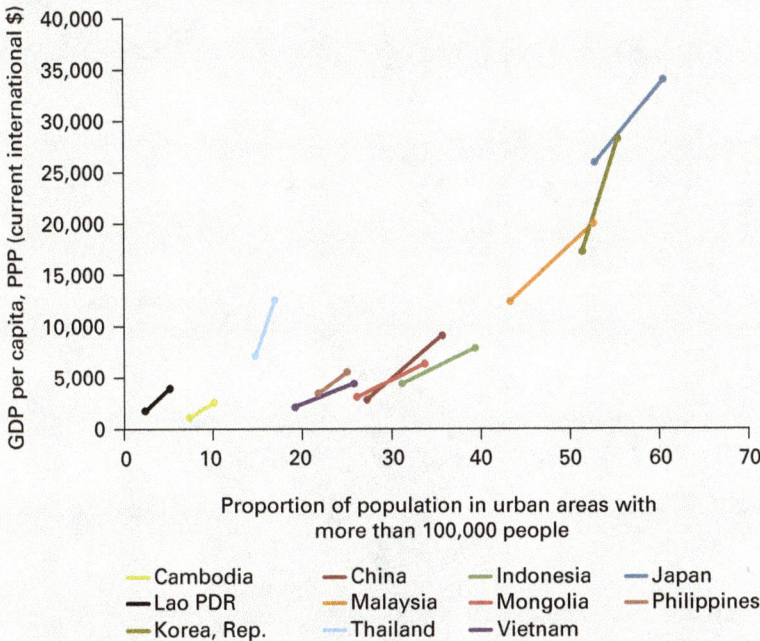

Source: Study team, incorporating WorldPop data, http://www.worldpop.org.uk/data/. Income figures from data.worldbank.org.
Note: PPP = purchasing power parity.

The type of urban expansion influences the risk for exposure to environmental and natural hazards. The countries that have had the greatest increases in urban expansion are also likely to see large gains in the consumption of fossil fuels (Satterthwaite 2009). International evidence suggests that environmental degradation increases with income in the initial stages of economic development (Stern 2004). The rate of environmental degradation slows at higher incomes, but most countries in East Asia, particularly the large, rapidly urbanizing ones, are still at the stage at which income growth, urban expansion, and environmental degradation go hand in hand. Land use and transportation decisions can have long-term impacts on the environmental sustainability of cities. The urban poor may settle on land that is especially prone to hazards such as flooding, landslides, and earthquakes. Unplanned growth in coastal areas may leave cities susceptible to threats of subsidence (as in Shanghai and Surabaya) as well as climate-related risks such as rising sea levels. Poorly planned urban expansion that results in low densities and segmented land use increases the cost of extending infrastructure to outlying areas and can worsen traffic congestion and air pollution (as evidenced by Beijing and Ulaanbaatar).

Tianjin is among the largest urban areas in China.

This study attempts to expand the knowledge of urbanization by defining and measuring the physical extent of urban areas and their populations in a consistent manner, across the entire East Asia and Pacific region, using built-up areas as observed from satellites.[2] This introduction includes an overview of key issues and briefly outlines the methodology used to carry out the analysis. Chapter 2 covers the main findings from the analysis in three sections: changes in urban land and population, trends related to population density, and issues of metropolitan fragmentation. Chapter 3 includes a set of recommendations and options for policy makers and urban planners.

A New Approach to Measuring Urban Expansion

Cities are notoriously hard to define in physical terms. Each country defines urban areas and populations differently (box 1.1). There is no consensus on how big a settlement needs to be or what characteristics it needs to have for it to be defined as a city or urban area. It is equally difficult to define where a city begins and ends; in most places a continuum of dispersed peri-urban settlements extends into the countryside rather than stopping at a firm edge. In some cases, what one person might describe as one multipolar urban area, someone else might think of as a group of separate cities. Administrative boundaries and official definitions are not a good guide either. Urban areas rarely fall neatly within an administrative boundary.

Urban leaders, policy makers, and researchers trying to understand or respond to urbanization have always been hampered by the lack of internationally comparable data. It has been difficult to consistently calculate whether one country is more or less urbanized than another, whether a country's urbanization path is similar to or different from that of other countries, and what effect urbanization policies have had on various development outcomes. As urbanization increasingly becomes a central development challenge, and as governments rely more and more on data as an input into policy decisions, comparable data on urbanization become increasingly necessary. Recent advances in technology, including satellite imagery and

---

Box 1.1   Defining "urban"

The criteria used to define what is urban in East Asia vary widely from one country to another. For example, the Philippines' definition combines administrative, population, and density criteria. Meanwhile, the Lao People's Democratic Republic uses a definition based on population as measured by individuals and households, as well as physical characteristics. In Indonesia, the definition of urban is circular, given that it includes "other places with urban characteristics." In Vietnam, it is simply "places with 4,000 inhabitants or more," with no definition of what counts as a single "place."

These country-based definitions may be suitable in their local contexts, but clearly they do not facilitate international comparability. The United Nations *World Urbanization Prospects* is a very useful compilation of urban demographic information (United Nations 2012). The most commonly cited source of data on urban populations, it prompted countless headlines about the world crossing the "50 percent urban" milestone in 2008. However, all the discrepancies referred to above are carried over into the UN figures. According to the UN Population Division, they "do not use [their] own definition of 'urban' population but follow the definition that is used in each country" (United Nations 2012).

Researchers have attempted to address this issue by crafting a standard definition of urban, notably the technique outlined by Chomitz, Buys, and Thomas (2005) and elaborated on by Uchida and Nelson (2010), which was used in *World Development Report 2009: Reshaping Economic Geography* (World Bank 2009). This definition uses thresholds based on minimum population size, minimum population density, and maximum travel time by road. However, this definition has not been found to be universally applicable; for example, when applied to Indonesia in unmodified form, it was found to define nearly all of the island of Java (home to 140 million people) as one large urban area (World Bank 2012). This method also requires reliable and consistent data on road networks and travel times, which do not currently exist on a regional or global scale.

techniques for modeling population distribution, allow us for the first time to map all human settlements and arrive at a common understanding of urbanization trends.

This study attempts to provide such data and develop this kind of understanding for the East Asia region, using satellite imagery and demographic data to measure expansion and population change in urban areas of 100,000 people and more, between 2000 and 2010.[3] To create maps of built-up areas throughout the region, change-detection methods were applied to analyze Moderate Resolution Imaging Spectroradiometer (MODIS) satellite data (Mertes and others, forthcoming). These maps rely on a geophysical definition of built-up areas: built-up land refers to places dominated by the "built environment," which includes all nonvegetative, human-constructed elements (for example, roads and buildings) with greater than 50 percent coverage of a landscape unit (here, a 250-meter pixel, that is, a square area of land with sides measuring 250 meters).[4] These built-up areas were combined with the AsiaPop map,[5] which models population distribution using census and other data as inputs. In brief, the 2000 and 2010 MODIS-derived built-up areas described above were integrated with detailed land cover data derived from the "Landsat" remote sensing project run by the U.S. Geological Survey and NASA. These refined land cover data sets were then combined with land cover–based population density weightings derived from fine resolution census data, and used to disaggregate the administrative-unit-level population counts to a 100 meter × 100 meter grid.[6] (See appendix C.)

The study builds on previous work, particularly by Angel (2012); Angel, Sheppard, and Civco (2005); and Angel and others (2010), who pioneered the use of satellite imagery in the measurement of urban extents. However, this study modifies past methodologies in two important ways. First, past studies have drawn on samples of selected urban areas, but this study mapped artificial land cover across the entire surface of the East Asia region before identifying urban areas, giving a more complete picture of urban growth in the region. Second, whereas other studies have had to use population figures of entire administrative units as a proxy for the population of built-up areas, this study used disaggregated population distribution maps, providing a better sense of where urban populations live.[7]

Although most of the built-up land observed by satellites is in urban areas, that built-up land also includes many small settlements (as long as they are built with artificial construction materials) that are commonly thought of as rural.[8] For these reasons, "urban land" in the report is defined as just the built-up land in urban areas with populations of 100,000 or more, as opposed to all built-up land. Similarly, "urban population" refers to just the population mapped to this urban land, that is, built-up land in urban areas with more than 100,000 people.

This report uses the term "urban area" to differentiate an area with a largely contiguous built-up footprint, which is the report's unit of analysis, from "cities," which may be confused with administrative definitions. For example, when the "Jakarta urban area" is discussed, it refers to the built-up area with Jakarta at its primary original center, but it also includes a large part that now lies outside the administrative boundaries of "Jakarta," and includes other centers, such as Bogor (see appendix C for details on how urban areas were defined).

This approach has allowed us for the first time to answer questions about urbanization across the entire region in a consistent manner so as to systematically establish where urbanization is occurring, how much, and how fast; how urban population growth relates to urban spatial expansion; and the relationship between urbanization, income growth, and inequality. The spatial data on urban growth being released alongside this report will allow other researchers to build on this study using a consistent set of definitions, further enhancing the understanding of urbanization in East Asia and its implications.

Notes

1. According to national estimates of urban population, the region passed urbanization rates of 50 percent in 2009 with an average GDP per capita of $5,300. In contrast, Latin America and the Caribbean crossed the same threshold in 1961 at a GDP per capita of $2,300, and Sub-Saharan Africa is currently 37 percent urban with an average GDP per capita of $992 (figures in 2005 U.S. dollars; World Bank, World Development Indicators). Note that, as discussed in the following section, urbanization rates defined according to national definitions, which lead to the urbanization figure of 50 percent as of 2009, differ significantly from those defined according to this study, which are much lower.
2. The World Bank defines the East Asia and Pacific (EAP) region to include countries stretching from Mongolia to the Pacific Islands. This study concentrates on Brunei Darussalam, Cambodia, China, Indonesia, Japan, the Democratic People's Republic of Korea, the Republic of Korea, the Lao People's Democratic Republic, Malaysia, Mongolia, Myanmar, the Philippines, Singapore, Thailand, Timor-Leste, and Vietnam. Because the report does not address urbanization in the Pacific Islands specifically, the study area is referred to as East Asia.
3. Because missing observations frequently occur within or near cities due to cloud cover, three full years of monthly satellite data were selected for each time point (2000–02 for circa 2000 data, and 2008–10 for circa 2010 maps). While the input data covered multiple years, feature selection, testing, and analysis were all conducted using year 2000 and 2010 data (Mertes and others, forthcoming).
4. Although the resolution of the imagery used to map the urban areas in this study (250 meters) is higher than has been used in previous studies conducted at this large scale, measuring smaller changes in urban area at a local scale would require even higher resolution imagery.

5. The AsiaPop map may be found at www.worldpop.org.uk.

6. The population distribution maps used publicly available census data. They are more reliable for places where the available census data were highly disaggregated relative to the size of a settlement, that is, where census units are small, as in Vietnam, and for larger urban areas. Where the available census figures were for administrative units that are much larger than urban areas, for example, in Mongolia and parts of Indonesia, estimates of urban populations relied more heavily on modeling.

7. This difference may partly explain why this study found increasing population densities while others have found declining densities. If people move from rural to urban areas within an administrative unit as the built-up area expands within it, the increase in urban population by this number of people will not be registered, even though all the increase in urban area will be calculated. This approach would give the impression, perhaps incorrect, of declining densities.

8. The amount of land picked up in these smaller settlements would vary by country. Satellite images would pick up fewer villages as "built-up" land in countries like Myanmar or Thailand, where dwellings are built from bamboo or thatch, than in countries like China, where such traditional materials are not in great use.

References

Angel, S. 2012. *Planet of Cities*. Cambridge, MA: Lincoln Institute of Land Policy.

Angel, S., J. Parent, D. L. Civco, and A. M. Blei. 2010. *Atlas of Urban Expansion*. Cambridge, MA: Lincoln Institute of Land Policy. http://www.lincolninst.edu/subcenters/atlas-urban-expansion/.

Angel, S., S. C. Sheppard, and D. L. Civco. 2005. *The Dynamics of Global Urban Expansion*. Washington, DC: World Bank.

Chomitz, K. M., P. Buys, and T. S. Thomas. 2005. "Quantifying the Rural-Urban Gradient in Latin America and the Caribbean." Policy Research Working Paper 3634, Development Research Group, Infrastructure and Environment Team, World Bank, Washington, DC.

Ciccone, A., and R. E. Hall. 1996. "Productivity and the Density of Economic Activity." *American Economic Review* 86 (1): 54–70.

Glaeser, E. L., and A. Joshi-Ghani. 2013. "Rethinking Cities: Toward Shared Prosperity." *Economic Premise* 126, World Bank, Washington, DC.

Glaeser, E. L., and D. Maré. 2001. "Cities and Skills." *Journal of Labor Economics* 19 (2): 316–42.

Mertes, C., A. Schneider, D. Sulla-Menashe, A. Tatem, and B. Tan. Forthcoming. "Detecting Change in Urban Areas at Continental Scales with MODIS Data." *Remote Sensing of Environment*.

Satterthwaite, D. 2009. "The Implications of Population Growth and Urbanization for Climate Change." *Environment and Urbanization* 21 (2): 545–67.

Stern, D. 2004. "The Rise and Fall of the Environmental Kuznet Curve." *World Development* 32 (8): 1419–39.

Uchida, H., and A. Nelson. 2010. "Agglomeration Index: Towards a New Measure of Urban Concentration." Background paper for *World Development Report 2009: Reshaping Economic Geography*. World Bank, Washington, DC.

United Nations, Department of Economic and Social Affairs, Population Division. 2012. *World Urbanization Prospects: The 2011 Revision*. CD-ROM edition, United Nations, New York.

World Bank. 2009. *World Development Report 2009: Reshaping Economic Geography*. Washington, DC: World Bank.

World Bank. 2012. "Indonesia: The Rise of Metropolitan Regions: Towards Inclusive and Sustainable Regional Development." World Bank, Washington, DC. http://documents.worldbank.org/curated /en/2012/08/16587797/indonesia-rise-metropolitan-regions-towards-inclusive-sustainable-regional-development.

CHAPTER 2

Key Findings: Urban Expansion in East Asia, 2000–10

Rapid Urban Expansion and Population Growth

Regional and Country Trends

East Asia experienced large amounts of urban expansion during the past decade.[1] The East Asia region had 106,000 square kilometers of urban land in 2000, which grew at an average rate of 2.4 percent a year to 135,000 square kilometers in 2010. Past studies suggest that the proportion of the total land area that is urbanized is higher in East Asia than in other regions (Angel and others 2010). Still, less than 1 percent of the region is urbanized (0.64 percent in 2000, increasing to 0.81 percent in 2010). Apart from the city-state of Singapore, the highest proportions of urban land were in Taiwan, China (which is considered a distinct economy; 5.3 percent); Japan (4.3 percent); Brunei Darussalam (3.1 percent); and the Republic of Korea (2.5 percent).

Two-thirds of the total urban land in the region in 2010 was in China (figure 2.1). Urban expansion in China has also consumed the most land in absolute terms (23,600 square kilometers). This is not surprising given the size of the country's population and land area. Nonetheless, as map 2.1 shows, the amount of new urban land in China dwarfs that of other rapidly urbanizing, large countries like Indonesia. The large impact of Chinese urban expansion on regional trends is evidenced by the fact that while the average annual rate of increase of urban land for the region as a whole was 2.4 percent, this figure drops to just 1.1 percent when China is excluded (see appendix B). The second-highest increase in urban land between 2000 and 2010 occurred in Indonesia (1,100 square kilometers). Although Japan continued to have the second-largest amount of urban land, its urban area expanded less (630 square kilometers) than Malaysia's (650 square kilometers) or Vietnam's (710 square kilometers).

Figure 2.1 Proportion of total urban land in East Asia by country, 2000 and 2010

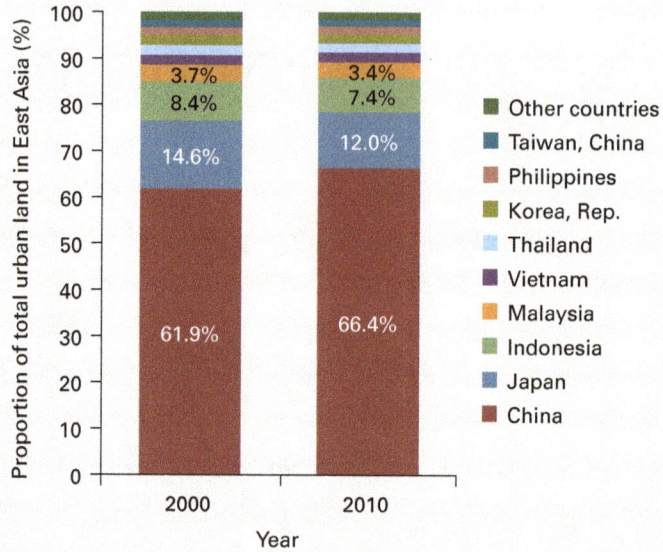

Source: Study team, incorporating WorldPop data, http://www.worldpop.org.uk/data/.

Rates of spatial expansion varied widely across countries in the region (figure 2.2). The Lao People's Democratic Republic and Cambodia, still mostly rural countries just beginning to urbanize, had the fastest rates of urban spatial expansion, 7.3 percent and 4.3 percent, respectively (very small absolute amounts of urban spatial expansion were involved, as map 2.1 shows). These countries were followed by China, in which urban areas expanded an average of 3.1 percent a year, Vietnam (2.8 percent), Mongolia (2.6 percent), and the Philippines (2.4 percent). Although Japan has the second-largest total amount of urban land, it had the lowest rate of increase in urban land among the countries studied (0.4 percent).

Urban population in the region grew even faster than urban land. The rapid expansion of urban areas in the region occurred in response to the even faster growth of an already large urban population. The total urban population of the region increased from 579 million in 2000 to 778 million in 2010 (map 2.2), an average annual growth rate of 3.0 percent. (To put this in perspective, if this new urban population of nearly 200 million people were a country unto itself, it would be the world's sixth largest.) Much of this growth was driven by China, which has the largest urban population in the region (and the world)—477 million urban inhabitants in 2010, more than the urban population of the rest of the region combined. The growth in China's urban population, 131 million people, was twice that of the rest of the region combined. However, China was not alone in its urban population growth; even excluding China, the urban population growth rate for

Map 2.1 Urban land by country, 2000 and 2010

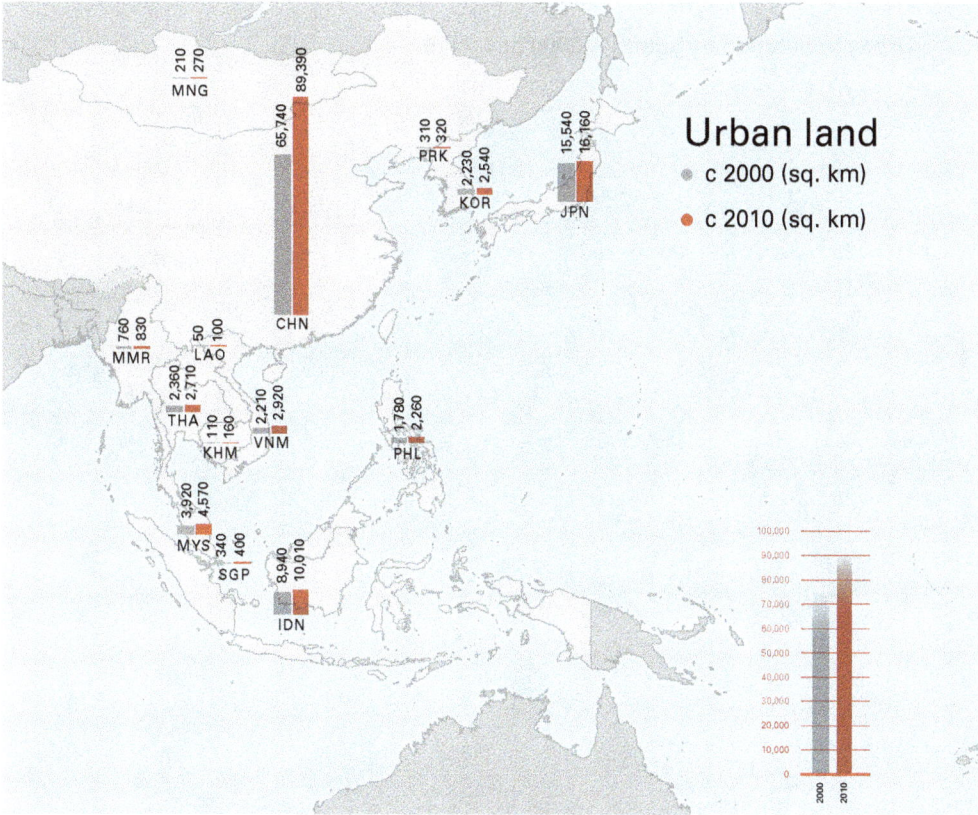

Source: Study team, incorporating WorldPop data, http://www.worldpop.org.uk/data/.
Note: CHN = China; IDN = Indonesia; JPN = Japan; KHM = Cambodia; KOR = Republic of Korea; LAO = Lao People's Democratic Republic; MNG = Mongolia; MMR = Myanmar; MYS = Malaysia; PHL = Philippines; PRK = Democratic People's Republic of Korea; SGP = Singapore; THA = Thailand; VNM = Vietnam.

Figure 2.2 Annual rate of urban spatial expansion by country, 2000–10

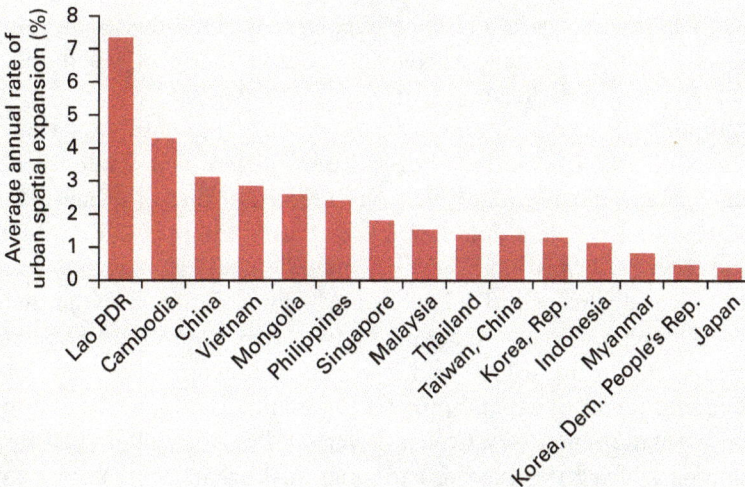

Source: Study team, incorporating WorldPop data, http://www.worldpop.org.uk/data/.

Map 2.2   Urban population by country, 2000 and 2010

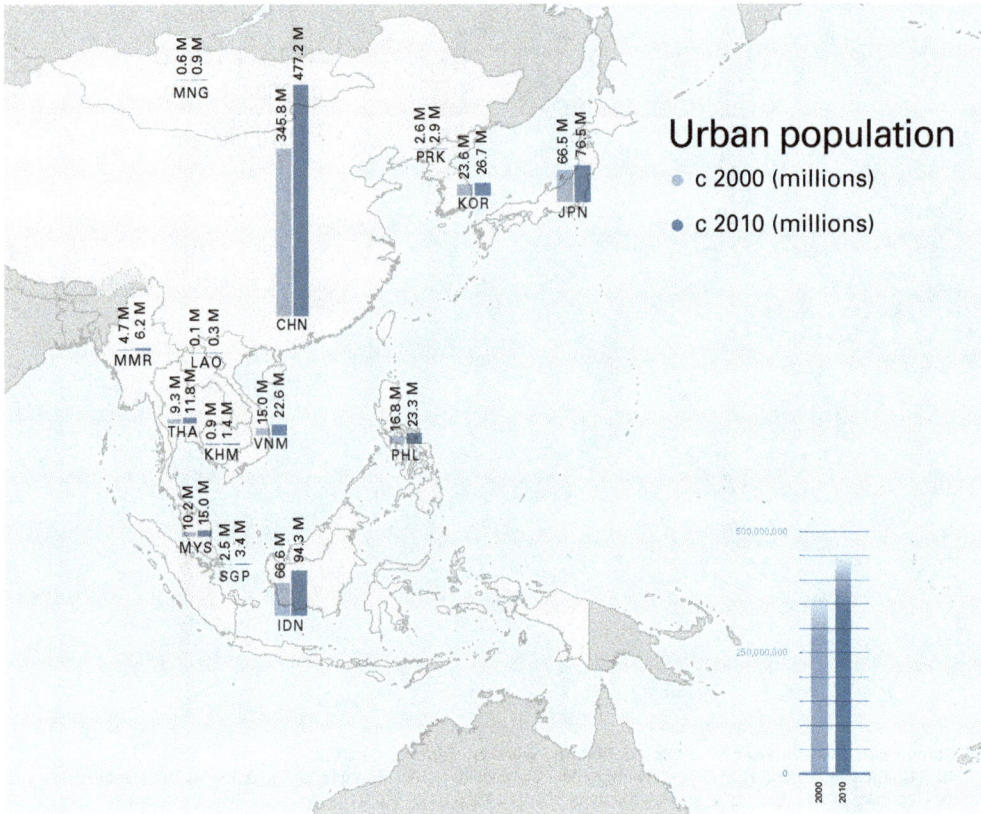

Source: Study team, incorporating WorldPop data, http://www.worldpop.org.uk/data/.
Note: For country names, see the note to map 2.1.

the region was 2.5 percent a year. Vietnam's urban population overtook Thailand's and the Republic of Korea's during this period. As figure 2.3 shows, China, Indonesia, and the Philippines increased their shares of the regional urban population, whereas the relative shares of Japan and the Republic of Korea declined.

Although China's urban population was largest in absolute terms, the urban populations of several smaller countries grew at faster rates. As figure 2.4 demonstrates, Lao PDR had the fastest rate of urban population growth, more than doubling its small urban population during this period. Lao PDR was followed by Cambodia and Vietnam, which both had between 4 percent and 4.5 percent urban population growth rates per year. As discussed in the following section, this rapid urban population growth is occurring in low- and lower-middle-income countries, which lack the resources to expand infrastructure and housing to keep up with these population increases. China, despite adding 131 million new urban inhabitants during this period, had an annual urban population growth rate of 3.3 percent, only slightly higher than the region as a whole (3.0 percent).

Figure 2.3   Proportion of total urban population in East Asia by country, 2000 and 2010

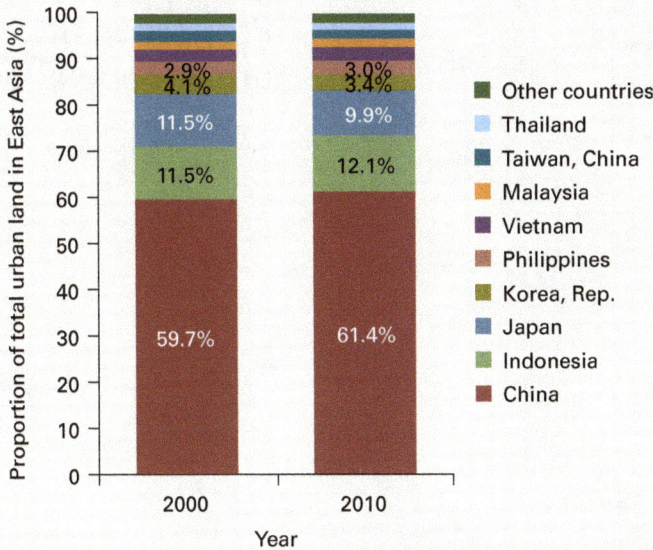

Source: Study team, incorporating WorldPop data, http://www.worldpop.org.uk/data/.

Figure 2.4   Rate of urban population growth by country, 2000–10

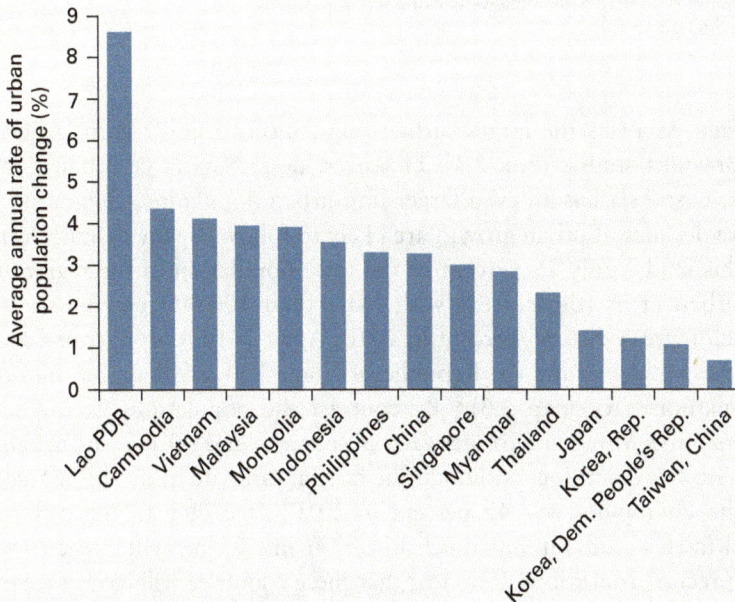

Source: Study team, incorporating WorldPop data, http://www.worldpop.org.uk/data/.

Map 2.3   Proportion of urban population by country, 2000 and 2010

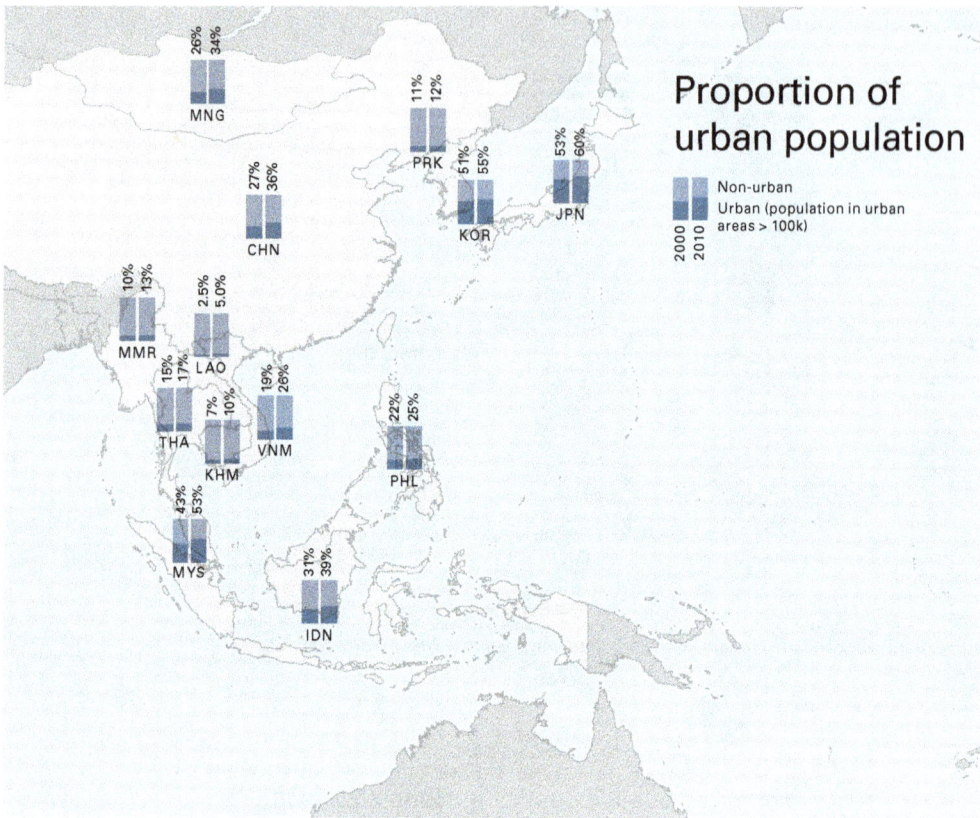

Proportion of urban population

- Non-urban
- Urban (population in urban areas > 100k)

2000
2010

MNG 26% 34%
PRK 11% 12%
JPN 53% 60%
KOR 51% 55%
CHN 27% 36%
MMR 10% 13%
LAO 2.5% 5.0%
THA 15% 17%
KHM 7% 10%
VNM 19% 26%
PHL 22% 25%
MYS 43% 53%
IDN 31% 39%

Source: Study team, incorporating WorldPop data, http://www.worldpop.org.uk/data/.
Note: For country names, see the note to map 2.1.

East Asia has the largest urban population of any region, according to previous studies (box 2.1). However, despite its large urban population, East Asia has an even larger non-urban population, suggesting that more decades of urban growth are likely to follow. By the definitions used in this study, only 29 percent of the total population of the region lived in urban areas (those areas with more than 100,000 people) in 2000, which increased to 36 percent in 2010. As of 2010, only Japan; Taiwan, China; Malaysia; and the Republic of Korea had larger urban than rural populations (see map 2.3).[2] By contrast the populations of Indonesia, China, and Mongolia are between 30 percent and 40 percent urban, by this study's definition. Although the official estimate of urban population in the Philippines was 49 percent in 2010, according to the definitions used in this study, it was much lower, at just 25 percent. Regardless of the precise proportions, it is clear that these countries will likely face more decades of rapid urban population growth, which will require proactive policies to provide land, housing, and services to accommodate these new urban residents (see chapter 3).

Box 2.1   Comparing urbanization in East Asia to that in the rest of the world

No global studies have been completed using the same approach and data as in this study, making cross-regional comparisons with these data difficult. However, Angel and others (2010) follow a similar approach, using maps of urban areas with more than 100,000 people (which they term "large cities") for the years 1990 and 2000, thus providing a sense of how urbanization in East Asia differs from that in other regions.[a] According to their study, countries in East Asia and the Pacific (EAP) had 1,190 large cities in 2000, the highest number of any region (Europe had 696; South and Central Asia had 539). Although Europe and the group of land-rich developed countries (Australia, Canada, New Zealand, and the United States) had more urban land by area, EAP had by far the world's largest urban population. By their figures, the urban population of EAP was twice that of Europe (which had the second-largest urban population). Their figures suggest that urban population density in EAP was equivalent to or slightly less than that in Sub-Saharan Africa, Northern Africa, and South and Central Asia, but 1.3 times that in Western Asia (the Middle East), more than 1.5 times that in Latin America and the Caribbean, more than twice that in Europe, and nearly four times that in the land-rich developed countries (Angel and others 2010).

a. The World Bank definition of EAP includes the "Eastern Asia and the Pacific" and "Southeast Asia" regions used by Angel and others (2010), and Japan. Totals in this box are presented according to the World Bank definition.

The dominant role of China in East Asia's urbanization is the result not only of its large size and rapidly growing economy, but also its approach to urbanization as a key national priority. Urbanization in China is unique, not just in its magnitude but also because, unlike anywhere else in the region or the world, it is not simply a phenomenon, but a deliberate, ambitious project. Rapid urbanization is a feature of many countries as their economies make the transition from agriculture to industry and services, but never before has a government been so proactive in leading this change by acquiring land, building cities, and moving people into them. The China Development Bank, a state-owned financial institution, lent US$168 billion to projects related to urbanization in 2013, two-thirds of its total loans that year.[3] The Chinese government has made urbanization, along with the increase in incomes and consumption it hopes it will stimulate, a keystone of its economic transition, and as such, the success or failure of this effort will have a long-lasting impact on the economy of China and the world (Johnson 2013). Another World Bank study prepared concurrently with this one looks in detail at various facets of urbanization in China and finds that it has been successful so far in lifting people out of poverty and avoiding the common pitfalls of slums and lack of infrastructure (World Bank and Development Research Center of the State Council, P.R. China 2014). However, it also notes that the country is increasingly faced with challenges relating to barriers to migration, unequal access to services, conflicts related to land acquisition, and environmental degradation. Data from this study illustrate some of the concerns related to misplaced investments in urban construction: even though on the whole urban population density in China increased slightly, more than 50 counties in the country experienced spatial urban expansion even though their populations dropped (see box A.2 in appendix A).

Trends by Income Group

High-income countries in East Asia are the most urbanized.[4] In absolute terms, most of the urban land and population in the region were in the upper-middle-income category, which is unsurprising, given that China belongs to this group. However, high-income countries had a much larger portion of their land in urban areas (4.1 percent in 2010) compared with upper-middle-income, lower-middle-income, or low-income countries (0.9 percent, 0.3 percent, and 0.1 percent respectively; see figure 2.5). High-income countries also had higher proportions of urban population (60 percent in 2010) compared with these other groups (35 percent, 33 percent, and 12 percent, respectively). Figure 2.6 shows the relationship between per capita incomes and urbanization rates, reinforcing the well-established idea that urbanization is important for economic growth. However, urban growth does not necessarily contribute to reducing income inequality within cities. Special attention must be paid to ensuring that urbanization is equitable and inclusive (see chapter 3).

Differing rates of urban spatial expansion and urban population growth among the country income groups suggest a general pattern of urbanization and economic growth. The urban population growth rate was slightly higher in lower-middle-income countries (3.6 percent) than in upper-middle-income countries (3.3 percent; figure 2.7). However, the rate of urban spatial expansion was highest in upper-middle-income countries (3.0 percent), followed by lower-middle- and low-income countries (1.7 percent and 1.1 percent; figure 2.8).[5] High-income countries had the lowest rates of increase for both spatial expansion and population growth. That higher levels of urbanization are associated with higher national incomes suggests a

Figure 2.5 **Proportion of urban land by income group, 2000 and 2010**

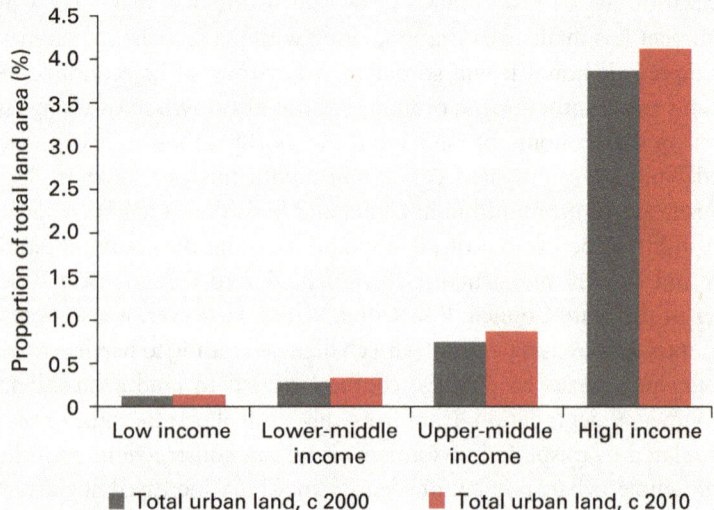

Source: Study team, incorporating WorldPop data, http://www.worldpop.org.uk/data/.

Figure 2.6   Changes in proportion of urban population (urbanization rate) and GDP per capita, 2000–10

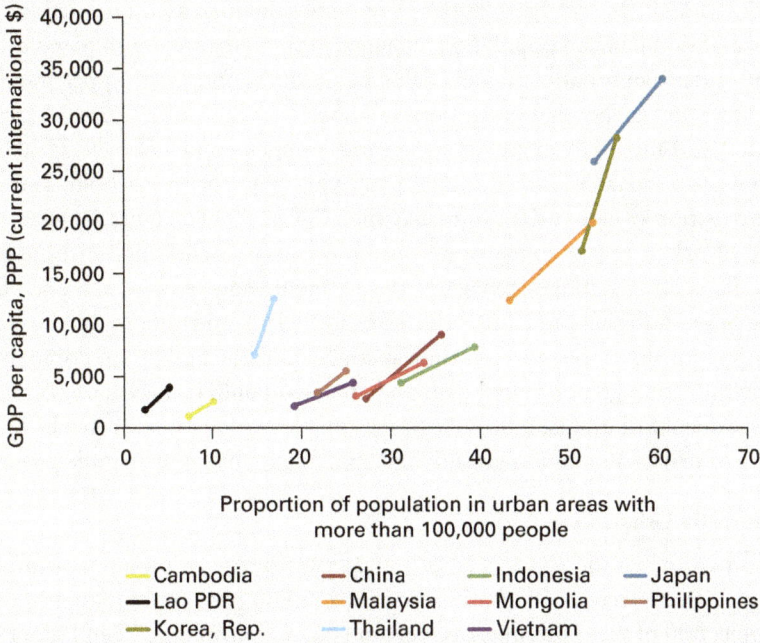

Proportion of population in urban areas with
more than 100,000 people

— Cambodia   — China   — Indonesia   — Japan
— Lao PDR   — Malaysia   — Mongolia   — Philippines
— Korea, Rep.   — Thailand   — Vietnam

Sources: Study team, incorporating WorldPop data, http://www.worldpop.org.uk/data/.
Income figures from data.worldbank.org.
Note: PPP = purchasing power parity.

Figure 2.7   Rate of urban population growth by income group, 2000–10

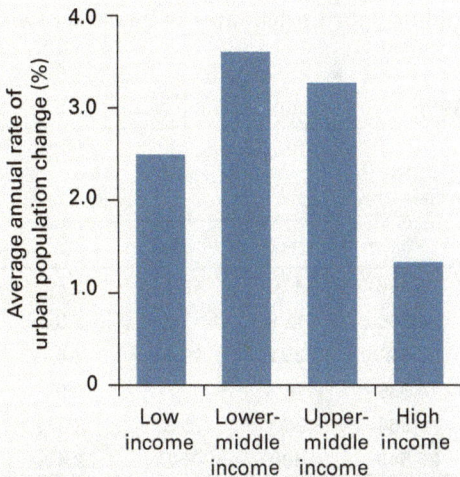

Source: Study team, incorporating WorldPop data,
http://www.worldpop.org.uk/data/.

Figure 2.8   Rate of urban spatial expansion by income group, 2000–10

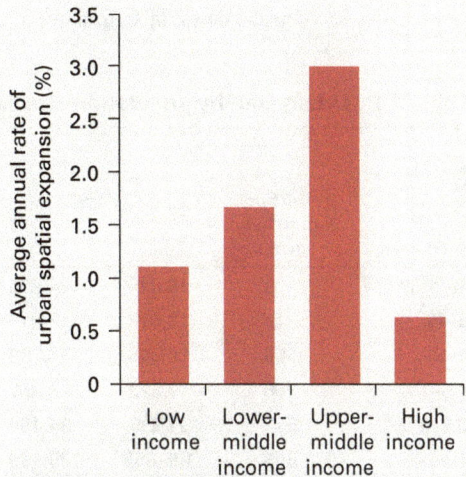

Source: Study team, incorporating WorldPop data,
http://www.worldpop.org.uk/data/.

likely general pattern of urbanization: First, people in lower-middle-income countries move in large numbers to urban areas. Initially, because of limited resources, urban areas are not able to expand quickly enough to accommodate them all (World Bank 2009). Eventually the increased productivity of this additional urban population, engaged in small manufacturing and other labor-intensive urban activities, helps boost the economy to upper-middle-income status. This change in status is associated with a move to more large-scale, land-intensive manufacturing, and rising incomes also bring about more car ownership, larger amounts of living space per household, and the construction of new urban infrastructure. All of these changes increase the rate of urban spatial expansion. Once a country reaches high-income status, its economy moves toward service-related industries, which are both less labor intensive and less land intensive (Seto and others 2011). This adjustment slows the rates of urban spatial expansion and urban population growth. Although additional data and analysis would be necessary to verify this sequence of events, it provides a reasonable explanation for the differing rates of urban population growth and spatial expansion by income group.

Trends by Urban Area

The majority of the region's largest and fastest-growing urban areas are in China. There were 869 urban areas in the region with more than 100,000 people; 600 of these urban areas were in China, followed by 77 in Indonesia and 59 in Japan (table 2.1). Of the region's 25 largest urban areas by land area, 15 are in China, 3 in Japan, 2 in Vietnam, and 1 each in Indonesia, the Republic of Korea, Malaysia, the Philippines, and Thailand (map 2.4; figures 2.9 and 2.10).[6] Given the large amount of public investment in urban construction in China, it is unsurprising that among large cities of more than a million people, those expanding the fastest were in China, with 12 doubling in area during the decade as a result of average annual growth of 7 percent, led by Changshu, Jiangyin, and Hangzhou. The fastest-growing urban areas outside China were the Johor Bahru urban area in Malaysia (which

Table 2.1   Urban land by population size category

Population size category (millions)	Total number of urban areas	Urban land (sq. km)		Increase in urban land, 2000–10 (sq. km)	Proportion of total urban land (%)		Average annual rate of urban expansion (%)
		2000	2010		2000	2010	
10 or more	8	18,820	24,876	6,056	17.6	18.4	2.8
5–10	17	13,673	18,013	4,340	12.8	13.3	2.8
1–5	106	26,845	34,288	7,442	25.2	25.4	2.5
0.5–1	166	19,529	23,868	4,338	18.3	17.7	2.0
0.1–0.5	572	27,790	34,154	6,364	26.1	25.3	2.1
Total	**869**	**106,658**	**135,199**	**28,540**	**100**	**100**	**2.4**

Source: Study team, incorporating WorldPop data, http://www.worldpop.org.uk/data/.
Note: Numbers may not add to totals because of rounding.

Map 2.4   East Asia: The 25 largest urban areas by population, 2010

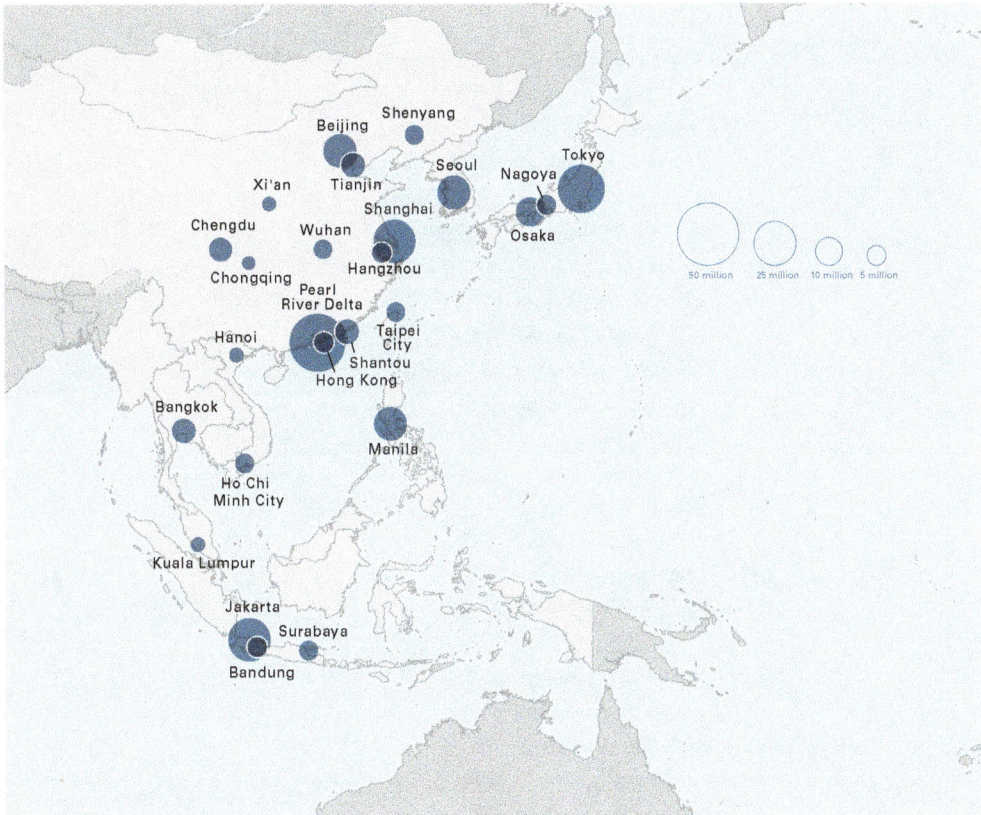

Source: Study team, incorporating WorldPop data, http://www.worldpop.org.uk/data/.

is close to Singapore), and the Phnom Penh urban area in Cambodia. In absolute amounts of new urban land, urban areas in China again dominate, with 19 of the top 25. Vietnam's two large urban areas, Ho Chi Minh City and Hanoi, expanded rapidly during this period, with both growing more in absolute land area than any other urban areas in the region other than China. As with urban spatial expansion, urban population growth rates among large urban areas were highest in China, with Hefei and Changshu urban areas having doubled in population during this period. In the region as a whole, 50 urban areas had growth rates that, if continued, would lead them to double in population between 2000 and 2020.

If considered a single urban area, the Pearl River Delta in China became the largest in the world as measured by both area and population. Although Tokyo has long been considered the largest metropolitan area, and has been expected to retain that position for the next few decades (United Nations Human Settlements Programme 2010; Hoornweg and Freire 2013), this study finds that it has been surpassed by the Pearl River Delta urban area, which includes Dongguan, Foshan, Guangzhou, and Shenzhen (map 2.5).[7] In 2000, the Pearl River Delta covered 4,500 square kilometers, and grew very rapidly (4.5 percent a year) to nearly 7,000 square kilometers in 2010.

Figure 2.9   East Asia: The 25 largest urban areas by land area, 2000 and 2010

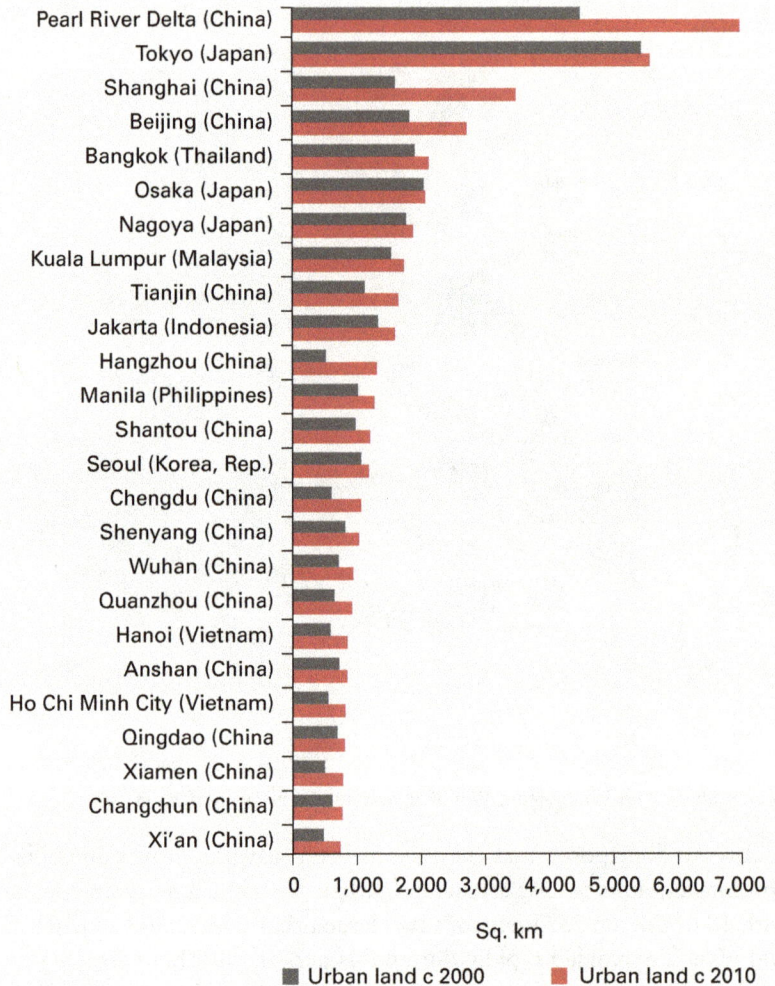

Source: Study team, incorporating WorldPop data, http://www.worldpop.org.uk/data/.

Map 2.5 shows that the built-up areas in 2000 (shown in gray), which may previously have been considered several distinct urban areas, appear to be merging into one continuous, if scattered, urban region. It is more than twice as large as the Shanghai urban area, four times the size of the Jakarta urban area, and five times the size of the Manila urban area, each of which are massive in their own right. The Pearl River Delta urban area had 42 million inhabitants in 2010, more than some entire countries, including Argentina, Australia, Canada, and Malaysia.

Trends by Size Category

Despite their global visibility, East Asia's "megacities" represent only a part of the overall urban landscape.[8] Discussion of urbanization in East Asia

Figure 2.10   The 25 largest urban areas by population and land area, 2010

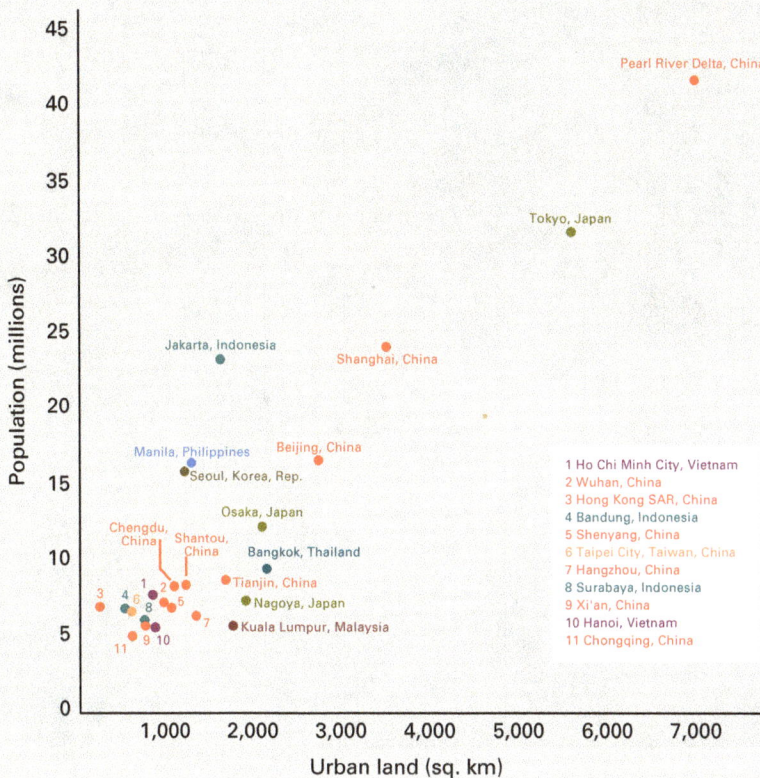

1 Ho Chi Minh City, Vietnam
2 Wuhan, China
3 Hong Kong SAR, China
4 Bandung, Indonesia
5 Shenyang, China
6 Taipei City, Taiwan, China
7 Hangzhou, China
8 Surabaya, Indonesia
9 Xi'an, China
10 Hanoi, Vietnam
11 Chongqing, China

Source: Study team, incorporating WorldPop data, http://www.worldpop.org.uk/data/.

tends to focus on its massive megacities of 10 million or more people, such as the large and rapidly expanding Pearl River Delta urban area. Megacities are internationally recognizable; exemplify extreme versions of urban problems like traffic congestion and urban poverty; and are often the seat of government, private enterprise, and educational institutions. However, only 8 urban areas in the region are megacities; in contrast, 572 urban areas are in the smallest population size category of 100,000 to 500,000 people and account for two-thirds of the urban areas in the region (table 2.1).

The largest amount of the region's urban land and urban expansion is in small and medium-sized urban areas.[9] Although the average megacity is spatially more than 50 times as large as the average of the smallest category, there is, in fact, more land in urban areas in the smallest category and in the category of 1 million to 5 million people (both categories have about 34,000 square kilometers, about a quarter of the total urban land each) than in the megacity category (25,000 square kilometers) (table 2.1 and figure 2.11). Both of these categories also acquired more absolute amounts of new urban land area than the megacity category. The larger categories grew at slightly faster rates than the smaller ones, but this resulted in only a very

Map 2.5   China's Pearl River Delta urban area has surpassed Tokyo

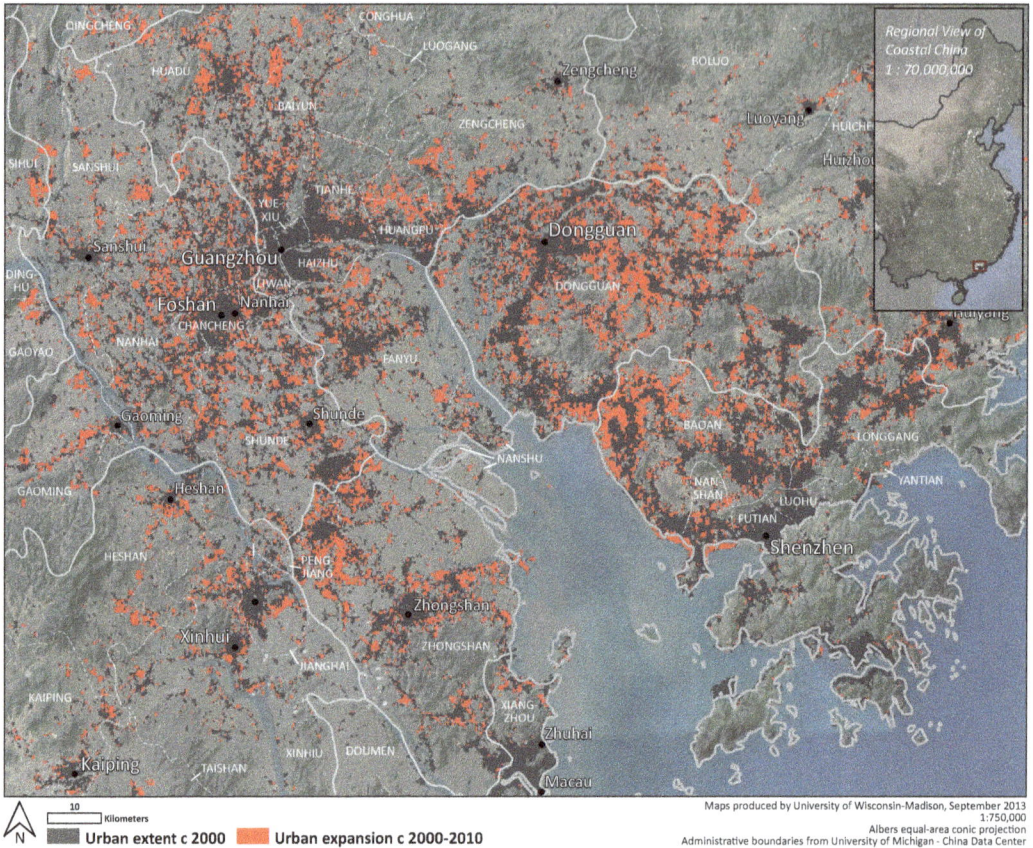

Regional View of
Coastal China
1 : 70,000,000

Urban extent c 2000   Urban expansion c 2000-2010

Maps produced by University of Wisconsin-Madison, September 2013
1:750,000
Albers equal-area conic projection
Administrative boundaries from University of Michigan - China Data Center

small shift in the relative proportions of urban land toward the larger size categories, as indicated in table 2.1. In middle-income countries, most of the urban land was in the smallest three categories, that is, in urban areas with fewer than 5 million people. However, in lower-middle-income countries, urban areas with 5 million to 10 million people expanded fastest, whereas in upper-middle-income countries, the megacities expanded fastest.

The largest amount of both urban population and urban population growth in the region was in medium-sized urban areas and megacities. The 106 urban areas in the 1 million to 5 million category had the largest urban population among the five categories (212 million people in 2010), followed by the eight megacities, which together had 183 million people in 2010 (table 2.2 and figure 2.12). These two categories also added the most population, 57 million people and 50 million people, respectively. As with urban land, population growth rates in larger urban areas grew slightly faster, resulting in a slight shift in the proportion of urban population toward larger urban areas. In lower-middle-income countries, the megacities had the largest urban population, although it was the 5 million to 10 million people category that grew fastest. By contrast, in upper-middle-income

Figure 2.11   Urban land by population size category, 2000 and 2010

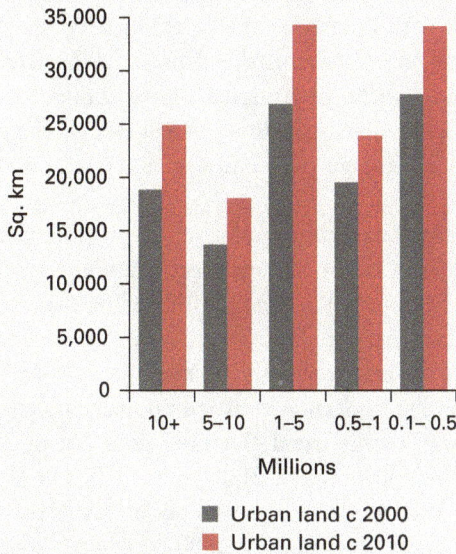

Source: Study team, incorporating WorldPop data, http://www.worldpop.org.uk/data/.

Figure 2.12   Urban population by population size category

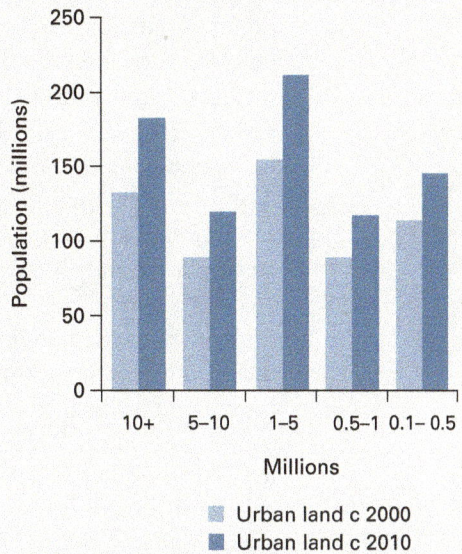

Source: Study team, incorporating WorldPop data, http://www.worldpop.org.uk/data/.

Table 2.2   Urban population by population size category

Population size category (millions)	Urban population (millions)		Increase in urban population, 2000–10 (millions)	Proportion of total urban population (%)		Average annual rate of increase in urban population (%)
	2000	2010		2000	2010	
10 or more	132.72	182.58	49.86	22.9	23.5	3.2
5–10	88.98	119.83	30.84	15.4	15.4	3.0
1–5	154.65	211.89	57.24	26.7	27.3	3.2
0.5–1	88.93	117.44	28.51	15.4	15.1	2.8
0.1–0.5	114.05	145.78	31.73	19.7	18.7	2.5
Total	**579.33**	**777.51**	**198.18**	**100**	**100**	**3.0**

Source: Study team, incorporating WorldPop data, http://www.worldpop.org.uk/data/.
Note: Numbers may not add to totals because of rounding.

countries, the urban areas with 1 million to 5 million people had the largest total urban population, though the megacities grew fastest. This slight shift toward larger urban areas could be associated with a shift toward higher value added industries, in the direction of the pattern seen in high-income countries, which were dominated by their megacities, with 50 percent of their urban population residing in them (see chapter 3).

Density: High and Increasing, on Average

Population density in urban areas in East Asia was more than 1.5 times greater than the average for the world's urban areas. Comparisons of urban population and densities with the rest of the world in 2000 suggest that although East Asian urban areas are not the densest in the world, they are much denser than those in Latin America, Europe, and North America (box 2.1). This high urban density is an asset to East Asian cities that potentially gives them an advantage over cities in other regions (as discussed in chapter 3).

Overall, East Asia's cities have maintained relatively high population density while they have expanded. One of the unexpected findings of this analysis is that, despite the large amount of urban growth leading to perceptions of sprawl and declining densities, population density in urban areas in the region, in fact, appears to be increasing slightly, on average. Past studies have found a global trend of long-term decline in urban population density (Angel and others 2010). However, this trend generally does not appear to hold true for the East Asia region between 2000 and 2010. On average, total urban population density in the region was about 5,400 people per square kilometer in 2000, which increased to 5,800 people per square kilometer in 2010 (if China is excluded, average density for the region is even higher: 5,800 in 2000 and 6,600 in 2010). With the exception of the Republic of Korea and Taiwan, China, population density in urban areas everywhere rose during this period.

Urban population density—the total population of an urban area divided by its total land area—is a simple concept that can indicate general trends.

Box 2.2   Projecting future urban expansion

This report does not project urban spatial expansion into the future on the basis of expansion between 2000 and 2010. It is unlikely that future urban growth will continue in a simple linear fashion at the same rate as during 2000–10, which for many of the countries in the region has been a unique period of economic and demographic transition. The future rate of urban expansion will depend on a number of factors: demographic changes, economic policies, climate change, investments in housing and transportation infrastructure, and a range of policy decisions. Even if it were possible to project each of these variables, the exact relationship between them and urban spatial expansion, for different countries at different stages of development, would require complex modeling that lies beyond the scope of this study, and might rely on too many assumptions to be useful. Although it is possible to apply a relationship observed in other regions of the world to East Asia, care must be taken in doing so. The scale, pace, and mode of urbanization of East Asia are unprecedented in history, and have been driven by a unique set of political, economic, and technological forces. For these reasons, this report does not make the assumption that East Asian countries are destined to follow a standard urbanization trajectory. The dangers of forecasting urban growth are illustrated by the attempt of a team of urban experts in 1974 to predict the sizes of world cities in 2000. As noted in the World Bank's *World Development Report 2009,* their forecasts were "way off," with population projections for several cities being 50–100 percent higher than actual populations in 2000 (World Bank 2009, 198–99).

However, at a local level, density measures often mask much complexity, which needs to be carefully understood. See box 2.3.

The majority of urban areas in the region became denser during this period. In the region as a whole, more than half (56 percent) of all urban areas increased in density (table 2.3). Nearly all of the urban areas with declining densities were in China, which may have to do with mismatches in the location of the supply of and demand for urban construction in China (see box A.2 in appendix A), and with rising incomes leading to the demand for more residential space per capita. However, if China is excluded, density was on the rise in 92 percent of the remaining urban areas. Larger urban areas were denser, but medium-sized urban areas saw the greatest

---

Box 2.3   The urban population density metric

An important feature of the urban population density metric is that it represents *built-up area density*, that is, the population density of only the built-up areas within an urban area. It does not reflect how those pixels are arranged, or how dispersed the urban fabric is. This means that an urban area with "leapfrog" development, in which there are several clusters of development separated by expanses of unbuilt land (a common situation on the transitional, urbanizing edge of East Asian cities) would show the same density as one in which the same development was contiguous. The urban population density metric does not reflect these different kinds of urban growth, one likely to be more desirable than another. These differences might be better captured by other metrics, such as *urbanized area density* or *city footprint density*, both of which take into account some of the unbuilt areas surrounding the built-up areas (Angel and others 2010). Measures other than density, such as the *contiguity index, compactness index,* and *openness index,* reflect these characteristics of urban form more directly (Angel, Sheppard, and Civco 2005).

Even when only taking into account built-up areas, density figures for the same place can vary greatly depending on what area the figures are averaged over, an issue referred to as the "modifiable areal unit problem." Usually the unit is an administrative boundary, but the size of these jurisdictions vary, so to say that a small district A is denser than a larger district B on average may hide the fact that district B has pockets that are denser than A. Perhaps the most famously high-density piece of land in the region is Pudong in Shanghai, whose towering skyline is the emblematic image of East Asian urban density. However, the figure for the district of Pudong does not capture this intense population density because the boundary covers a much wider area, including some low-density, semirural areas, resulting in a much lower average population density than might be expected. This is not to say that the density figure is incorrect, simply that it does not capture internal variations, and may be misleading if not examined closely.

As some East Asian urban areas, such as Ho Chi Minh City, develop more manufacturing, their overall densities decline because of large industrial developments on their outskirts. However, these developments often create jobs that draw additional residents into the city; these new residents live in older, inner areas that are, in fact, becoming denser. That overall density figures may not capture this variation is another example of the modifiable areal unit problem. It also illustrates another important point about population density figures—they represent residential population density, not economic density or density of the built environment. Needless to say, an area with low population density may still require a large amount of infrastructure and services if it is home to jobs or other activities. However, despite these caveats, the overall urban population density figures that emerge from this study do indicate broad trends in East Asian urbanization.

Table 2.3   Changes in the population density of urban areas, by country, 2000–10

Country/economy	Change in average density (people per sq. km)	Number of urban areas with increasing density	Proportion of urban areas with increasing density (%)	Number of urban areas with decreasing density	Proportion of urban areas with decreasing density (%)	Total number of urban areas
China	+78	236	39	364	61	600
Indonesia	+1,974	74	96	3	4	77
Japan	+454	59	100	0	0	59
Vietnam	+894	28	93	2	7	30
Philippines	+851	19	90	2	10	21
Malaysia	+684	19	100	0	0	19
Korea, Rep.	-73	9	56	7	44	16
Thailand	+386	11	100	0	0	11
Myanmar	+1,347	10	100	0	0	10
Taiwan, China	-519	3	30	7	70	10
Korea, Dem. People's Rep.	+515	9	100	0	0	9
Brunei Darussalam	+198	1	100	0	0	1
Cambodia	+49	1	100	0	0	1
Lao PDR	+359	1	100	0	0	1
Mongolia	+411	1	100	0	0	1
Papua New Guinea	+846	1	100	0	0	1
Singapore	+928	1	100	0	0	1
Timor-Leste	+2,285	1	100	0	0	1
All countries	**+321**[a]	**484**	**56**	**385**	**44**	**869**
All excluding China	*+864*	*248*	*92*	*21*	*8*	*269*

Source: Study team, incorporating WorldPop data, http://www.worldpop.org.uk/data/.
a. Total urban population of the region divided by the total urban land of the region.

density gains (figure 2.13). Among medium-sized and large urban areas, density declined mainly in those with the fastest rates of spatial growth, in excess of 7 percent a year (that is, those that doubled in size between 2000 and 2010), as seen in figure 2.14.

However, this high, increasing density is not a uniform trend across all countries in the region (figure 2.15). The Republic of Korea and the Philippines had the highest urban population densities, more than 10,000 people per square kilometer. Indonesia's urban population density jumped sharply between 2000 and 2010, to approximately 9,400 people per square kilometer from 7,400. Myanmar, the Philippines, and Vietnam also experienced large absolute gains in urban population density. Japan, Lao PDR, Malaysia, Mongolia, and Thailand had the lowest densities. These differing densities mean that Japan has much more urban land than Indonesia, despite having a smaller urban population. Similarly, Malaysia and Thailand have

Figure 2.13   Urban population density by population size category, 2000 and 2010

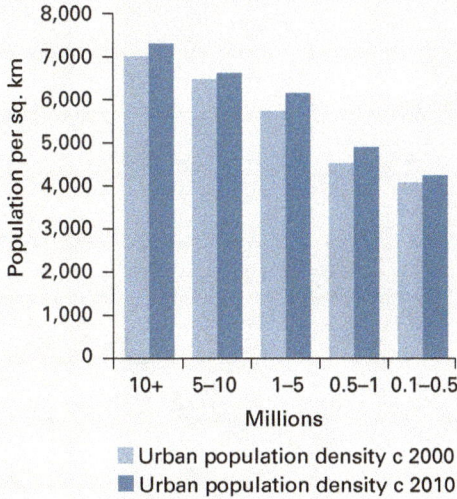

Source: Study team, incorporating WorldPop data, http://www.worldpop.org.uk/data/.

Figure 2.14   Rates of population growth and spatial expansion in urban areas with more than 1 million people, 2000–10

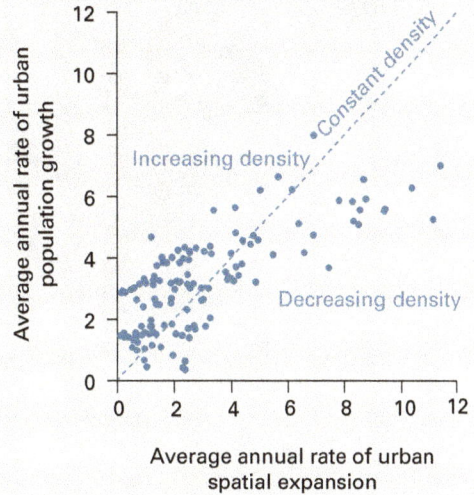

Source: Study team, incorporating WorldPop data, http://www.worldpop.org.uk/data/.

Figure 2.15   Urban population density by country, 2000 and 2010

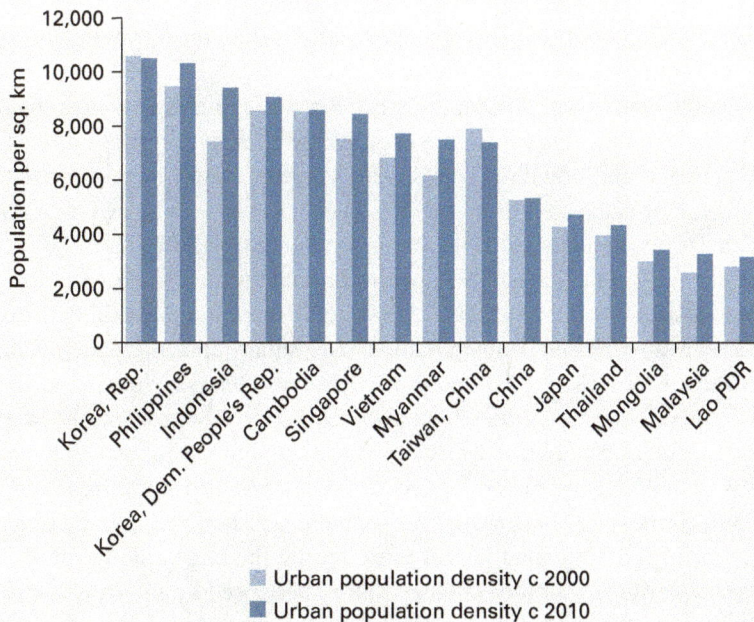

Source: Study team, incorporating WorldPop data, http://www.worldpop.org.uk/data/.

Figure 2.16   Urban spatial expansion per additional urban inhabitant, 2000–10

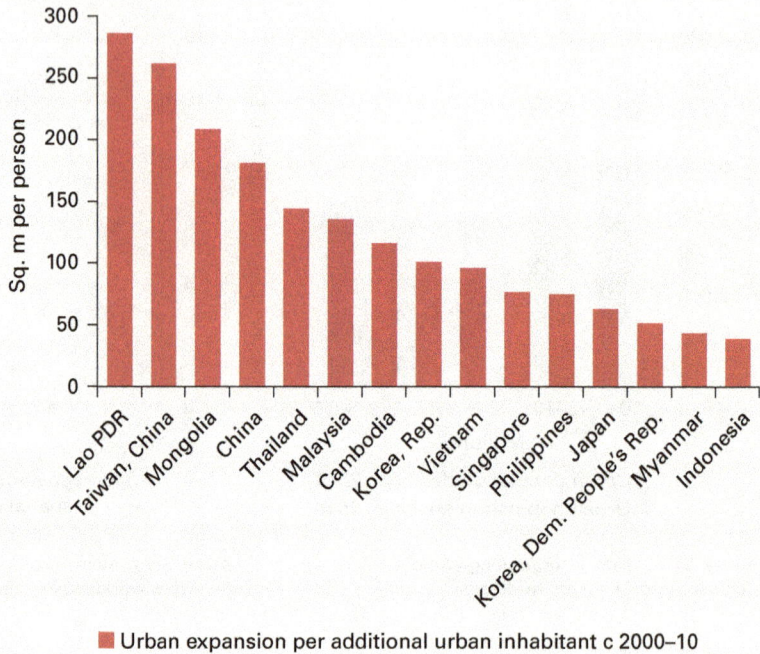

■ Urban expansion per additional urban inhabitant c 2000–10

Source: Study team, incorporating WorldPop data, http://www.worldpop.org.uk/data/.

more urban land but smaller urban populations than the Republic of Korea and the Philippines.

The amount of new urban construction per capita also varies greatly across the region. This measure compares, by country, the amount of new land per each additional urban resident. There is, however, no clear determining factor (such as country income level or urban area size category) for this variation (figure 2.16). The amount was the highest in Lao PDR (280 square meters of new urban area per additional urban resident) and lowest in Indonesia, although both are lower-middle-income countries. Per capita expansion was high in Taiwan, China (260 square meters), which is land constrained, but also in Mongolia (200 square meters) which is not land constrained. Urban areas in China also grew relatively expansively, at 180 square meters per additional urban inhabitant. Indonesia saw an average of less than 40 square meters of new urban land built per additional urban resident, indicating that urban development has been relatively compact when measured per capita (a fact disguised by the large amount of visible urban expansion). Another country that experienced an increase in urban population without the construction of large amounts of new urban area was Myanmar, a trend that may change suddenly as its economy opens up. Understanding the exact determinants across these countries of these differing types of urban expansion would require further analysis of land and housing markets, infrastructure construction, and various urban policies on a country-by-country basis.

Even though China has undergone massive urban population growth, density gains have been modest. Despite the huge growth in its urban population, China's urban population density (5,300 people per square kilometer in 2010) remained stable, and lower than the average for the region, as a result of the accompanying rapid urban spatial expansion. Contrasting this to a country like Indonesia, which saw a large jump in urban population density, is telling. In China, new urban construction is plentiful; the barriers have been to the movement of population, due in part to the *hukou* system of urban registration, which regulates access to urban public services and social security.[10] By contrast, in Indonesia, and many other countries, the situation is the opposite: populations migrate freely, while the constraint is on producing new urban area with infrastructure and housing. In China, more than 60 percent of the urban areas, including Chongqing, Shanghai, Tianjin, and other large urban areas, declined in density, as table 2.3 shows. Indeed, as noted previously, more than 50 Chinese counties expanded spatially but simultaneously lost population. In contrast, despite a slight reduction in overall urban population density, Hong Kong SAR, China, remained the densest urban area in the region, with an extremely high average density of 32,000 people per square kilometer in 2010.

High-density growth patterns may be the result of infrastructure shortages. Indonesia's compact urban growth and sharply increasing density are likely due to constraints in investment in urban infrastructure and housing, rather than deliberate attempts at compact development. Recent studies of urbanization in Indonesia take this view, finding that capital expenditure on infrastructure is insufficient (World Bank 2012b) and that housing construction does not meet demand (World Bank 2012a). However, future urban investment need not inevitably result in urban expansion. With careful planning, Indonesian cities have an opportunity to maintain their already high density, which has its advantages, even while increasing housing and infrastructure. It is also important to note that density metrics are purely quantitative and do not describe the quality of new urban development. Compact development is not desirable if it lacks space for schools, parks, public transportation, and municipal infrastructure.

Low-density urban growth patterns can be the result of residents' lifestyle preferences or unintended consequences of land policies. Malaysia and Mongolia show similar urban population densities (3,300 and 3,400 people per square kilometer, respectively) despite being at very different stages of economic and urban development. Malaysia's urban development pattern is atypical for East Asia, taking the form of automobile-oriented suburban growth with single-family dwellings. In contrast, Mongolia's low-density urban development takes the form of neighborhoods of traditional *ger* dwellings on the outskirts of the city, fueled by a policy of distributing large plots of free land to all citizens. This makes the provision of infrastructure and services to these areas, including roads and transportation, prohibitively expensive. The municipality of the capital, Ulaanbaatar, is now trying

Figure 2.17   **Urban population density by income group, 2000 and 2010**

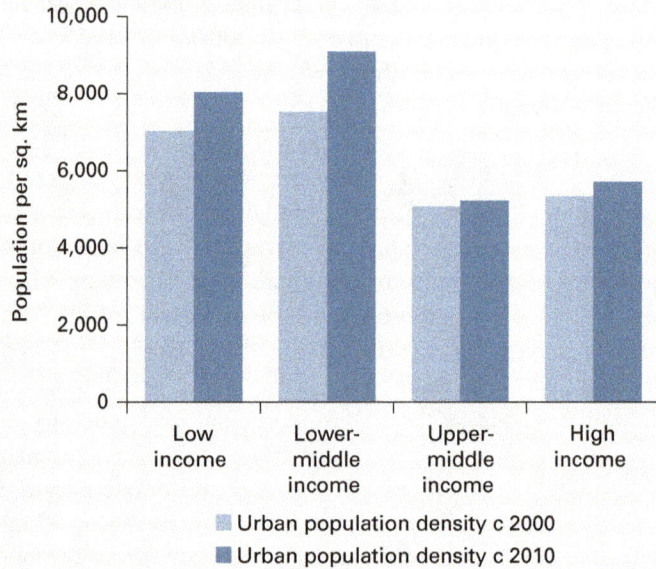

Source: Study team, incorporating WorldPop data, http://www.worldpop.org.uk/data/.

to increase density in existing settlements, which involves several challenges (Kamata and others 2010).

Low- and lower-middle-income countries had much higher densities and larger increases in density. As figure 2.17 shows, urban population densities in low- and lower-middle-income countries (8,000 and 9,100 people per square kilometer, respectively) were much higher than in upper-middle-income and high-income countries (5,200 and 5,700 people per square kilometer, respectively). The largest increase in urban density was in lower-middle-income countries, while density in upper-middle-income countries remained stable.

The challenge for most East Asian countries is to establish the right kind of density as cities grow and expand. Despite the numerous benefits of adequate urban population density, the findings of this study suggest that because density in most East Asian countries is already high and often increasing, the focus should not be simply on further densification, but on the appropriate location, coordination, quality, and design of density, as discussed in chapter 3.

Increasing Metropolitan Fragmentation

Metropolitan fragmentation has emerged as a significant challenge in the East Asia region. Fragmentation of metropolitan areas refers to the spillover of urban growth from original boundaries into neighboring jurisdictions, or the merging of multiple cities into a single entity, while they continue to be administered separately. Among the urban areas examined here, 521 were contained within a single municipal boundary, 213 were "spillover" urban areas (with up to half spilling over, but still mostly within one boundary), and 135 were "fragmented" urban areas (with no municipal boundary encompassing even half the total urban area).[11] For example, the Jakarta urban area was home to 23 million people in 2010, up from 16 million a decade earlier, and now covers more than 1,600 square kilometers (map 2.6). The overall Jakarta urban area crosses 12 municipalities and regencies in the provinces of Greater Jakarta, Banten, and West Java.

Administrative fragmentation takes on different forms, each of which requires a distinct approach to metropolitan governance. Smaller municipalities may have space to grow within a single administrative boundary (see "Contained Urban Areas" in box 2.4). The key challenge for governments in this scenario is to manage future urban growth efficiently and

Map 2.6 **The Jakarta, Indonesia, urban area covers 1,600 square kilometers and 12 jurisdictions**

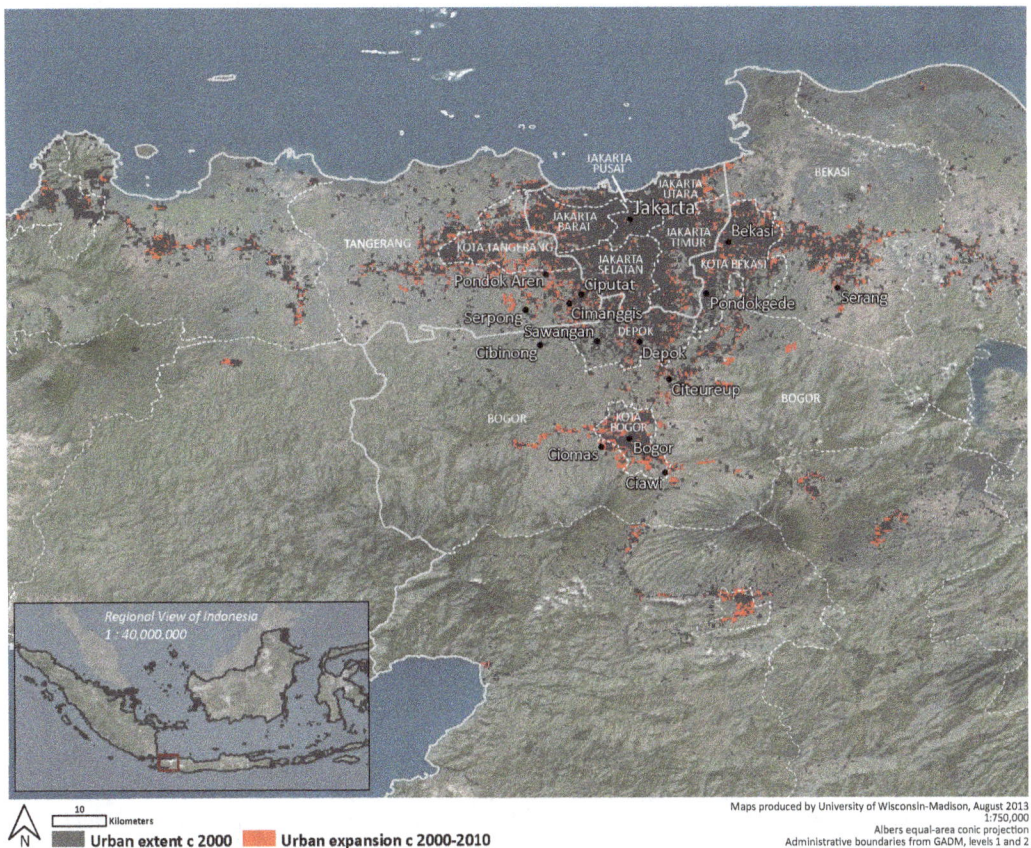

Note: In this map, only labeled areas are counted as part of the Jakarta urban area.

Box 2.4   A typology of urban areas based on administrative fragmentation

Although the size of urban areas is a frequent topic of discussion, another important consideration from the point of view of urban management is the way in which administrative boundaries are arranged in relation to built-up extents of the urban area, independent of size.

The maps accompanying this report show that administrative boundaries intersect with urban extents in a number of ways. There is no ideal arrangement in this regard. Even an administrative boundary that exactly "fits" the extents of an urban area today may not 10 years from now, as urban expansion continues. Instead of trying to somehow match the two perfectly, it is important to understand the benefits and challenges of different arrangements of urban extents and administrative boundaries, as a step toward devising appropriate urban governance institutions and policies. The following categorization, as used in this report, provides a framework for understanding some of these issues.

Contained Urban Areas

In "contained" urban areas, the entire built-up area falls within the relevant administrative boundary, that is, the boundary representing the unit of government responsible for urban management (figure B2.4.1). Some examples of urban areas of this type in East Asia include Hai Phong in Vietnam and Balikpapan in Indonesia.

Figure B2.4.1   Contained urban areas

The benefit of this arrangement is that a single government has the ability to address all the needs of the urban area in an integrated manner. In addition, some of the positive externalities associated with urbanization, such as increased land values, as well as negative externalities, such as pollution, may be contained within one jurisdiction, which provides incentives to that jurisdiction to manage these externalities.

However, the administrative boundary also may encompass rural areas, which means that the government has to balance the differing needs of rural and urban populations. If local governing bodies are selected by popular election, one constituency may dominate, which results in the needs of the minority being neglected.

Another potential challenge of this arrangement, particularly in larger urban areas, is that the main decision-making level of government is removed from the needs of communities within the urban area. This situation could require the creation of smaller district bodies to empower local communities, although if decision-making power is decentralized to this lower level, the urban area is no longer a contained urban area but a fragmented urban area, described later.

(Box continues next page)

Box 2.4   A typology of urban areas based on administrative fragmentation *(continued)*

Spillover Urban Areas

In a "spillover" urban area, urbanization extends beyond the boundary of the jurisdiction in which urban activity originated, into surrounding jurisdictions. For the purposes of this study, a spillover urban area is defined as one in which one jurisdiction still has more than 50 percent of the total built-up area, but less than 100 percent (figure B2.4.2).

Figure B2.4.2   Spillover urban areas

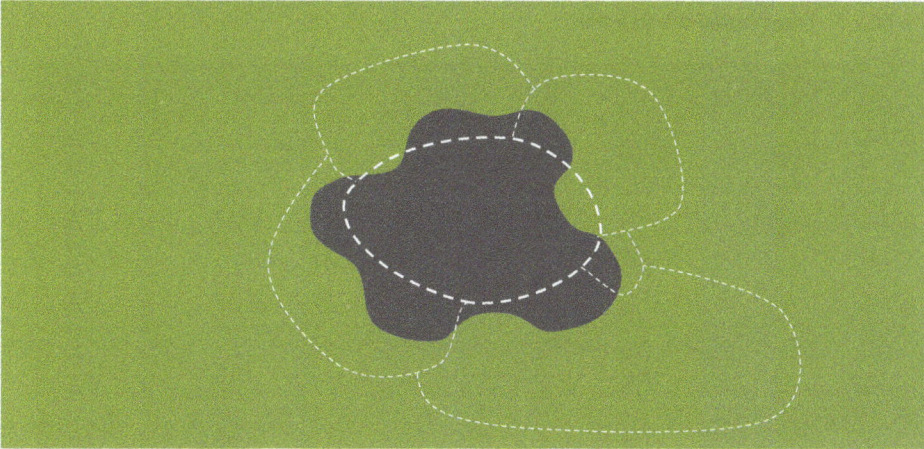

Urban areas of this type include Hangzhou in China, Nha Trang in Vietnam, Bandung in Indonesia, and Ipoh in Malaysia. The entire urban region is usually referred to by the name of the original city at its center, which sometimes obscures the need for additional administrative areas to be involved in its management.

A spillover urban area mostly continues to act as a single entity with regard to its economy, ecology, transportation patterns, and land and housing markets. However, common needs can no longer be met by a single governing body because peri-urban areas are administered separately. The dominant city at the core of this kind of urban area often does not or cannot influence what happens in the peri-urban areas that are located in other jurisdictions.

Public choice theory argues that this arrangement has the advantage of allowing households to choose the municipality that provides the combination of services and taxes that best suits its needs (Tiebout 1956). However, this administrative fragmentation typically leads to inefficient use of resources. For example, if public transportation systems are not coordinated between jurisdictions, the residents of peripheral areas may be forced to take long trips in private vehicles to reach the city center, leading to increased congestion and carbon emissions. If secondary business districts emerge in peri-urban areas, transportation patterns within the original center may change in a way that its transportation system cannot handle. Negative externalities generated by the central city, such as water pollution, may fall on peri-urban jurisdictions that are unable to curtail them.

In many cases, the poor cannot afford expensive land or housing at the center, and are forced to move to the peri-urban areas. These jurisdictions may not have significant own-source revenue and therefore have difficulties providing for the poor. In some cases, the opposite may occur: wealthy households and industries may move out of the central city, leaving the poor in the center, leading to similar problems.

(Box continues next page)

Box 2.4   **A typology of urban areas based on administrative fragmentation** *(continued)*

Fragmented Urban Areas

Administratively fragmented urban areas are similar to spillover urban areas in that they are divided between several administrative jurisdictions. However, fragmented urban areas have not one but several original centers that over time merge across boundaries (figure B2.4.3). Unlike spillover urban areas, fragmented urban areas have no dominant central city, and instead form an extended, sprawling urban region. This study defines those urban areas in which no single jurisdiction has more than 50 percent of the built-up area within it as fragmented urban areas.

Figure B2.4.3   Fragmented urban areas

Multijurisdictional urban areas of this type in East Asia include the Pearl River Delta urban area in China, which incorporates the large cities of Dongguan, Foshan, Guangzhou, and Shenzhen; the Manila urban area in the Philippines, which includes 85 municipalities and cities in seven provinces; and the Tokyo urban area in Japan, which includes 240 municipalities in seven prefectures.

The economies of these large urban areas benefit from their size, through economies of scale and knowledge spillovers, but are often too large to be administered as single entities with no subdivisions. Several additional challenges are involved in managing these fragmented urban areas, many of which are also common to spillover urban areas. In fact, because they are essentially groups of spillover urban areas, these challenges are multiplied. The lack of a distinct center also has disadvantages. Each jurisdiction in this type of region might compete for centrality, leading to uncoordinated infrastructure planning and a "tragedy of the commons." This may take the form of overinvestment: for example, a region that would be best served by a single airport or seaport may instead have several competing ones built in different jurisdictions. Conversely, competition may also lead to underinvestment: for example, no individual jurisdiction may want to bear the expense and externalities of a landfill for the region. Lack of metropolitan coordination may also cause such urban areas to miss opportunities to benefit from economies of scale in financing and maintaining infrastructure and basic services.

In addition, protecting ecological systems, such as rivers, forests, and coastal regions, that may be threatened by urban activities requires consensus and cooperation among neighbors, which is particularly difficult in fragmented urban areas. In theory, a higher level of government, such as a state or province, may take on some of these responsibilities. However, these higher levels are often too large, extending far beyond the urbanized area, encompassing several separate cities, towns, and villages.

Figure 2.18   Fragmentation by size category

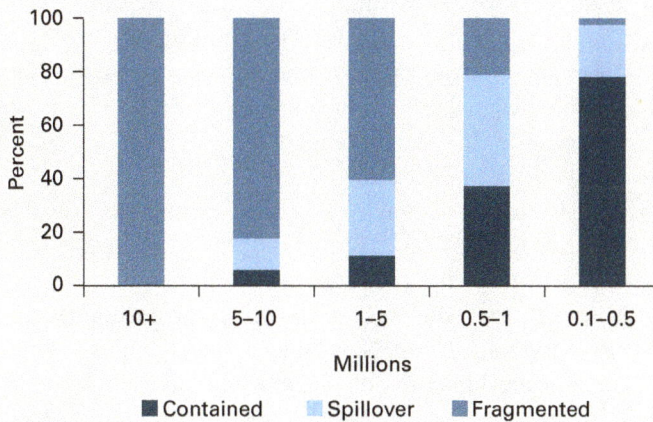

Source: Study team, incorporating WorldPop data, http://www.worldpop.org.uk/data/.

provide equitable access to services to residents within the administrative boundaries that may be physically distant or who lack adequate representation. A second scenario (see "Spillover Urban Areas" in box 2.4) occurs when an urban area expands across several administrative boundaries. This scenario poses challenges to fringe municipalities that have to provide services for residents that are economically integrated into the spillover municipality. A third scenario (see "Fragmented Urban Areas" in box 2.4) requires a great amount of policy coordination and cooperation between various administrative jurisdictions to provide and maintain adequate infrastructure that may cross multiple administrative boundaries.

The challenges that large urban areas encounter as the result of metropolitan fragmentation are soon likely to be faced by medium-sized urban areas, where the majority of population growth and land consumption has occurred. Figure 2.18 shows that fragmentation increases steadily with increasing population size, as one might expect. The majority of urban areas with fewer than 500,000 people are contained within their boundaries, whereas all the megacities are fragmented. As observed previously, the largest amount of urban spatial expansion—that is, increase in absolute land area—has occurred in the small and medium-sized urban areas, many of which are on the cusp of becoming spillover or fragmented urban areas. These urban areas can prepare in advance for the challenges of fragmentation by putting in place mechanisms for collaboration across administrative boundaries, as discussed in chapter 3.

Notes

1. See summary tables in appendix D: Changes in Urban Land, Population, and Density by Country and appendix E: Changes in Urban

Land, Population, and Density in Urban Areas with Population Greater than 1 million; see appendix C for information on how to access the data in digital formats. Because of the large size and population of China, regional averages for East Asia are often skewed by trends in China. Trends in urbanization in the rest of the region, that is, East Asia excluding China, are examined in appendix B.

2. This excludes the city-state of Singapore, which may be considered to have a fully urban population.

3. "CDB's Urbanization Loans Near 1 Trillion in 2013," Xinhua News Agency, January 26, 2014.

4. As of 2014, Cambodia, the Democratic People's Republic of Korea (North Korea), and Myanmar are low-income economies; Indonesia, Lao PDR, Mongolia, Papua New Guinea, the Philippines, Timor-Leste, and Vietnam are lower-middle-income economies. China, Malaysia, and Thailand are upper-middle-income economies. Brunei Darussalam; Japan; the Republic of Korea; Singapore; and Taiwan, China, are high-income economies. All analysis in this report uses this classification regardless of whether their status was different in 2000 or 2010.

5. Note that this is specifically a function of China's high spatial growth rate. When China is excluded, the rate of spatial growth in lower-middle-income countries is higher than in upper-middle-income countries. See figure B.2 in appendix B.

6. The urban areas are usually named after the largest local jurisdiction within them, but they may incorporate other neighboring "cities" as well.

7. The definition of the Pearl River Delta sometimes includes Hong Kong SAR, China, but in this report Hong Kong SAR, China, is considered a distinct urban area. No definitive claim as to largest metropolitan area can be made because there are no directly comparable data for other regions of the world. However, if Tokyo was the largest in the world in 2000, and if no other urban area surpassed Tokyo during this period, the Pearl River Delta is the largest urban area in the world as of 2010.

8. Urban areas are categorized throughout according to their 2010 population, that is, they are not reclassified between 2000 and 2010. For example, the smallest category would include an urban area that had fewer than 100,000 people in 2000 if it crossed the 100,000 threshold by 2010.

This study uses the same population size categorization as the United Nations World Urbanization Prospects, (500,000 to 1 million, 1 million to 5 million, 5 million to 10 million, and more than 10 million), and adds a category for urban areas between 100,000 and 500,000. These size categories are therefore well established, and are easy to grasp. Still, it is important to note that the analysis in this section applies only to this particular classification, and is influenced by the small number of urban areas in the largest size category and the large number in the smallest. How the urban areas are grouped can affect the analysis significantly. For example, the urban areas may be grouped by quantiles (with equal numbers of urban areas in each category), ordered either by urban population or by urban land, each of which emphasizes different trends in the data. Readers interested in experimenting with alternate groupings are encouraged to download the data in spreadsheet form (see appendix C).

9. These land and population trends are heavily influenced by patterns in China. When China is excluded, there is more urban land and urban population in the megacity category than in other categories. See appendix B for figures for the rest of East Asia.

10. Even though the majority of migrant workers would like to settle in urban areas, only 20 percent migrate with their families, and the average stay in the urban area is seven to nine years. This suggests that the hukou system continues to restrict permanent relocation of people. (World Bank and Development Research Center of the State Council, P.R. China 2014)

11. Other than in China, there are, in fact, more spillover urban areas than contained urban areas in East Asia (see appendix B).

References

Angel, S., J. Parent, D. L. Civco, and A. M. Blei. 2010. *Atlas of Urban Expansion*. Cambridge, MA: Lincoln Institute of Land Policy. http://www.lincolninst.edu/subcenters/atlas-urban-expansion/.

Angel, S., S. C. Sheppard, and D. L. Civco. 2005. *The Dynamics of Global Urban Expansion*. Washington, DC: World Bank.

Hoornweg, D., and M. Freire. 2013. *Main Report*. Vol. 1 of *Building Sustainability in an Urbanizing World: A Partnership Report*. Washington, DC: World Bank. http://documents.worldbank.org/curated/en/2.

Johnson, I. 2013. "China's Great Uprooting: Moving 250 Million into Cities." *New York Times*, June 15. http://www.nytimes.com/2013/06/16/world/asia/chinas-great-uprooting-moving-250-million-into-cities.html.

Kamata, T., J. Reichert, T. Tsevegmid, Y. Kim, and B. Sedgewick. 2010. *Managing Urban Expansion in Mongolia: Best Practices in Scenario-Based Urban Planning*. Washington, DC: World Bank.

Seto, K. C., M. Fragkias, B. Güneralp, and M. K. Reilly. 2011. "A Meta-Analysis of Global Urban Land Expansion." *PLOS ONE* 6 (8): e23777.

Tiebout, C. 1956. "A Pure Theory of Local Expenditures." *Journal of Political Economy* 64 (5): 416–24.

United Nations Human Settlements Programme. 2010. *The State of the World's Cities 2010/2011: Bridging the Urban Divide*. London: Earthscan. http://site.ebrary.com/id/10392045.

World Bank. 2009. *World Development Report 2009: Reshaping Economic Geography*. Washington, DC: World Bank.

World Bank. 2012a. "Housing in Indonesia: Expanding Access, Improving Efficiency." World Bank, Washington, DC.

World Bank. 2012b. "Indonesia: The Rise of Metropolitan Regions: Towards Inclusive and Sustainable Regional Development." World Bank, Washington, DC. http://documents.worldbank.org/curated/en /2012/08/16587797/indonesia-rise-metropolitan-regions-towards-inclusive-sustainable-regional-development.

World Bank and Development Research Center of the State Council, P.R. China. 2014. *Urban China: Toward Efficient, Inclusive, and Sustainable Urbanization*. Washington, DC: World Bank.

CHAPTER 3

Recommendations: What Policy Makers Can Do to Facilitate Efficient, Sustainable, and Inclusive Urban Growth

Despite appearances, urban expansion in East Asia has been relatively compact. Despite what may seem like vast sprawl and uncontrolled expansion, East Asian cities are an efficient form of settlement, with an urban population twice the size of that of Europe residing in a smaller amount of urban land (box 2.1). The entire urban population of East Asia, 778 million people, resides on urban land that could fit comfortably within the area of the Lao People's Democratic Republic, Cambodia, or the United Kingdom. All the new urban expansion in the entire region between 2000 and 2010, nearly 200 million people, would fit on the island of Taiwan, China (which is home to just 23 million people). Urban expansion in the region is a means of accommodating vast new urban populations and supporting economic transformation, and as such should be facilitated by both the public and private sectors.

Policy makers at the national and municipal levels have important roles to play in ensuring that urbanization proceeds in an economically efficient, sustainable, and inclusive manner. Urbanization in the region has been largely driven by market forces, which are sensitive to demand for urban growth and adept at responding to this demand. However, market forces left to themselves do not always appropriately manage the positive and negative externalities of urbanization, or provide the public goods that are necessary to support urbanization. A lack of government support to urbanization can lead to uncoordinated and inefficient development and irreversible spatial patterns that result in congestion, pollution, lost productivity, and inequality. Cities and countries need to consider priority investments and policy reforms that will allow urbanization to provide the foundation for long-term growth. Long-term growth is linked to policy options that create jobs, improve living conditions, and expand basic services for urban

Guangzhou is one of the cities in the vast Pearl River Delta urban area in China.

residents, and each of these issues has an important connection to the pattern and physical form of urban growth.

Cities and countries have choices about their urban futures. As noted previously (box 2.2), this study does not attempt to predict future urbanization trends in a deterministic manner, but rather seeks to emphasize that different policy and investment decisions made today can have a range of outcomes. There are many different ways to urbanize. A city can decide to restrict growth, grow in a compact manner, or expand rapidly. A country may decide to spend more on building urban schools, clinics, or parks than on highways and industrial zones. Each society has choices for its urban future, and must base those choices about how to grow and what kind of infrastructure to build on its goals and values. Assuming that economic efficiency, sustainability, and inclusiveness are shared values, policy makers can use their influence over urban form to help urban growth develop in line with these values.

The findings of this study raise a series of questions about how governments can help facilitate economically efficient, sustainable, and inclusive urbanization. The main findings, as discussed in the previous chapter, are the following:

- Despite rapid urban expansion and urban population growth in East Asia, the population of the region is still mostly nonurban, which suggests a large amount of urbanization is still to come.
- The largest amount of urban population growth is occurring in medium-sized urban areas of 1 million to 5 million people, and the largest amount of spatial expansion is occurring in small and medium-sized urban areas with fewer than 5 million people.
- As national incomes rise, urban populations grow first, while countries are at lower-middle-income levels, followed by rapid urban spatial

expansion as they reach upper-middle-income levels, after which their urban form is "locked in" as they move toward high-income levels.

- Increasing urbanization and economic growth are strongly related, but urbanization can exacerbate income inequality within a city if not well planned.
- Urban population densities are high and increasing, although not uniformly.
- Urban areas become increasingly administratively fragmented as they grow, with hundreds of urban areas in the region already crossing local administrative boundaries.

These observations raise the following questions for policy makers:

- How can governments prepare for future urban expansion?
- How can policy makers ensure that their system of cities is economically efficient?
- How can countries ensure that the prosperity that urbanization brings is inclusive?
- How can urban areas grow in an environmentally sustainable way?
- How can large, fragmented urban areas better coordinate among their jurisdictions?
- How can smaller urban areas prepare for future administrative fragmentation as they grow beyond local boundaries?

Preparing for Future Spatial Expansion

In lower-middle-income countries, governments should facilitate access to land for future urban growth. Between 2000 and 2010, 28,000 square kilometers of land in East Asia became urbanized. The fact that the population of East Asia is still not even 50 percent urban suggests that it is likely that much more land will be required for urban expansion in coming decades. Governments have an important role in facilitating the supply of urban land so that urban expansion can occur efficiently and smoothly. This role is particularly important in lower-middle-income countries, which have experienced increasing urban populations and are likely to undergo rapid spatial expansion as incomes increase. In these countries, the alternative to anticipating urban expansion would not be less urban expansion, but haphazard, fragmented, and inefficient urban expansion.

In upper-middle-income countries, cities should support the efficient use of existing built-up urban land. Vacant land on the urban fringe has a lower initial acquisition cost, but the investment needed to extend roads, water, sewage, and other public facilities to new developments presents large, long-term costs to governments. China was home to 80 percent of the new urban expansion in East Asia, and local governments have acquired large amounts of land for urbanization in a short time. However, they have done so in a way that has provoked much resistance on the part of rural land-owners. Municipalities have also tended to rely on the conversion of land

Vietnam's two large urban areas, Hanoi (shown here) and Ho Chi Minh City, expanded rapidly during this period, with both growing more in absolute land area terms than any other urban areas in East Asia outside China.

© Chandan Deuskar, 2012. Used with permission. Further permission required for reuse.

from rural to urban use for revenue, which is considered unsustainable in the long term. As discussed previously, the government has also acquired and built on land in areas where there may not be market demand for urban construction. Urban development plans should identify underutilized or infill sites within or proximate to built-up areas and help bring them into the urban land market.

Expanding cities will require different strategies to integrate surrounding municipalities. For example, the maps from this study show that Beijing, China, and Hanoi, Vietnam, are both surrounded by rural areas with hundreds of very small settlements. By contrast, their respective southern counterparts, Shanghai and Ho Chi Minh City, are surrounded by fewer, larger, and more widely spaced settlements. The infrastructure required in these two different types of regions may need to be different. As Beijing and Hanoi expand, they will need to find ways to integrate the residents of these existing settlements into the larger urban areas, without disrupting their livelihoods or creating pockets of urban poverty that are cut off from the urban economy.

Governments in the region can use a number of potential mechanisms to facilitate access to new urban land while still allowing the private sector to lead construction. Cities can acquire and reserve rights-of-way for the orderly development of a vast area to be developed over several subsequent

The famous Gangnam district in Seoul, Republic of Korea, was created using land readjustment.

decades. Among the most successful examples of this process, known as "guided land development," was the creation of the New York City street grid in the early nineteenth century, which remained reserved for streets even if they took generations to be developed. Similarly, Barcelona and Buenos Aires have historically made advance provisions for future urban expansion (Angel 2012). Cities in India, Japan, the Republic of Korea, and elsewhere have used land pooling/readjustment to acquire land for the expansion of cities, a mechanism that shares the benefits of urban development with the original owners of the land. Other tools such as land sharing and transferable development rights are available to governments to use where appropriate to smooth the conversion of rural to urban land (box 3.1).

Ensuring That Urbanization Is Economically Efficient

National governments can help foster the economic benefits of urbanization through national urbanization strategies that address the country's entire system of cities at once. Across East Asia, national governments are coming to terms with the importance of urbanization to their overall economic growth, and are therefore starting to think about urbanization strategies on a national scale. An important question they face is how to support public investment in a range of cities to foster a diversity of economic activity. It is important for national and regional governments to address the entire system of cities in a coordinated manner because welfare gains in a single city may be crowded out by new migrants. This is less likely to happen if equivalent improvements are made in a range of cities (Duranton 2014). Additionally, efficiencies are to be gained by encouraging different types of industries among cities of different sizes. Research suggests that a system in which large cities focus on services and high-technology manufacturing while small and medium-sized cities specialize in lower-technology manufacturing and agriculture-related industries is more economically efficient. Outside East Asia, manufacturing has initially been concentrated in large cities of countries in the early stages of economic development, then becomes dispersed evenly across the urban system (for example, Brazil), and finally becomes specialized in small cities and rural areas of mature systems (for example, the United States) (Lall and Wang 2012).

Economic differentiation between cities of different sizes can benefit the entire system of cities. Larger cities can support greater economic diversity because of the lower fixed costs associated with setting up a business, scale economies in providing nontraded intermediate inputs, and the

---

Box 3.1   Innovative land tools for urban expansion

In addition to some of the more commonly used policy levers for managing urban land—land regulation, property taxation, and public-private partnerships—city leaders can explore the potential for deploying some innovative land instruments in their cities. Some of these are briefly described below.

Guided Land Development

Guided land development (GLD) refers to the process by which cities and municipalities prepare for anticipated—and likely inevitable—expansion. The experience of many cities in the developing world is that most urban development is occurring in the urban fringes where rural land is converted to urban uses. GLD is a technique for guiding the conversion of privately owned land on the urban periphery from rural to urban use so that development occurs less haphazardly and informally. GLD entails providing a pathway for future infrastructure to steer urban development. The infrastructure itself may not be built until later when population density justifies making those investments. The appeal of GLD to local governments is that it is less expensive than outright land acquisition, and landowners contribute toward the cost. The landowners' contribution is twofold. First, they contribute by donating land for roads and rights-of-way for infrastructure. Second, they may contribute by paying betterment levies—justified because of the increased value of the land from the infrastructure and the conversion from rural to urban use. Individual landowners can then subdivide and service their own land. GLD tackles the inevitability of urban growth head-on.

Land Pooling/Readjustment

Urban land pooling/readjustment (LP/R) is a technique normally used for managing and financing the subdivision of selected urban fringe areas for urban development. Sometimes it is also used for inner-city redevelopment. In each LP/R project, a group of separate land parcels are consolidated for unified design, servicing, and subdivision into a layout of roads, utility service lines, open spaces, and building plots. The sale of some of the plots is then used for project cost recovery, and the now smaller—but higher-value—lots are distributed back to the landowners in exchange for their rural

(Box continues next page)

Box 3.1   Innovative land tools for urban expansion *(continued)*

land. The approach is widely used in Japan; the Republic of Korea; and Taiwan, China, and is being transferred to the developing countries of Southeast and South Asia. LP/R projects are mainly undertaken by local governments. The attraction of LP/R for landowners is that they can share in the land value gains from urbanization. For local governments, the technique ensures efficient urbanization of land at reduced cost because the project site and infrastructure rights-of-way do not have to be purchased or compulsorily acquired.

Transfer of Development Rights

Although development rights are usually linked with a physical piece of land, the right to develop land can be separated from the land itself. This separation and transfer of development rights can provide local governments with an innovative way to meet certain social and economic goals and channel development to specific locations in the process. Referred to as transfer of land development rights, this mechanism involves purchasing development rights—usually from areas where development is to be discouraged—and using them to develop land in another location—in areas where more development or density is desired. In effect, the owner is being paid to not develop in one location and to develop somewhere else.

Land Sharing

Land sharing is an agreement between the unauthorized occupants of a piece of land and the landowner. It essentially involves the occupants moving off the high-value portion of land in return for being allowed to either rent or buy a part of the land at a price below its market value. The advantage to landowners is that they are able to regain control of the site, proceed with development plans, and realize higher commercial returns from the land without having to evict the occupants. In return, residents are rehoused in better-quality housing with services, gain legitimate tenure, and are able to continue living close to their established livelihoods.

Source: Lipman and Rajack 2011.

---

fact that larger cities have a higher propensity to produce high-tech and experimental items that require a diversity of skills and production types to thrive (Jacobs 1969; Duranton and Puga 2001). A significant share of the population in the high-income countries in East Asia, as well as in other developed countries such as the United States, is in large metropolitan areas. However, this is not yet the case in China, where, despite the massive size of its megacities, most of the population remains in small and medium-sized urban areas, in part because of migration restrictions that have only recently been eased (Au and Henderson 2006; World Bank and Development Research Center of the State Council, P.R. China 2014). In lower-middle-income countries, the largest proportion of the population is in megacities, but their economic growth may be stifled by the lack of dispersal of manufacturing. The agglomeration effects mentioned above are much more important for services and high-tech industries than for more traditional manufacturing or other industries, which are land intensive and benefit more from the lower costs of locating in small and medium-sized cities instead. However, these industries often remain in large cities because of the inadequate infrastructure or access to labor in other cities, or limited connectivity between cities. This lack of dispersal of manufacturing makes it difficult for large cities to develop industries that add higher value. Addressing the needs of small and medium-sized cities and making it easier for them to specialize while simultaneously fostering positive agglomeration effects in large cities can help bring about a more efficient distribution of industries in cities.

Governments should support investment in small and medium-sized cities. As shown in chapter 2, the largest amount of urban growth is occurring in small and medium-sized cities. Evidence suggests that differentiation of economic activity is occurring in some countries in the region. For example, in Vietnam manufacturing employment is still concentrated in larger cities, but growth in manufacturing employment between 1999 and 2009 was higher in small and medium-sized cities, suggesting that the dispersal described above is occurring (World Bank 2011). In Indonesia, productivity growth has actually been highest in smaller cities in recent years. However, given their lack of technical and financial capacity, small and medium-sized cities may face a rapid deterioration in service levels and quality of life unless they effectively address the challenges posed by rapid growth (World Bank 2012). China has a policy of moving rural residents to towns close to their original homes rather than to megacities, a process known as *chengzhenhua* (which has been translated as "city- and town-ification," as opposed to *dushihua*, or "urbanization"). This shift in focus of the urbanization strategy, from megacities to small and medium-sized cities, is intended to narrow regional gaps in economic growth (Yinan 2014). However, concerns about the economic viability of these rural towns suggest that rather than directing people to certain types of cities, governments may achieve more by fostering the right environment for economic development of a range of city sizes (Johnson 2013a; Shih 2013). Through national urban development grants, revolving funds, financial intermediaries, and other means, national governments can play a role in channeling private and public investment to small and medium-sized cities, where the private sector may be reluctant to invest on its own.

Ensuring That Urbanization Is Inclusive

Spatial planning can help reduce inequality in access to urban opportunities and amenities. As discussed in the previous chapter, urbanization has been associated with economic growth, but not necessarily with reducing inequality. The pattern of urban form is one of many factors that affect the ability of the urban poor to access economic opportunities in their cities. Ensuring a spatial match between jobs, affordable retail, public transportation, health and education services, recreational areas, and affordable housing is among the means of fostering such access. Areas with shorter commutes and lower travel costs have significantly higher upward mobility, as evidenced in research in the United States (Chetty and others 2014). In spatially efficient cities, time that the poor would otherwise spend commuting can instead be spent generating income, and household resources that would have been spent on commuting to work or accessing other services can otherwise be spent on food or education. Research also suggests that the distances people must travel to work directly influence their subjective well-being, with shorter commutes being associated with greater self-reported levels of happiness (Stutzer and Frey 2004). In large East Asian cities, commutes may be relatively short, as in Hanoi, where people often live above their places of work, or several hours long, as in Jakarta.

Land acquisition for urban expansion can be disruptive, but it can also help bring opportunities to peri-urban residents. How to bring peri-urban land into the urban land market in ways that respect the rights of the original occupants of the land and does not disrupt their livelihoods is a concern faced by governments throughout the region. There is evidence in China that taking land from rural farmers and relocating them to high-rise towers in new towns causes social and psychological damage, with reports of high unemployment and frequent suicides (Johnson 2013b). As the authors of a World Bank report on urbanization in China note:

> Land lies at the heart of China's urbanization challenges and is the highest priority for reform. . . . Strengthening property rights on rural land and clarifying collective ownership arrangements would also increase the compensation that accrues to farmers in land transactions, thus making urbanization more inclusive (World Bank and Development Research Center of the State Council, P.R. China 2014, 38).

Land pooling/readjustment and land sharing (box 3.1) are among the mechanisms that governments in the region have used to allow original land users to share in the benefits of extending urban infrastructure and services to peri-urban areas, by allowing them to retain some of the land in the newly developed areas. Within East Asia, Japan and the Republic of Korea used land pooling/readjustment extensively during the twentieth century, and Indonesia and Vietnam have also experimented with forms of this tool.

New housing must be affordable. International evidence suggests that housing investment takes off at income levels of about $3,000 per capita (that is, the lower-middle-income range) and then slows at income levels of about $36,000 per capita (well into the high-income range). Consistent with these trends, housing investment in developing East Asia has grown by 9 percent between 2001 and 2011, with aggregate housing investment keeping pace with urbanization (Dasgupta, Lall, and Lozano 2014). However, most countries in the region face severe challenges in providing affordable housing to their residents. The cost of homeownership in cities across much of the region exceeds 50–60 percent of annual household incomes, significantly higher than the internationally recognized affordability level of 30 percent. Public homeownership subsidies, public rental programs, and private housing provisions have all struggled to deliver affordable housing to the poorest, instead favoring middle-income households. The poor

*Adequate housing and transportation remains unaffordable in many of East
Asia's urban areas, including Jakarta, Indonesia, forcing the urban poor to live
in informal settlements.*

© Jonathan McIntosh, 2004. Used via a Creative Commons license, creativecommons.org
/licenses/by-sa/2.0.

are left with no choice but to seek housing in informal areas, despite their
lack of tenure security, exposure to environmental hazards, and unhealthy
physical environment (World Bank 2014).

Addressing the vulnerabilities of recent rural-to-urban migrants can help
ensure that rapid urbanization is inclusive. Mishra (2014) suggests that
"the urbanized villager may turn out to define the future of Asia." Nearly
200 million people became urban residents between 2000 and 2010. These
newly urban residents, and the millions that will follow them, are economically and socially vulnerable as they adapt to new industries and lifestyles,
often without traditional social and economic support networks. The large
influx of migrants to Chinese cities, where migrants outnumber local residents in some cases, has been accompanied by social tensions, sometimes
leading to violent riots (World Bank and Development Research Center
of the State Council, P.R. China 2014). Household dynamics also change
in cities, often in ways that can restrict employment options for women,
who, in the absence of extended family networks for child care, have to
become full-time housewives or must work at home (Hew 2003). Poor
women who live in slums and informal settlements are more vulnerable
to the health hazards and other environmental stressors recurrent in these
neighborhoods, including crime, contamination of water, and exposure to
communicable diseases (United Nations Human Settlements Programme
2013). Cultural traditions rooted in centuries of rural life are often lost

in the new urban societies, where rural culture is often seen as backward (Johnson 2014). In rapidly urbanizing countries worldwide, strong anti-migrant sentiment often erupts in cities, leading to social exclusion and even violence, particularly if this sentiment is exploited by political interests.[1] Evidence from China and India suggests that migrants who do not find economic opportunities in cities often are forced to return to less productive, rural occupations (Anderlini 2014; Zhong and Dutta 2014). By paying special attention to these vulnerable recent migrants and helping them gain a foothold in urban society and the urban economy, local governments, together with civic organizations and nongovernmental organizations, can help make urbanization more inclusive.

Smaller cities are important from the point of view of targeting the poor. Despite the high visibility of urban poverty in large cities, residents of smaller cities are often the most deprived of economic opportunity. For example, in China, more than 80 percent of the urban "underclass" (the relatively poor who live on less than twice the World Bank poverty line) live in smaller (prefectural or lower-level) cities (Lall and Wang 2012).

Ensuring That Urbanization Is Sustainable

The high population densities of East Asia's urban areas are a valuable asset that potentially gives them a considerable advantage over urban areas elsewhere in the world. Sufficiently high urban densities can result in a range of positive outcomes. In addition to economic advantages, such as more efficient provision of services, lower shipping costs for goods, and knowledge spillovers, high density can also result in lower carbon emissions from reduced vehicular trips and lower energy consumption for heating and cooling, along with healthier lifestyles and the conservation of nature (Dodman 2009; Glaeser 2013; Glaeser and Kahn 2003). Although higher density is often popularly associated with traffic congestion, in fact, congestion may be caused or exacerbated by low-density development, which results in a greater number and length of vehicular trips (CEOs for Cities 2010). High-density destinations take the blame for traffic congestion, even though they are paying the price for the traffic generated by widely dispersed origins.

Although sufficient urban density is important for sustainability, simply adding more density is not a key priority in already dense East Asian urban areas. In many parts of the world the need to increase urban densities is critical, but this is not the case everywhere. As others have noted, the focus on densification alone may not be as relevant for many developing countries, where "densities are already high and associated with a range of problems including infrastructure overload, overcrowding, congestion, air pollution, severe health hazards, lack of public and green space and environmental degradation" (Burgess 2000, 9). As Angel and others (2010, 109) put it, "Urban containment and compact city policies may be less relevant in rapidly growing cities with much higher densities than those prevailing in the U.S. . . . In some developing-country cities, densities are

Hong Kong SAR, China, remains the densest urban area in East Asia.

© Hamedog, 2005. Used via a Creative Commons license, creativecommons.org/licenses /by-sa/3.0.

too high, and calling for containing their expansion so as to increase densities is misplaced."[2]

Ensuring that density is well located, coordinated, and designed can help ensure that it contributes to sustainability. The majority of urban areas in East Asia are already dense and becoming denser. To ensure that this density contributes to sustainable outcomes, planners, policy makers, and developers in these areas should allow density to locate where there is demand for it; support density by coordinating it with the location of jobs, services, and public transportation; and design density so that it produces a walkable, livable urban environment. Such coordination of origins, destinations, and transportation corridors can result in fewer, shorter trips; more trips made by nonmotorized transportation modes (walking and bicycling); and more use of public transportation modes, all of which reduce the carbon footprint of a city. Although vehicle ownership is increasing rapidly in East Asian countries, most still have lower rates of vehicle ownership than more economically advanced regions, which means that the opportunity to take a relatively low-carbon approach to urban growth is still available.[3]

The sustainability of urban form can be enhanced by improving road networks and transportation options and mixing allowable land uses. Not all density is equally beneficial. For example, "superblocks" of purely residential high-rise buildings surrounded by multilane highways, a common type of development in China, have high density without many of the benefits of well-designed urban spaces, and have been criticized as "high-density sprawl" (Dumaine 2012). This urban development model is increasingly seen elsewhere in the region. A recent study of walkability in China found that blocks immediately surrounding metro stations in Beijing were 4 times larger than equivalent blocks in New York and 2.5 times larger than in

Table 3.1   Comparison of connectivity in Chinese and other cities

	Turin, Italy	Barcelona, Spain	Paris, France	Pudong, Shanghai	Hutong in Beijing	New areas in Beijing
Urban grid						
Intersections per square kilometer	152	103	133	17	119	14
Distance between intersections	80	130	150	280	75	400

Source: World Bank and Development Research Center of the State Council, P.R. China 2014.

London (table 3.1). Large blocks like this may have high average population densities, but they reduce the frequency of intersections and make transportation nodes and other amenities less accessible to residents, counteracting the benefits of population density (Qu and others 2014).

As a World Bank study on urbanization in China puts it:

> Density (demographic or FAR [floor area ratio]) is not the only characteristic of compact sustainable cities. Proximity and accessibility, mixed-use, [and] connectedness are also preconditions for the formation of agglomeration economies for addressing social inclusiveness and environmental wellbeing. They should be enhanced in an adaptive strategic planning process by increasing progressively the number of intersections per square kilometer and the linear density of streets to develop the connectivity and create a more fine-grain urban fabric.

The density of public amenities such as public parks and health care, child care, and education facilities should be increased, to create a city where most daily amenities are available within a five minute walk. Finally, cities should mix commercial space, offices, and residential areas to reduce the distance residents have to travel to their jobs or recreational space. Articulated densities will allow more efficient and cleaner transport modes to become viable and affordable, such as biking, walking, and public transit systems. Densification is not an end in itself, but a means of improving the sustainability, connectivity, accessibility, and diversity of the city as well as its vitality (World Bank and Development Research Center of the State Council, P.R. China 2014, 142).

The coordination of land use and transportation can increase land values, the benefits of which can be used to enhance accessibility. Cities in which public transportation is convenient, affordable, and well coordinated with land use can reduce commute times (for both public and private vehicles) and carbon emissions. Transportation access can enhance land values, provided that transit corridors are coordinated with population centers,

"Superblocks" of high-rise residential towers surrounded by highways are a common form of construction in Chinese cities like Xi'an. While providing high density, they do not provide many of the benefits usually associated with density, like walkability.

© miumiu熊, 2011. Used via a Creative Commons license, creativecommons.org/licenses /by-sa/2.0.

locations of jobs, and other important destinations. Governments can capture the increases in land value brought about by public transportation investments and use this revenue to enhance the accessibility of surrounding urban areas (box 3.2).

Box 3.2   Creating and sharing higher land value in transit development

By changing land use regulations, such as allocating higher floor area ratios and converting land from single to mixed use, governments can increase densities in transit station areas for diverse uses while increasing revenues. By using proceeds for investments—such as parks, street lights, bike lanes, and pedestrian sidewalks—in station areas; governments, transit agencies, developers, and communities can jointly develop efficient, attractive, and safe public places, further increasing property values.

Consider the Rail + Property Program of Hong Kong SAR, China, implemented by the Mass Transit Railway Corporation (MTRC). Under the mechanism, the government gives exclusive property development rights on government-owned land at a before-rail market price. MTRC then captures the land value increment created, such as accessibility and agglomeration benefits, by partnering with private firms to develop the land and by selling the completed development at an "after-rail" market price; it recoups the capital, operating, and maintenance costs of railway projects through profit sharing. That process also allows MTRC to integrate different phases of rail and property development projects, ensuring smooth project implementation and reducing transaction costs.

Source: Suzuki, Cervero, and Iuchi 2013.

A pedestrianized street in Singapore ensures that people can take advantage of the density of destinations in the city.

Although most urban areas in the region have high and increasing densities, this is not the case for all urban areas in the region. Urban densities in upper-middle-income and high-income countries are lower than in low- and lower-middle-income countries, which means that as incomes rise, densities are likely to level off and possibly fall in future decades, as vehicle ownership increases and residents are able to afford more living space per capita. In particular, Malaysia and Mongolia face difficulties typically associated with low urban density and widely dispersed urban growth. In these cases, governments may need to create or maintain a certain level of density, using the location of infrastructure and regulation as levers of influence in local land markets, to avoid the environmental costs and the inefficiencies in service provision associated with urban expansion at low density.

Risk-sensitive land use planning can guide future development to reduce exposure to climate and disaster risks. Rapidly growing cities in developing countries often expand into unsafe areas such as floodplains, water catchments, and steep hillsides, exposing those who live in these areas, typically the urban poor, to hazards, and weakening the resilience of the city as a whole. Ensuring that new urban growth skirts high-risk areas can save lives and prevent property damage. Risk-sensitive land use planning and management, which takes into account flood, seismic, and other risks, has been described as the most effective means of integrating climate change and disaster-risk-reduction policies into urban planning and management (Baker 2012). Natural disasters are a particularly important problem for

Low-density development in Ulaanbaatar, Mongolia, makes the provision of services difficult. It also makes accessibility to jobs and schools expensive and time-consuming for the urban poor.

© Chandan Deuskar, 2012. Used with permission. Further permission required for reuse.

urban areas in this region: a ranking of world cities by size of population vulnerable to a range of natural disasters found that the six most vulnerable urban areas in the world were in East Asia.[4]

Overcoming Metropolitan Fragmentation

The prosperity of East Asia's urban areas in coming decades will depend in large measure on tackling the challenge of governing metropolitan regions effectively. Almost 350 urban areas in East Asia are already multi-jurisdictional, with 135 of them having no dominant local jurisdiction. For example, the Pearl River Delta urban area in China incorporates the large cities of Dongguan, Foshan, Guangzhou, and Shenzhen. The Manila urban area in the Philippines includes 85 municipalities and cities in seven provinces. The Greater Tokyo urban area in Japan includes 240 munici-palities in seven prefectures. Although municipal governments will continue to have an important role in providing transportation, health, and edu-cational infrastructure to support economic activity, in fragmented urban areas like these, the coverage and quality of services and infrastructure are often uneven. For governments, donor agencies, and international develop-ment institutions, addressing issues relating to urban transportation, land and housing markets, or infrastructure deficits without working at the level of the whole urban area will be nearly impossible. In fact, working with

Tokyo, Japan, has developed elaborate institutional arrangements to deliver services across its large metropolitan area.

only one municipality in isolation within an urban area could even cause new problems or exacerbate existing weaknesses. Resolving this challenge will not be easy because it will involve tackling the logistical and political complexities of forging multijurisdictional coalitions, some of which may have conflicting priorities.

International experience suggests that regional governmental authorities and other mechanisms can help coordinate urban service provision across municipal boundaries. Box 3.3 reviews examples. In many countries, single-sector or limited-subject metropolitan agencies may be created by national law, as with the Syndicat des transports d'Île-de-France (STIF), or by provincial law, as in Vancouver, Canada. Such agencies may be formed by voluntary associations of municipalities, as in most French metropolitan areas and in Recife, Brazil. In France, the formation of an *autorite organizatrice* (AO), though voluntary, is strongly encouraged in national law, which gives an area setting up an AO the right to levy an employment tax specifically earmarked for public transportation. There are even cases, such as the Washington Metropolitan Area Transit Authority in the United States, in which the parties to the agreement (the District of Columbia and some districts in the states of Maryland and Virginia) have different legal status and special powers.

Decentralization, despite its many benefits, carries with it a particular set of challenges for metropolitan coordination. Proponents of fiscal federalism strongly favor decentralization of power to the local level, which they argue

Box 3.3   Some models of metropolitan governance

Several metropolitan areas across the world have attempted some form of metropolitan governance:

- In 1970, the province of Manitoba, Canada, combined the Corporation of Greater Winnipeg and its districts into a single town, Winnipeg. Similarly, Toronto created a metropolitan government in 1998, dissolving the lower tier of government; and the province of Quebec in 2000 created the new, enlarged municipal areas of Montreal and Quebec.
- The Community of Madrid and the Grand Paris Region have greater powers than their constituent municipalities.
- Cape Town consolidated various local governments into a single "unicity" in 2000.
- The Greater London Authority is a slightly weaker form of metropolitan governance, with power mostly over transport and police functions.
- Parastatal bodies in India created by state governments, such as the Mumbai Metropolitan Region Development Authority, are more technocratic than political institutions, and are growing in importance, but have had mixed success so far.
- Other metropolitan areas have created special bodies to provide specific services to the entire area, for example, the metropolitan areas of Sydney, Australia, and Lima-Callao, Santiago de Chile, and Bogotá in South America, as well as metropolitan transit agencies in several metropolitan areas in the United States.
- The Regional Plan Association provides long-term integrated planning for the metropolitan region of New York, and despite being a nongovernmental organization, has a strong influence on planning decisions for the region.

Several metropolitan areas in East Asia have some form of metropolitan governance:

- The urban wards within the Tokyo prefecture deliver services on behalf of the Tokyo Metropolitan Government, which is one of many players involved in regional governance, along with prefectures, regional ministerial offices, Japan Railway, and private companies.
- The Bangkok Metropolitan Administration was created by merging Bangkok and Thonburi. Similar absorption of at least some functions and responsibilities of lesser towns has occurred in Seoul, Kuala Lumpur, Surabaya, and Jakarta.
- The Seoul Metropolitan Government is run by a mayor and an elected assembly, and encompasses 25 districts.
- The Chinese government created metropolitan towns directed by powerful mayors who are appointed by the state in Beijing, Chongqing, Guangzhou, Shanghai, and Tianjin. On the inframetropolitan level, districts still exist, but with reduced authority and budgets. This situation sometimes leads to friction between the metropolitan level and the affected areas.
- The Metro Manila Development Authority (MMDA) was created by Filipino legislation in 1995. The MMDA, which is under the direct control of the president of the Philippines, is responsible for planning, monitoring, and coordination tasks. However, its budgetary resources and regulatory powers remain limited.

Sources: Bahl, Linn, and Wetzel 2013; Sellers and Hoffmann-Martinot 2008.

increases efficiency of service delivery and promotes healthy competition between municipalities to attract residents to live, work, and invest within their jurisdictions. However, the applicability of fiscal federalism to developing countries has also been challenged for a number of reasons (Oates 2006; Smoke 2001). For example, the urban poor and recent migrants often face constraints on where they can locate and what information they have access to. Decentralization may also fail to take into account either economies of scale in provision of services, as with electricity and transportation, or the existence of interjurisdictional externalities such as poverty, crime, or traffic, which make the total cost of certain services more expensive or redundant.[5]

Overcoming issues related to metropolitan fragmentation requires trade-offs between localized and centralized administrative authority. Solutions to metropolitan fragmentation include creating new metropolitan government structures, annexing adjacent territories, and dissolving the lowest tier of government. However, these actions usually face great political resistance from entrenched interests, including some who would legitimately lose a voice if authority were less decentralized. Equity might also be attained at the expense of efficiency (and vice versa). The desire for greater representation and "home rule" brings decision making closer to local residents and allows for investments that match local priorities. Yet the wealthy and the poor could end up segregated in different local jurisdictions because the poor may lack the resources or organization to effect change, reinforcing fiscal and social disparities (Sellers and Hoffmann-Martinot 2008). A more centralized metropolitan governance approach aims for equitable outcomes for particular services across the entire metropolitan area. Yet ultimately, as Bahl, Linn, and Wetzel (2013, 5) observe, "there is no good evidence to prove the better results from one system than from another, and, of course, 'better' also depends on what local voters want from their government." Cities must therefore adopt a flexible approach that can adapt to urban growth and evolve with the changing needs of citizens.

Conclusions and Areas for Further Research

This study used data that are available at the regional scale (data on built-up areas, populations, administrative boundaries, and national-level income and income inequality) to allow consistent comparison of urbanization trends across all of East Asia. Analysis using these data sources alone already constitutes a step forward in the understanding of urbanization trends in the region, which have not previously been examined at this scale in a consistent manner. The analysis has yielded a few key insights. First, it has drawn attention to the importance of small and medium-sized urban areas in a region in which megacities often dominate the discourse on urbanization. The study highlights the need for policy makers to support the development of these smaller urban areas in ways that can benefit the entire system of cities. Second, the analysis has shown that despite concerns about urban sprawl of the kind commonly observed in many other parts of the world, urban areas in East Asia are, on the whole, dense and becoming denser in most countries, and in every national income group and size category. This observation underscores the need for not just high density, but density that is well coordinated, located, and designed. Last, overlaying administrative boundaries on urban extents has confirmed that the management of large and medium-sized urban areas cannot be thought of as

Urban areas in the Republic of Korea are among the densest in the region, but cities like Seoul are taking steps to ensure that public spaces are available for recreation.

the domain of individual governments alone, calling attention to the need for mechanisms of metropolitan cooperation between neighboring jurisdictions and multiple tiers of government.

The use of region-wide data has deepened our understanding, but there are many fruitful directions for further research that can combine this data (which are being publicly released in several formats; see appendix C) with other data sets that may be available for individual countries or cities. Two areas of research in particular seem relevant: First, these additional data would allow researchers to examine the effects of policies (for example, tenure regularization, housing subsidies, or fuel subsidies) or the provision of infrastructure (such as highway or rail networks) on urban expansion, urban form, and population density. Second, the data from this study could be combined with national or local data to determine the impact of urban growth on the environment, including on carbon emissions, air pollution, energy consumption, and food security. Conducting analysis along these lines, and acting on the insights that it yields, can play a part in helping to improve the lives of hundreds of millions of people during the coming decades of East Asia's urban transformation.

Notes

1. "Chronology: MNS's Tirade against North Indians," *Hindustan Times*, February 2, 2010. http://www.hindustantimes.com/india-news /chronology-mns-s-tirade-against-north-indians/article1-504339.aspx.

2. The debate on the dangers of urban sprawl and low-density suburbanization has perhaps been most active in the United States, and it is important to note how different the densities in question are from those in East Asia. In 2010, the average population density of all Metropolitan Statistical Areas in the United States was about 110 people per square kilometer (Wilson 2012) compared with 5,800 people per square kilometer in all urban areas in East Asia, more than 50 times higher. Looking just at metropolitan areas of 5 million or more people, the average population density in the United States was 490 people per square kilometer as opposed to about 7,100 people per square kilometer in East Asia. The densest metropolitan area in the United States (New York–Northern New Jersey–Long Island) had an average density of 1,100 people per square kilometer (still less than the East Asia average), as opposed to the densest urban area in East Asia (Hong Kong SAR, China), at 32,100 people per square kilometer. Although, given different methods of defining metropolitan areas and urban populations, the U.S. data may not be perfectly comparable to the data from this study, they provide an indication of why the debates about density and sprawl in most of East Asia must differ from those in countries like the United States.

3. World Development Indicators (database), World Bank, Washington, DC, data.worldbank.org.

4. These were Tokyo-Yokohama, Manila, the Pearl River Delta, Osaka-Kobe, Jakarta, and Nagoya (Swiss Reinsurance Company 2013). These urban areas were defined differently by Swiss Re than in this study.

5. An example of higher cost and redundancies would include a group of contiguous municipalities that each have their own separate police services, rather than a single force that serves all jurisdictions under a joint agreement.

References

Anderlini, J. 2014. "FT Series The Fragile Middle: China's Migrant Workers Test Urbanisation Drive," *Financial Times*, April 14.

Angel, S. 2012. *Planet of Cities*. Cambridge, MA: Lincoln Institute of Land Policy.

Angel, S., J. Parent, D. L. Civco, and A. M. Blei. 2010. "The Persistent Decline in Urban Densities: Global and Historical Evidence of 'Sprawl'." Lincoln Institute of Land Policy, Cambridge, MA.

Au, C.-C., and J. V. Henderson. 2006. "Are Chinese Cities Too Small?" *Review of Economic Studies* 73 (3): 549–76.

Bahl, R. W., J. F. Linn, and D. L. Wetzel. 2013. *Financing Metropolitan Governments in Developing Countries*. Cambridge, MA: Lincoln Institute of Land Policy.

Baker, J. L., ed. 2012. *Climate Change, Disaster Risk, and the Urban Poor: Cities Building Resilience for a Changing World*. Washington, DC: World Bank.

Burgess, R. 2000. "The Compact City Debate: A Global Perspective." In *Compact Cities: Sustainable Urban Forms for Developing Countries,* edited by M. Jenks and R. Burgess, 9–23. London and New York: Spon Press.

CEOs for Cities. 2010. "Driven Apart." CEOs for Cities, Cleveland, OH.

Chetty, R., N. Hendren, P. Kline, E. Saez, and N. Turner. 2014. "Is the United States Still a Land of Opportunity? Recent Trends in Intergenerational Mobility." NBER Working Paper 19844, National Bureau of Economic Research, Cambridge, MA.

Dasgupta, B., S. Lall, and N. Lozano. 2014. "Urbanization and Housing Investment." Policy Research Working Paper 7110, World Bank, Washington, DC.

Dodman, D. 2009. "Urban Density and Climate Change." United Nations Population Fund, New York.

Dumaine, B. 2012. "Rethinking China's Cities," *Fortune*, December 3.

Duranton, G. 2014. *Growing through Cities in Developing Countries.* Washington, D.C.: World Bank.

Duranton, G., and D. Puga. 2001. "Nursery Cities: Urban Diversity, Process Innovation, and the Life Cycle of Products." *American Economic Review* 91 (5): 1454–77.

Glaeser, E. L. 2013. "A World of Cities: The Causes and Consequences of Urbanization in Poorer Countries." NBER Working Paper 19745, National Bureau of Economic Research, Cambridge, MA.

Glaeser, E. L., and M. E. Kahn. 2003. "Sprawl and Urban Growth." NBER Working Paper 9733, National Bureau of Economic Research, Cambridge, MA.

Hew, C. S. 2003. "The Impact of Urbanization on Family Structure: The Experience of Sarawak, Malaysia." *Sojourn: Social Issues in Southeast Asia* 18 (1): 89–109.

Jacobs, J. 1969. *The Economy of Cities.* New York: Random House.

Johnson, I. 2013a. "Pitfalls Abound in China's Push from Farm to City." *New York Times*, July 13. http://www.nytimes.com/2013/07/14/world/asia/pitfalls-abound-in-chinas-push-from-farm-to-city.html.

———. 2013b. "New China Cities: Shoddy Homes, Broken Hope." *New York Times,* November 9. http://www.nytimes.com/2013/11/10/world/asia/new-china-cities-shoddy-homes-broken-hope.html.

———. 2014. "In China, 'Once the Villages Are Gone, the Culture Is Gone'." *New York Times*, February 1. http://www.nytimes.com/2014/02/02/world/asia/once-the-villages-are-gone-the-culture-is-gone.html.

Lall, S., and H. G. Wang. 2012. "China Urbanization Review: Balancing Urban Transformation and Spatial Inclusion." World Bank, Washington, DC.

Lipman, B., and R. Rajack. 2011. *Memo to the Mayor: Improving Access to Urban Land for All Residents—Fulfilling the Promise.* Washington, DC: World Bank.

Mishra, P. 2014. "Urban Villagers Are Asia's New Force," *Bloomberg News,* January 14. http://www.bloomberg.com/news/2014-01-14/urban-villagers-are-asia-s-new-force.html.

Oates, W. 2006. "On the Theory and Practice of Fiscal Decentralization." Working Paper 2006-05, Institute for Federalism and Intergovernmental Relations, Lexington, KY.

Qu, L., Y. Gao, A. Salzberg, and G. Ollivier. 2014. "Walkability Analysis for Chinese Transit Oriented Development: A Case Study in Nanchang." World Bank, Washington, DC.

Sellers, J. M., and V. Hoffmann-Martinot. 2008. "Metropolitan Governance." In *Decentralization and Local Democracy in the World: First Global Report by United Cities and Local Governments*, 255–79. Washington, DC: World Bank and United Cities and Local Governments.

Shih, M. 2013. "Making Rural China Urban." *The China Story Journal.* http://www.thechinastory.org/2013/06/making-rural-china-urban/.

Smoke, P. J. 2001. *Fiscal Decentralization in Developing Countries: A Review of Current Concepts and Practice.* Geneva: United Nations Research Institute for Social Development.

Stutzer, A., and B. S. Frey. 2004. "Stress That Doesn't Pay: The Commuting Paradox." IZA Discussion Paper 1278, Institute for the Study of Labor, Bonn.

Swiss Reinsurance Company. 2013. *Mind the Risk: A Global Ranking of Cities under Threat from Natural Disasters.* Zurich: Swiss Reinsurance Company.

Suzuki, Hiroaki, Robert Cervero, and Kanako Iuchi. 2013. *Transforming Cities with Transit: Transit and Land-use Integration for Sustainable Urban Development.* Washington, DC: World Bank.

United Nations Human Settlements Programme. 2013. *State of Women in Cities 2012–2013: Gender and the Prosperity of Cities.* Nairobi, Kenya: UN-HABITAT.

Wilson, S. G. 2012. *Patterns of Metropolitan and Micropolitan Population Change, 2000 to 2010.* Washington, DC: U.S. Department of Commerce, Economics and Statistics Administration, U.S. Census Bureau.

World Bank. 2011. *Vietnam Urbanization Review: Technical Assistance Report.* Washington, DC: World Bank.

———. 2012. "Indonesia: The Rise of Metropolitan Regions: Towards Inclusive and Sustainable Regional Development." World Bank, Washington, DC. http://www.worldbank.org/en/news/feature/2012/08/13/towards-inclusive-and-sustainable-regional-development.

————. 2014. "Access to Affordable and Low-Income Housing in East Asia and the Pacific." Unpublished, World Bank, Washington, DC.

World Bank and Development Research Center of the State Council, P.R. China. 2014. *Urban China: Toward Efficient, Inclusive, and Sustainable Urbanization*. World Bank: Washington, DC.

Yinan, Z. 2014. "China's Urbanization Plan Awaits Approval," *China Daily*, January 22.

Zhong, R., and S. Dutta. 2014. "Growth in India Suffers as Workers Leave Cities," *Wall Street Journal*, April 15.

Urban Expansion in East Asia, 2000–10, by Country

Cambodia

Cambodia has a very small amount of urban area and urban population, although it is starting to urbanize. Phnom Penh, with more than a million people, remains the only major urban area in the country.

Cambodia has the fourth-smallest amount of urban land among the countries studied (after the Lao People's Democratic Republic, Papua New Guinea, and Timor-Leste). By the measures used in this study, the only urban area with more than 100,000 people was Phnom Penh, so all the urban land and population of the country for this report's purposes was in the Phnom Penh urban area (map A.1).[1] The amount of urban area grew from 110 square kilometers in 2000 to 160 in 2010. Only 0.1 percent of its total land mass was urban, the lowest proportion in East Asia after Lao PDR, Mongolia, and Papua New Guinea. Although the absolute amount of new built-up area was small, the rate of urban spatial expansion was the second fastest after Lao PDR: 4.3 percent a year, on average.

Cambodia also has among the smallest but fastest-growing urban populations, growing at 4.4 percent a year from 920,000 people to 1.4 million between 2000 and 2010. The proportion of the total population defined as urban for this study's purposes, also the second lowest in the region after Lao PDR, grew from 7 percent to 10 percent during this period.

Cambodia shares many of these urbanization characteristics with its neighbor Lao PDR, but there is a striking difference in average urban population density, which was much higher in Cambodia than in Lao PDR: 8,600 people per square kilometer in Cambodia in 2010, in contrast to 3,200 in Lao PDR.

More than 90 percent of the built-up area, urban population, and urban expansion of the Phnom Penh urban area was within the boundaries of the

Map A.1   Urban expansion in the Phnom Penh, Cambodia, urban area, 2000–10

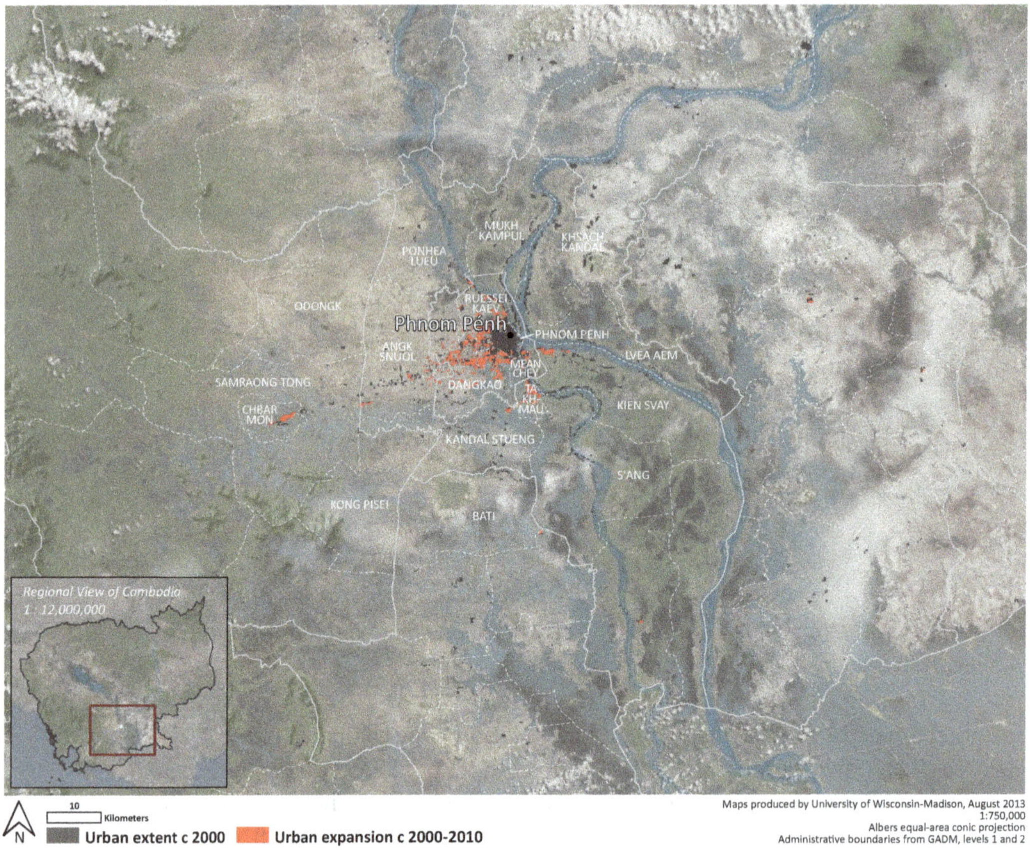

Maps produced by University of Wisconsin-Madison, August 2013
1:750,000
Albers equal-area conic projection
Administrative boundaries from GADM, levels 1 and 2

Urban extent c 2000   Urban expansion c 2000-2010

municipality of Phnom Penh, although urbanization has spilled over, particularly to the south and west.

The two other settlements in Cambodia sometimes considered cities are Baat Dambang and Siem Reap, though the urban populations of both were less than 100,000 people in 2010. Although both remained spatially and demographically very small, they grew very rapidly during this period, with Siem Reap doubling in size and tripling in population between 2000 and 2010.

China

Chinese urbanization is characterized not just by its immense scale and rapid pace, but also by the strong push toward urbanization exerted by the Chinese government at various levels, in the form of a vast amount of urban construction. As a result, despite the urban population increasing by more than 130 million people between 2000 and 2010, the density of urban areas has remained almost constant, in contrast with the rapidly increasing urban density seen in other countries in the East Asia region. In some parts of China the authorities have attempted to direct urbanization where it is not naturally occurring, with a large amount of construction in places with declining populations.

If thought of as a single entity, the Pearl River Delta would now be the largest, most populated urban area in the world. During this period, the Shanghai urban area overtook the Beijing urban area in size and population.

The scale of urbanization in China in the early twenty-first century is unprecedented. China dominates East Asia's urbanization trends—more than two-thirds of the region's total urban land as well as more than 80 percent of the new urban land added between 2000 and 2010 is located in China. The amount of urban land in China increased from 66,000 square kilometers in 2000 to 89,000 in 2010. By comparison, the country with the next largest amount of urban land, Japan, had 16,000 square kilometers in 2010, while the third, Indonesia, had 10,000 square kilometers. This means that the amount of new built-up land in China during this single decade, about 24,000 square kilometers, is more than double the *total* urban land in Indonesia (which itself has much more urban land than most other East Asian countries). Still, this massive amount of urban land is proportional to the vast size of the total land mass of China. In fact, less than 1 percent of the total land area of China was in urban areas of more than 100,000 people, which is only slightly greater than the average for the countries studied in the region (0.8 percent in 2010), and a smaller proportion than in Japan, the Republic of Korea, or Malaysia.

Urban expansion in China occurred rapidly during the 2000–10 decade, with urban spatial expansion occurring at 3.1 percent a year, on average. The only countries in the region with higher rates of increase in urban land are Lao PDR and Cambodia, which are tiny by comparison (only adding 50 and 60 square kilometers of new built-up land, respectively, during this period, as opposed to China's 24,000 square kilometers). Most of the increase in built-up land, 87 percent, occurred on arable land, which resulted in 1 percent of the country's total arable land being lost during this 10-year period.[2] Box A.1 describes the transition of peri-urban land from rural to urban use.

China's urban population is also much larger than that in other East Asian countries. Its urban population (the population in urban areas of more than 100,000 people) grew from 346 million (27 percent of its total

Box A.1   A snapshot of urbanization in progress

Even in rapidly urbanizing China, peri-urban areas often experience a transitional phase as they gradually transform from primarily rural to primarily urban. Angel, Valdivia, and Lutzy (2011, 141) describe
what this process looks like in the urbanizing areas around Zhengzhou, in Henan province, based on
field observations and interviews in 2007:

> A significant portion of the growth in the built-up area of Zhengzhou arises from the urban-
> ization of rural villages. . . . [T]hese villages are now undergoing rapid urbanization, albeit
> without the ownership of their land being transferred to the municipality. A patchwork of
> nonagricultural uses was apparent in these villages: industrial and commercial centers; new
> roads and bus lines; and local factories and small-scale industry established by outsiders
> and locals. Also evident [was] an increase in the importance of rental housing as a signifi-
> cant source of income for villagers and an influx of outsiders, including factory workers,
> construction workers, and college students.

population) to 477 million people (36 percent) between 2000 and 2010.
This 3.3 percent average annual rate of urban population growth was not
particularly large by East Asian standards, with 9 out of the 18 countries
included in this study having higher rates. However, even this modest rate
has resulted in a very large absolute number of new urban inhabitants (131
million).

A large amount of urban land, 180 square meters, was built per additional urban resident in China, among the highest in the region. (This figure
understates the amount of construction, given that it only captures hori-
zontal growth and not vertical growth.) Because of this heavy investment in
urban construction, China's rate of increase in built-up land (3.1 percent a
year, as noted earlier) is almost at par with its urban population growth rate
of 3.3 percent a year, resulting in a relatively stable urban population density. On average, urban areas are not particularly dense in China by East
Asian standards. The urban population density was approximately 5,300
people per square kilometer in both 2000 and 2010, which is lower than
the average for East Asian countries (5,800 people per square kilometer in
2010 for the countries studied).

China has three megacities of more than 10 million inhabitants: Beijing,
Shanghai, and the Pearl River Delta urban area (figures A.1 and A.2).
It has 9 urban areas of between 5 million and 10 million people, 69 of
1 million to 5 million, 104 of 500,000 to 1 million, and 415 of 100,000
to 500,000, as of 2010, for a total of 600 urban areas with more than
100,000 people.[3] The largest amount of urban land is concentrated in
small urban areas of 100,000 to 500,000 people (30 percent of the total
urban land in urban areas of more than 100,000), as well as those of 1 to
5 million (28 percent) (figure A.3). The population size category with the
highest amount of the urban population (31 percent) is the 1 million to
5 million category (figure A.4).

Figure A.1   China: The 25 largest urban areas by built-up area, 2000 and 2010

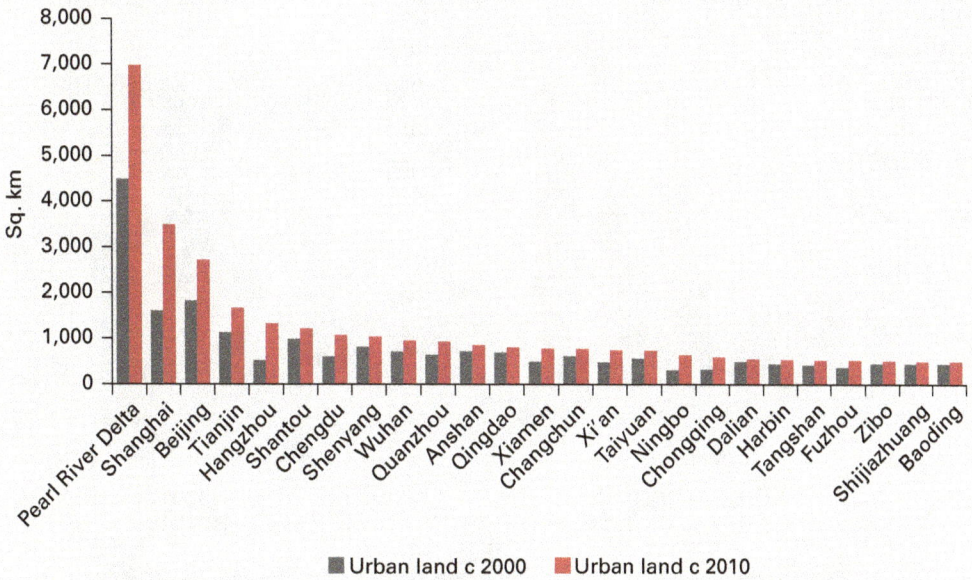

■ Urban land c 2000   ■ Urban land c 2010

Source: Study team, incorporating WorldPop data, http://www.worldpop.org.uk/data/.

Figure A.2   China: The 25 largest urban areas by population, 2000 and 2010

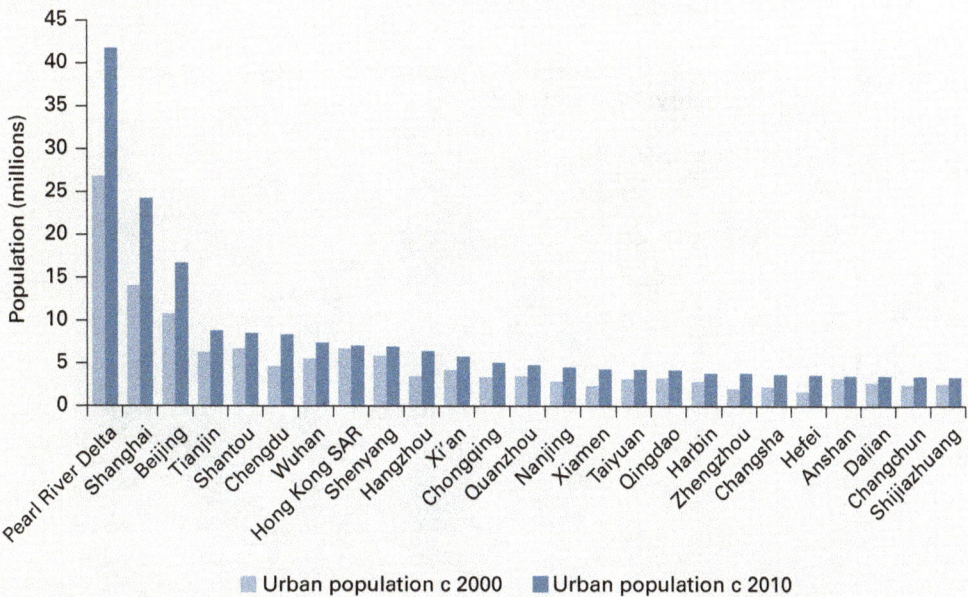

■ Urban population c 2000   ■ Urban population c 2010

Source: Study team, incorporating WorldPop data, http://www.worldpop.org.uk/data/.

Figure A.3   China: Urban land by population size category, 2000 and 2010

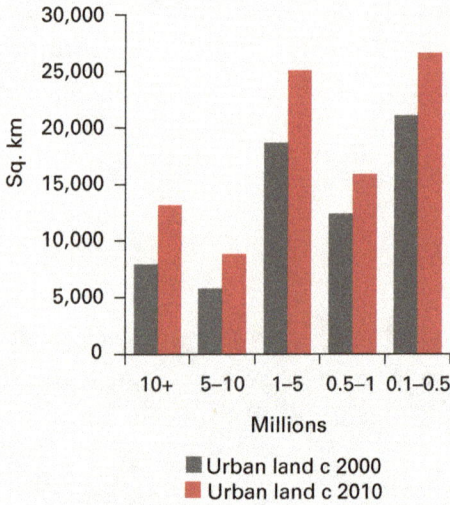

Millions

■ Urban land c 2000
■ Urban land c 2010

Source: Study team, incorporating WorldPop data, http://www.worldpop.org.uk/data/.

Figure A.4   China: Urban population by population size category, 2000 and 2010

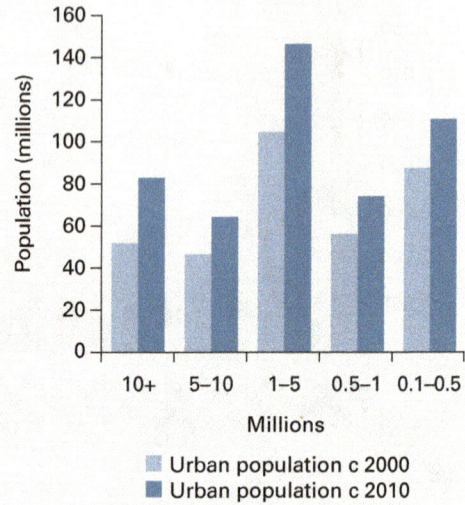

Millions

■ Urban population c 2000
■ Urban population c 2010

Source: Study team, incorporating WorldPop data, http://www.worldpop.org.uk/data/.

Of the 600 urban areas, more than 60 percent dropped in overall population density between 2000 and 2010 (figure A.5), and 54 of these urban areas actually lost population during this period (Box A.2). Almost all of these were small urban areas of fewer than 500,000 people.

Figure A.5   China: Urban population density by population size category, 2000 and 2010

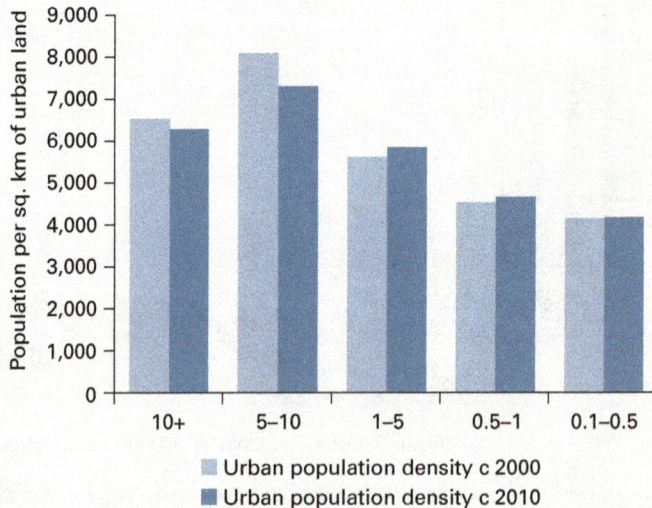

■ Urban population density c 2000
■ Urban population density c 2010

Source: Study team, incorporating WorldPop data, http://www.worldpop.org.uk/data/.

Box A.2   Ghost cities in China

Many news reports have drawn attention to the phenomenon of "ghost cities" in China, vast urban development projects that remain unoccupied (Day 2012; Young 2013).[a] The data from this study reveal a number of counties in China where a large increase in urban land was accompanied by a stagnation in or loss of population. In the country as a whole, more than 50 counties experienced an increase in urban land of 20 square kilometers that was accompanied by a population loss.

Ganyu, in Jiangsu province, lost 93,000 people, but continued to build large new urban areas (figure BA.2.1 and BA.2.2).

Figure BA.2.1   Ganyu in 2005

Source: Google Earth, map data © 2013 DigitalGlobe.

Figure BA.2.2   Ganyu in 2012

Source: Google Earth, map data © 2013 DigitalGlobe.

Guandu, in Kunming province, also lost more than half a million people between 2000 and 2010, while it added about 70 square kilometers of new urban land (figures BA.2.3, BA.2.4, and BA.2.5).

(Box continues next page)

Box A.2   Ghost cities in China *(continued)*

Figure BA.2.3   Guandu in 2002

Source: Google Earth, NASA map data © 2013 DigitalGlobe.

Figure BA.2.4   Guandu in 2013

Source: Google Earth, NASA map data © 2013 DigitalGlobe.

Mianyang, a prefecture-level city in Sichuan province, lost more than half a million people, dropping from 5.2 million inhabitants to 4.6 million between 2000 and 2010 (figure BA.2.6). However, during this same period it grew by more than 100 square kilometers.

The authors of the World Bank study of Chinese urbanization explain the context of this kind of growth:

> Urbanization has used land inefficiently. Rural land requisition and conversion for industrial use has been particularly inefficient because it has been largely driven by administrative decision rather than market demand. The incentives for local government to expand the city rather than develop existing underused urban land are strong: requisition of rural land

(Box continues next page)

Box A.2   Ghost cities in China *(continued)*

Figure BA.2.5   Guandu in 2013 (zoomed in)

Source: Google Earth, map data © 2013 DigitalGlobe.

Figure BA.2.6   Mianyang in 2012

Source: Google Earth, map data © 2013 DigitalGlobe.

and sale for commercial and residential purposes yields a large windfall gain for the city finances. In contrast, requisition of urban land is more expensive and cumbersome, because urban residents and enterprises have stronger property rights. Furthermore, national regulations that protect farmland from conversion have the unintended consequence of fragmenting the urban periphery because available land for conversion is often not adjacent to the core city (World Bank and Development Research Center of the State Council, P.R. China 2014, 10).

a. "The Ghost Towns of China: Amazing Satellite Images Show Cities Meant to be Home to Millions Lying Deserted." *Daily Mail,* December 18, 2010.

"China's Real Estate Bubble." *CBS News.* March 3, 2013.

Figure A.6   China: Provinces by urban land, 2000 and 2010

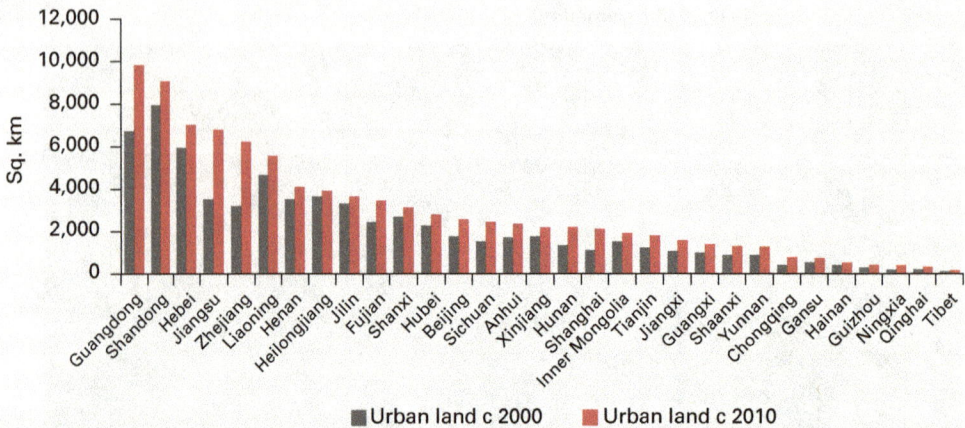

Source: Study team, incorporating WorldPop data, http://www.worldpop.org.uk/data/.

Of the 81 urban areas in China of more than 1 million people, 57 are "fragmented" urban areas, that is, no one county or district in the urban area has more than 50 percent of the overall urban land. Some 17 are "spill-over" urban areas that are at least 50 percent contained within one county but urban expansion has spilled over into others. Only seven are contained within a single county.

Breaking down urban land in the country by province, Guangdong (9,900 square kilometers), Shandong (9,100 square kilometers), and Hebei (7,000 square kilometers), all in eastern China, had the largest amounts of urban land in 2010 (figure A.6). Guangdong (61 million), Shandong (39 million), and Zhejiang (37 million) had the highest urban populations in 2010. Jiangsu and Zhejiang, the neighbors of Shanghai and also in eastern China, saw large increases in urban area and urban population.

The provinces with the highest proportion of urban land were Shanghai (33 percent), Beijing (16 percent), and Tianjin (15 percent), again all in eastern China. The populations of Shanghai and Beijing were both more than 80 percent urban, while Tianjin's population was more than 70 percent urban, by the definitions of this report.

The statistics above underscore the fact that provinces along the east coast of China are leading the urbanization trend (figures A.7 and A.8). Western China as a whole continues to urbanize slowly, particularly in proportion to its vast size. Grouping the provinces of China into four regions drives home this point.[4] The east coast region leads in every regard. Only a very small proportion of the land of the vast western region is urban, only 0.2 percent, as opposed to 5.4 percent of the land of east coast China, 1.6 percent of central China, and 1.7 percent of northeast China. About half

Figure A.7   China: Regions by urban land, 2000 and 2010

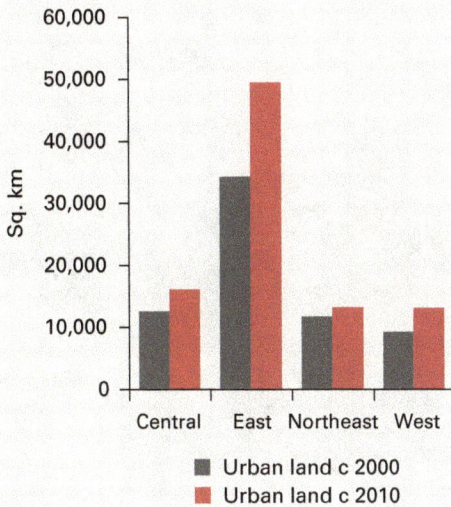

Source: Study team, incorporating WorldPop data, http://www.worldpop.org.uk/data/.

Figure A.8   China: Regions by urban population, 2000 and 2010

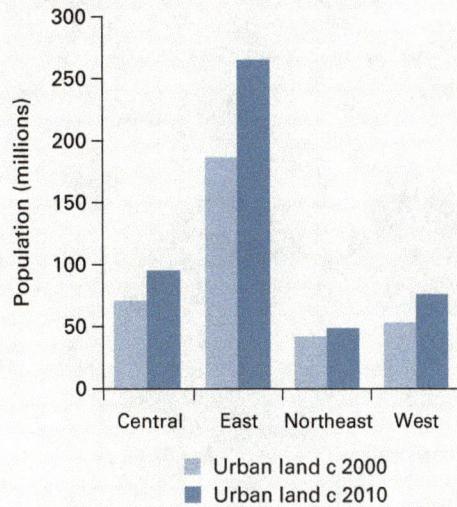

Source: Study team, incorporating WorldPop data, http://www.worldpop.org.uk/data/.

the population of east coast China is urban (264 million people), compared with slightly less than half of northeast China (which has a much smaller absolute population), and between 20 percent and 30 percent of central and western China.

The Pearl River Delta urban area, which includes Dongguan, Foshan, Guangzhou, and Shenzhen (but does not include Hong Kong SAR, China), is considered by this study to be a single entity, given that it is difficult to meaningfully distinguish one "city" from another in this interconnected urban mass. Defined this way, it is now the largest urban area in East Asia, and probably in the world, overtaking the Tokyo region sometime between 2000 and 2010. Its built-up area covered 4,500 square kilometers in 2000, and grew very rapidly (4.5 percent a year) to nearly 7,000 square kilometers in 2010. The enormous size of this built-up expanse is hard to overstate: it is more than twice as large as Shanghai, four times the size of Jakarta, and five times the size of Manila, each of which are massive urban areas in their own right.

The Pearl River Delta urban area, which began to merge into a unified entity during the 2000–10 decade, is a unique kind of settlement in its immense scale as well as its form. Vast and multinucleated with no clear center, its form arose from its unique economic origins in the 1980s and 1990s as the geographic center of the market reforms that subsequently transformed the Chinese economy, particularly the Shenzhen Special

Map A.2   Urban expansion in the Pearl River Delta, China, urban area, 2000–10

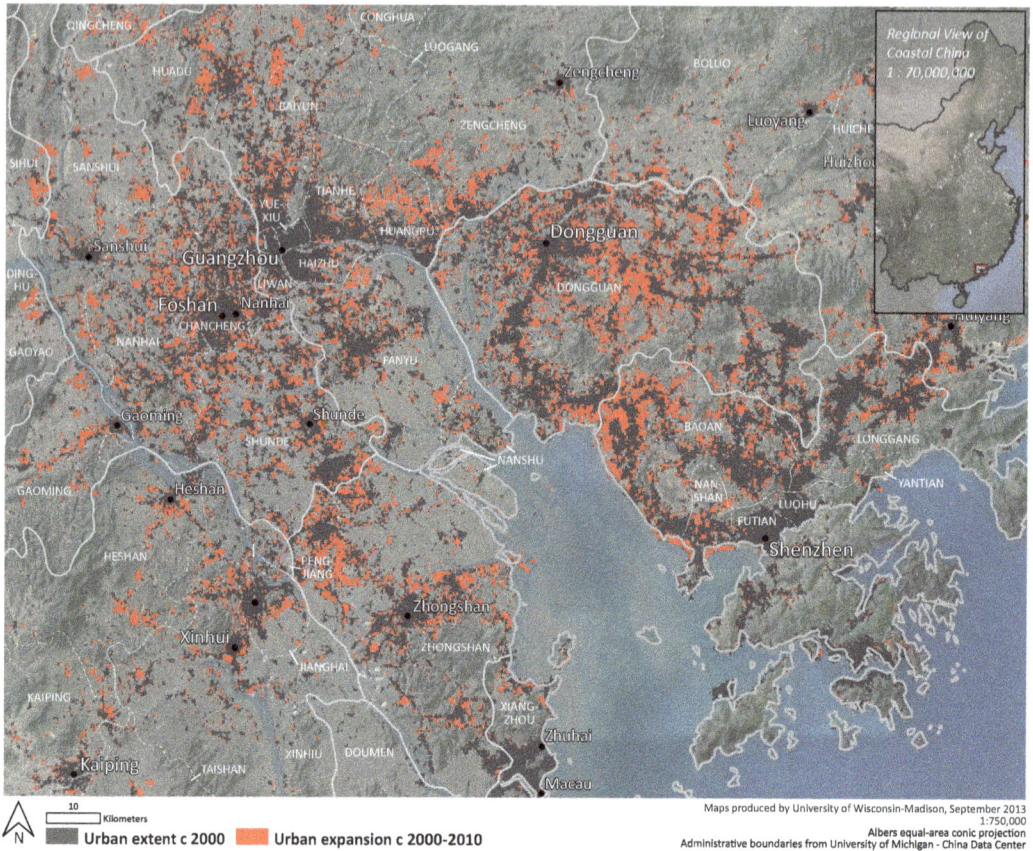

Maps produced by University of Wisconsin-Madison, September 2013
1:750,000
Albers equal-area conic projection
Administrative boundaries from University of Michigan - China Data Center

Urban extent c 2000   **Urban expansion c 2000-2010**

Economic Zone. This region thus has a very different, and more recent, urban growth trajectory than those of Beijing and Shanghai, which, despite their explosive recent growth, have grown around well-defined historic urban centers. The Pearl River Delta does have historic cities, but the present urban form cannot be understood as simply the outward expansion of these, as map A.2 makes clear.

The Pearl River Delta urban area, as defined by this study, spreads across 33 counties in 10 prefectures (map A.2). No single prefecture can claim the bulk of the urban land—Guangzhou has the highest proportion, 20 percent, or 1,400 square kilometers in 2010, followed by Foshan (18 percent), Dongguan (17 percent), and Shenzhen (13 percent). Urban spatial expansion between 2000 and 2010 in these prefectures was roughly proportional to these prefectures' existing urban areas.

The population of the Pearl River Delta urban area grew from 27 million in 2000 to an astounding 42 million people in 2010, overtaking Tokyo in this regard as well to become the most populous urban area in East Asia, and probably the most populous in the world. This rate of urban population growth, 4.5 percent a year, was identical to its rate of spatial

Map A.3   Urban expansion in the Shanghai, China, urban area, 2000–10

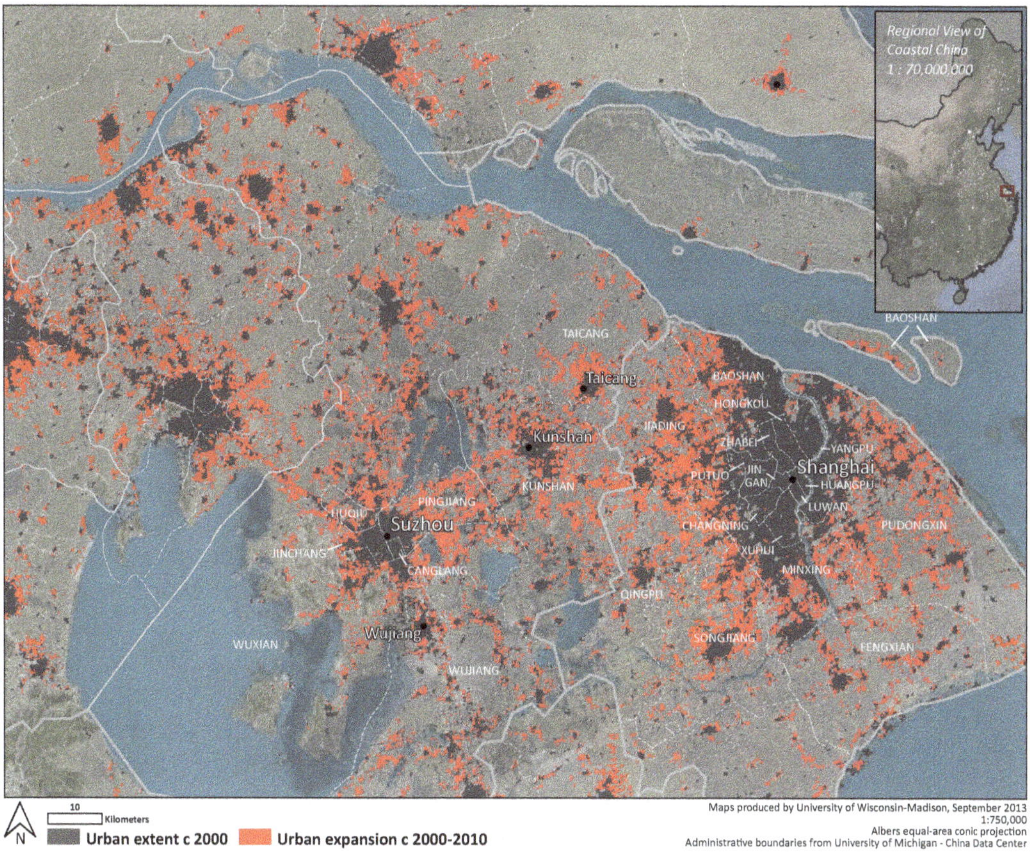

Note: In this map, only labeled areas are counted as part of the Shanghai urban area.

expansion, which means that its overall population density remained constant, at about 6,000 people per square kilometer, which was slightly lower than the average for the megacities in East Asia. The prefectures with the largest populations were Guangzhou (9.7 million people, or about 23 percent of the population of the overall urban area), and Shenzhen (9.3 million people, or 22 percent). These, along with Dongguan (7 million) and Foshan (5.8 million) would, of course, be major cities in their own right even if not part of the larger urban area. Ten individual counties in these prefectures have urban populations of more than a million people each.

The Shanghai urban area (map A.3) is hard to isolate from the broader Yangtze River Delta region, which is highly urbanized with a string of adjacent interconnected urban centers. For the purposes of this study, the Shanghai urban area is defined to also include Kunshan, Suzhou, Tiacang, and Wujiang (see "Defining Urban Areas" in appendix C).

Defined this way, the Shanghai urban area grew extremely quickly between 2000 and 2010, more than doubling in built-up area from 1,600 square kilometers to almost 3,500 square kilometers, overtaking Beijing in size. This average annual growth rate of 8.1 percent was faster than any city of more than 5 million people in East Asia, with the exception of Hangzhou, China. The pattern of expansion shows satellite towns being absorbed into the urban area, but new development was scattered and discontinuous.

The population of the urban area also grew very quickly, from 14 million people to 24 million between 2000 and 2010, an increase of 5.6 percent a year. Shanghai's population overtook Beijing's during this period, too. However, because of its much faster spatial growth, the urban population density decreased rapidly during this period, from 8,700 people per square kilometer to 6,900.

The district with the greatest area of urban land within the administrative boundary of Shanghai is Pudong, which doubled to 520 square kilometers from 260. Pudong and Minxing each gained more than 1.5 million people. At the same time, a number of the innermost districts of Shanghai in the historic center of Puxi, including Changning, Hongkou, Huangpu, Jingan, and Luwan, actually lost population. Other districts, like Qingpu, Suzhou, Taicang, and Wujiang, did not lose population but contracted in population density because of expansion of their built-up areas. Still, the inner districts of Shanghai remained extremely dense, with nine districts having more than 25,000 people per square kilometer. The densest district was Huangpu, whose population density decreased from 58,000 people per square kilometer to 43,000.[5]

The Beijing urban area (map A.4) grew from 1,800 square kilometers to 2,700 between 2000 and 2010, an average annual growth rate of 4.0 percent. In contrast to the Pearl River Delta region, Beijing shows a more traditional pattern of urban expansion, growing outward from a large, well-defined core, absorbing surrounding centers as well as the hundreds of small villages that dot the landscape of this region.

The population of the Beijing urban area increased from approximately 11 million people to 17 million during this period, growing 4.5 percent per year. Its overall urban population density increased slightly, from 5,900 people per square kilometer to 6,200.

The vast majority of the urban land (94 percent) and urban population (97 percent) lie within the urban districts of Beijing itself. The four innermost districts were already fully built up by 2000, and saw either a small amount of population increase or, in the case of Xicheng, a decrease in population by 2010. However, these four districts remained very dense, between 19,000 and 32,000 people per square kilometer, much denser than other districts in the urban area. The next ring of districts saw large population increases, with Chaoyang and Haidian adding more than a million people each. However, it was the next ring that saw the greatest increases in urban land, with Changping, Daxing, Shunyi, and Tongzhou adding more than 100 square kilometers each.

There are, of course, many large urban areas in China besides the three megacities described above. Of particular note is the Hong Kong urban

Map A.4   Urban expansion in the Beijing, China, urban area, 2000–10

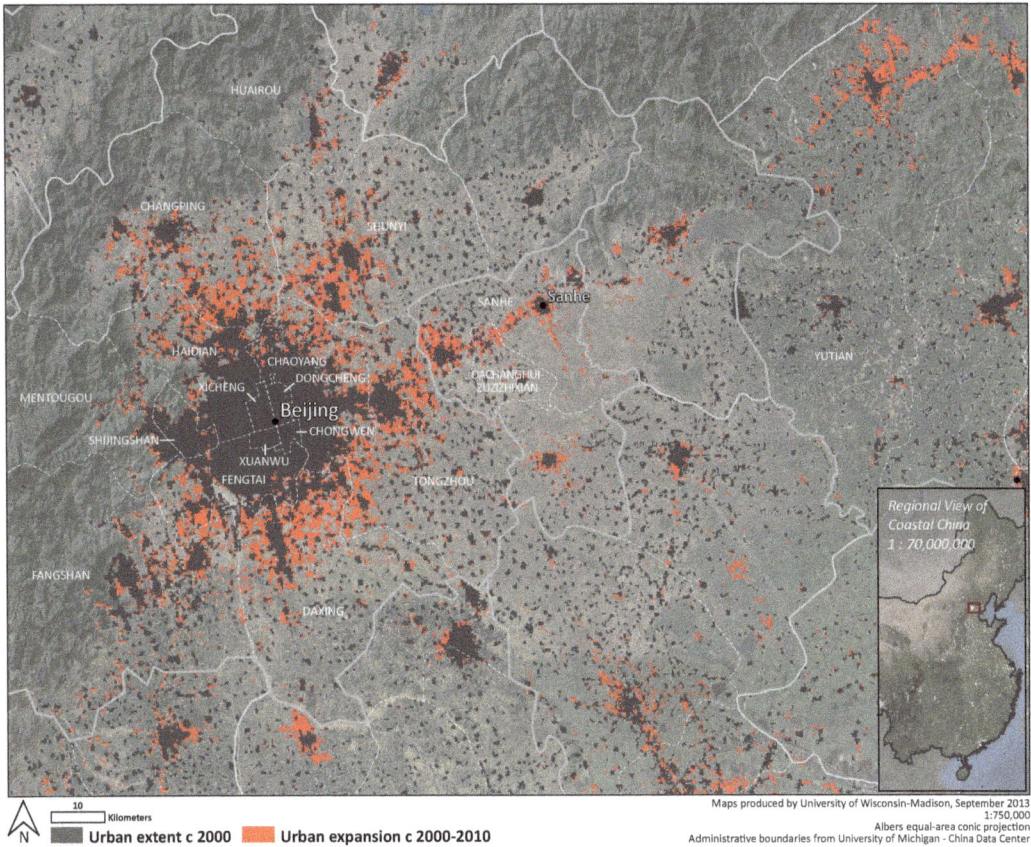

Maps produced by University of Wisconsin-Madison, September 2013
1:750,000
Albers equal-area conic projection
Administrative boundaries from University of Michigan - China Data Center

■ Urban extent c 2000   ■ Urban expansion c 2000-2010

Note: In this map, only labeled areas are counted as part of the Beijing urban area.

area (in Hong Kong SAR, China) whose urban population density was far greater than any other urban area of any size in East Asia: 33,200 people per square kilometer in 2000, dropping slightly to 32,100 in 2010. Chongqing is often erroneously described as the largest city in the world because the province of Chongqing is administratively considered a municipality, but in fact, only about a quarter of the population (about 5 million people) are part of the urban area, which covers just 1 percent of the administrative area of the municipality.

Figure A.9 expresses the amount of new built-up land in the five economic regions of China as compared with the area of Manhattan, underscoring the pace and scale of new construction in China. It shows that, for example, the Yangtze River Delta economic region (around Shanghai) has built-up land equivalent to 88 times the area of Manhattan in just this 10-year period. The figure also shows population growth in these areas, emphasizing that at the scale of the economic region, new construction has far exceeded population growth.[6]

Figure A.9   Change in population and built-up land in China's five economic regions, 2000–10, compared with the population and area of Manhattan

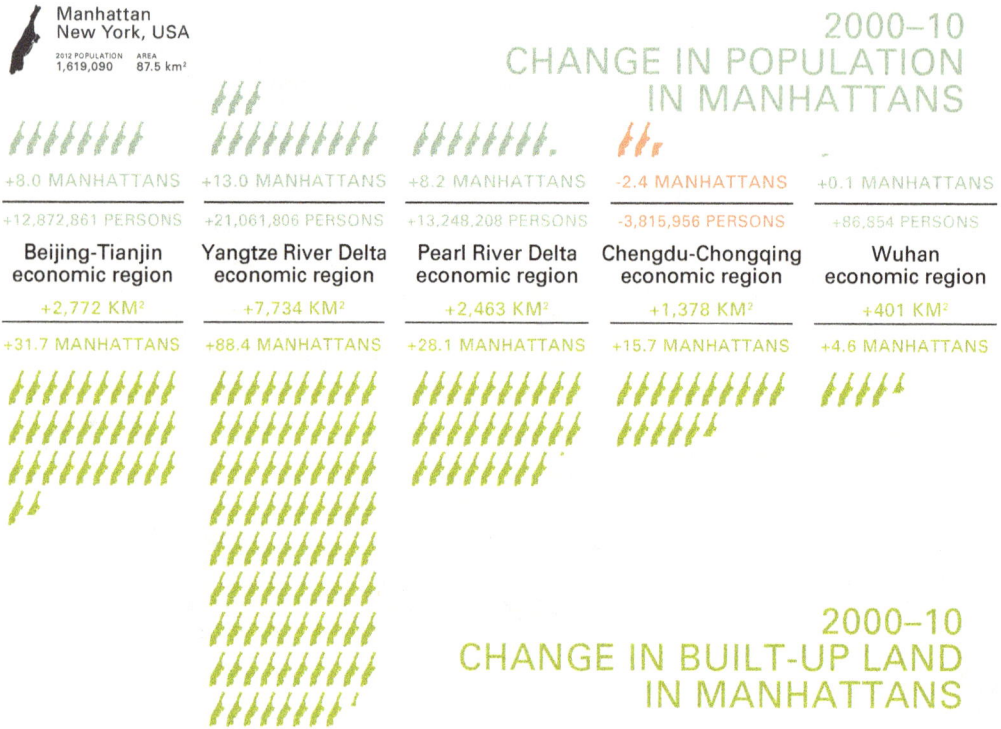

Manhattan
New York, USA
2012 POPULATION   AREA
1,619,090   87.5 km²

2000–10
CHANGE IN POPULATION
IN MANHATTANS

+8.0 MANHATTANS	+13.0 MANHATTANS	+8.2 MANHATTANS	-2.4 MANHATTANS	+0.1 MANHATTANS
+12,872,861 PERSONS	+21,061,806 PERSONS	+13,248,208 PERSONS	-3,815,956 PERSONS	+86,854 PERSONS
Beijing-Tianjin economic region	Yangtze River Delta economic region	Pearl River Delta economic region	Chengdu-Chongqing economic region	Wuhan economic region
+2,772 KM²	+7,734 KM²	+2,463 KM²	+1,378 KM²	+401 KM²
+31.7 MANHATTANS	+88.4 MANHATTANS	+28.1 MANHATTANS	+15.7 MANHATTANS	+4.6 MANHATTANS

2000–10
CHANGE IN BUILT-UP LAND
IN MANHATTANS

Note: The economic regions shown above are based on Chinese national definitions; they include urban and rural areas in several provinces, and not just the urban areas for which they are named. Figures include the population and built-up land of the entire economic region, and not just the urban population and land.

Indonesia

Indonesia is at a more advanced stage of urbanization than many of its neighbors, but still experienced a vast amount of urban expansion and urban population growth between 2000 and 2010. Indonesian cities have high population densities, and densities continue to increase. The Jakarta urban area remains dominant within Indonesia, but is highly fragmented administratively.

Indonesia has the third-largest amount of urban land in East Asia, after China and Japan. Between 2000 and 2010, the amount of land in urban areas in Indonesia increased from about 8,900 square kilometers to 10,000, an increase of 1.1 percent each year. Whereas this represented among the slowest average annual *rates* of increase in the region, it was still the second-largest increase in absolute amount of urban land, after China. For comparison, the amount of new urban land in Indonesia was more than twice that of the Philippines and three times that of the Republic of Korea.

Indonesia has the second-largest urban population in the region after China—94 million people in 2010, an increase of 28 million since 2000. This increase was also the second largest in the region after China. The proportion of people in Indonesia in urban areas of more than 100,000 people increased from 31 percent in 2000 to 39 percent in 2010. Its rate of urban population growth, 3.5 percent per year, was slightly higher than the Philippines' and China's (both 3.3 percent), but lower than Vietnam's (4.1 percent) and Malaysia's (4.0 percent).

Despite the large amounts of new urban land in Indonesia, the country has, in fact, been remarkably economical in its increase in urban land per person. The amount of new urban land added per new urban resident during the 2000–10 period was less than 40 square meters, which was the smallest amount of any country in the region. This compares to about 135 square meters per person in Malaysia and 180 square meters in China.

Total urban population density (total urban population divided by total urban land) increased sharply in Indonesia between 2000 and 2010, from 7,400 people per square kilometer to 9,400. This is the largest increase in urban population density of any country in the region. Urban population density in Indonesia is among the region's highest, more than double that of Malaysia or Thailand, though lower than that of the Republic of Korea and the Philippines. This increase in urban density is not driven by just a few densifying cities: 80 of the 83 urban areas studied in Indonesia showed an increase in urban population density.[7]

Because of the large land mass of the Indonesian archipelago, urban areas cover only 0.5 percent of its total land area, among the lowest in the region. Even though most of the increase in built-up land, 88 percent, was on arable land, this area amounted to just 0.3 percent of the total arable land in the country.[8]

Jakarta, Indonesia's capital, is one of the region's megacities (figure A.10). Indonesia also contains 2 urban areas with total populations

Figure A.10   Indonesia: The 25 largest urban areas by built-up area, 2000 and 2010

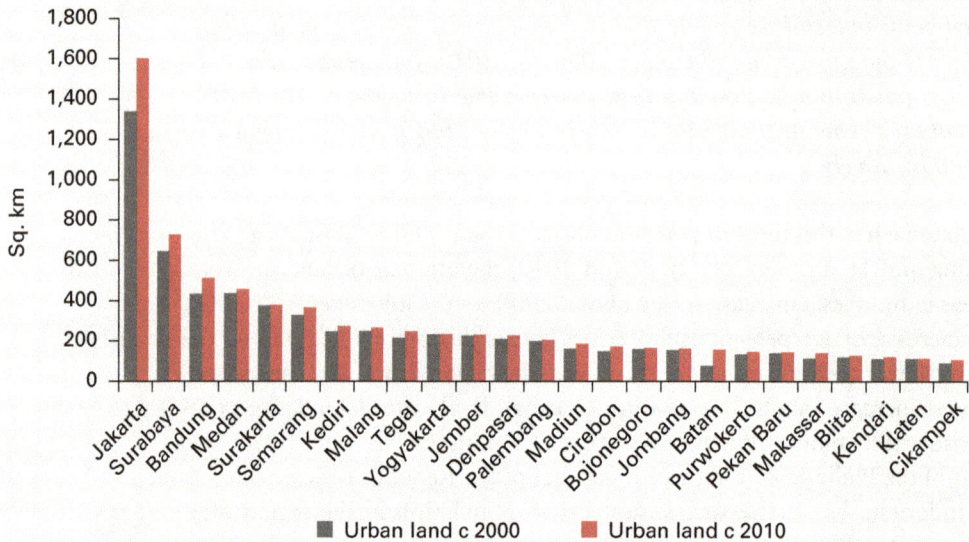

Source: Study team, incorporating WorldPop data, http://www.worldpop.org.uk/data/.

between 5 million and 10 million (Bandung and Surabaya), 18 of 1 million to 5 million, 27 of 500,000 to 1 million, and 29 of 100,000 to 500,000.

Of these size categories, the greatest proportion of urban land is in medium-sized urban areas: 27 percent is in urban areas of between 1 million and 5 million people, followed by 18 percent in the 500,000 to 1 million range (figure A.11). This is also roughly the same as those categories' shares of urban population (26 percent and 16 percent, respectively). All size categories of urban areas grew in population during 2000–10 at similar rates of between 3.5 and 3.7 percent per year, and as a result, in absolute terms the largest increase in population was in the category that already had the largest population, that is, the 1 million to 5 million category, which saw an increase of more than 9 million people (figure A.12).

Of the 21 urban areas in Indonesia with populations of more than 1 million people, only 4 are contained within a single administrative boundary. Of the remainder, 9 are "spillover" urban areas, that is, more than 50 percent within one jurisdiction, but urban expansion has spilled over into others; and 8 are "fragmented" urban areas, that is, no single jurisdiction has more than 50 percent of the overall urban land in the urban area.

The province with the greatest amount of built-up land is East Java (Jawa Timur), followed by West Java (Jawa Barat) and Central Java (Jawa Tengah) (figure A.13). These provinces also have the highest urban populations. The province of Greater Jakarta (Jakarta Raya) had the highest proportion of urban land (85 percent).

The island of Java remains the location of most of the urbanization in the country (figure A.14). Some 75 percent of the urban land in Indonesia in

Figure A.11   Indonesia: Urban land by population size category, 2000 and 2010

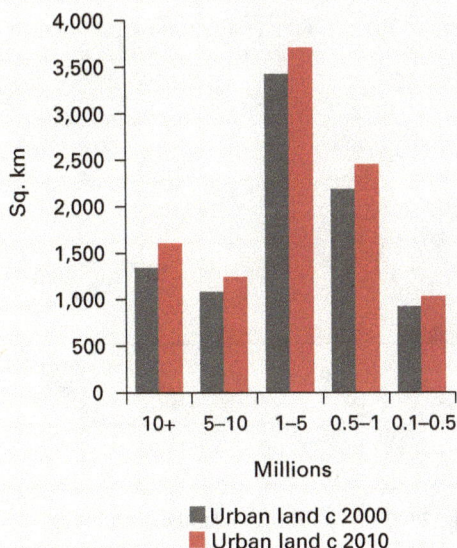

Source: Study team, incorporating WorldPop data, http://www.worldpop.org.uk/data/.

Figure A.12   Indonesia: Urban population by population size category, 2000 and 2010

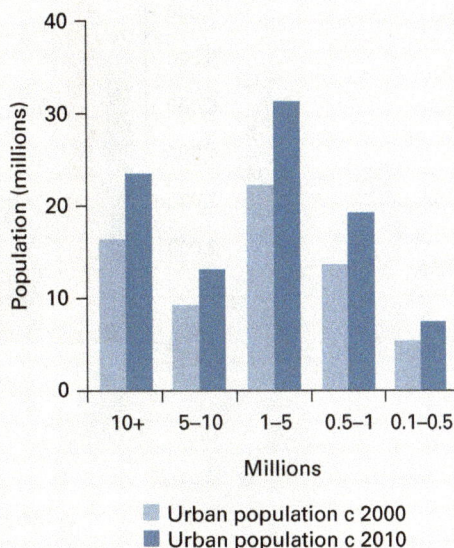

Source: Study team, incorporating WorldPop data, http://www.worldpop.org.uk/data/.

Figure A.13   Indonesia: The 10 most urban provinces by land, 2000 and 2010

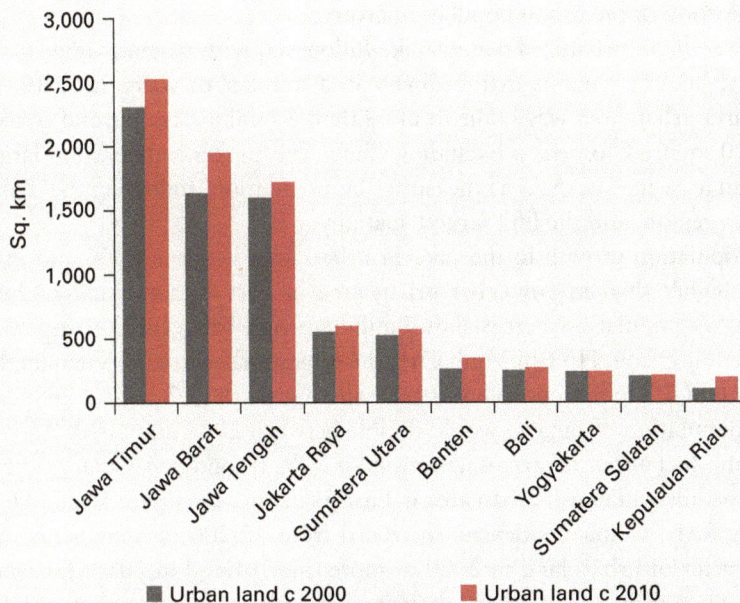

Source: Study team, incorporating WorldPop data, http://www.worldpop.org.uk/data/.

Figure A.14   Indonesia: Urban area by island group, 2000 and 2010

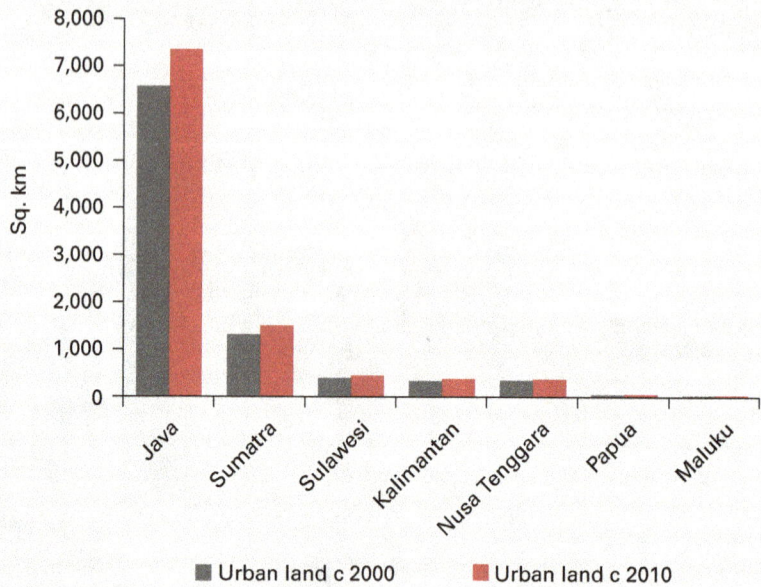

Source: Study team, incorporating WorldPop data, http://www.worldpop.org.uk/data/.

2010, as well as almost 75 percent of the increase in urban land since 2000, was on Java. Of the island's land, 5.5 percent was urban, whereas less than 1 percent of the land on every other island or island group was urban. Java had 80 percent of the urban population in the country, as well as the same proportion of the urban population growth.

Even in an urbanized country like Indonesia, with its many large urban areas, Jakarta remains extraordinary in a number of ways. In 2010, the Jakarta urban area was home to more than 23 million people and covered 1,600 square kilometers. Excluding China, this makes it the second-largest urban area in East Asia as measured by population, following the Tokyo urban region, and the fifth largest spatially.

Population growth in the Jakarta urban area between 2000 and 2010 was higher than in any other urban area in East Asia excluding China. Jakarta's population increased by 7 million people between 2000 and 2010. (By comparison, Ho Chi Minh City, the largest urban area in Vietnam, has a *total* of 7.8 million people.) At this rate of growth (3.7 percent per year), the population of Jakarta would double between 2000 and 2020. Another notable fact about Jakarta is its density: it is the second-densest large (5 million people and more) urban area in East Asia, after the urban area of Hong Kong SAR, China. Its density increased from 12,200 persons per square kilometer of urban land in 2000 to more than 14,600 in 2010. Jakarta is also much denser than other urban areas in Indonesia. It has about 12 percent of the country's built-up land, but 20 percent of its urban population.

The Jakarta urban area covers more than twice the area of its nearest Indonesian competitor, Surabaya. It is also expanding faster than other Indonesian urban areas: it grew by 1.8 percent per year, whereas the average rate of increase in all other urban areas in the country was 1.5 percent per year.

Jakarta is a prime example of metropolitan fragmentation. The built-up area of the Jakarta metropolitan region crosses 12 municipalities or regencies in the provinces of Greater Jakarta (Jakarta Raya), Banten, and West Java (Jawa Barat). As map A.5 shows, Greater Jakarta was already nearly completely built up by 2000, and subsequent growth has occurred along broad corridors toward the east, west, and south.

Although the Greater Jakarta province at the center of the metropolitan region remains highly populated and economically important, the distribution of urban land and population across the metropolitan region highlights the need to look beyond this core. Only 37 percent of urban land lies in Greater Jakarta, as of 2010, while 42 percent lies in West Java province (Jawa Barat) (figure A.15). The individual municipality or regency with both the largest amount of total urban land and the highest growth

Map A.5   **Urban expansion in the Jakarta, Indonesia, urban area, 2000–10**

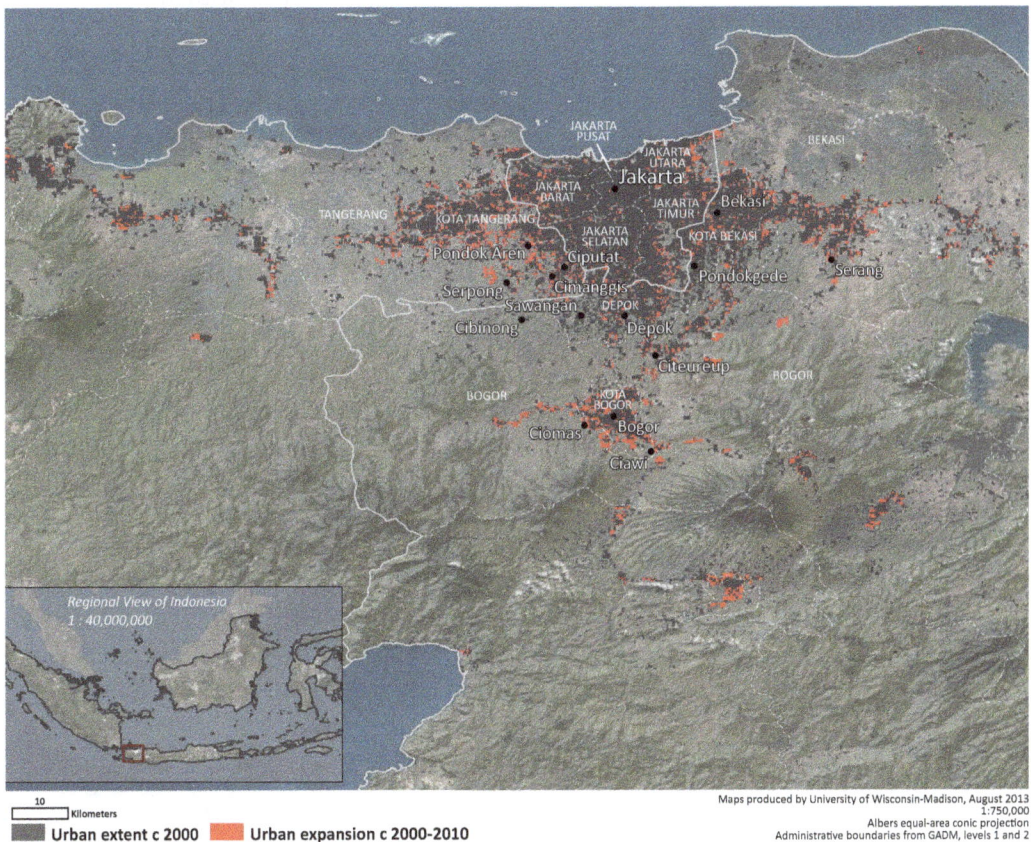

Note: In this map, only labeled areas are counted as part of the Jakarta urban area.

Figure A.15   Jakarta, Indonesia, urban area: Urban land, 2010

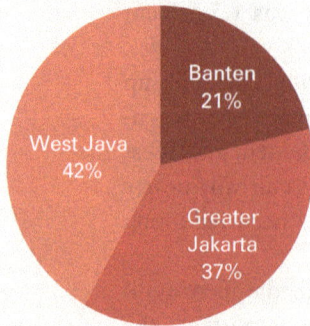

Banten 21%
West Java 42%
Greater Jakarta 37%

Source: Study team, incorporating WorldPop data, http://www.worldpop.org.uk/data/.

Figure A.16   Jakarta, Indonesia, urban area: Urban population, 2010

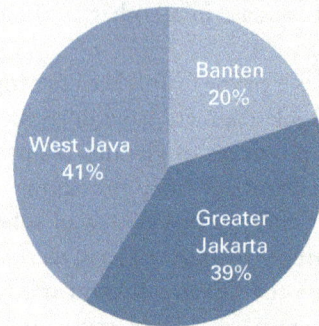

Banten 20%
West Java 41%
Greater Jakarta 39%

Source: Study team, incorporating WorldPop data, http://www.worldpop.org.uk/data/.

in urban land is Tangerang, which is in Banten province, again not in the province of Greater Jakarta. Half of all new increase in built-up land took place in West Java, and almost a third was in Banten, with the remainder in Greater Jakarta province.

Less than half the population of the metropolitan area lives in Greater Jakarta (figure A.16). The jurisdiction with the highest population, as well as the one with the highest population growth between 2000 and 2010, was Bogor in West Java (not including the municipality of Kota Bogor, which is a distinct jurisdiction). Bogor added more than a million people during this period.

The Bandung urban area in West Java and the Surabaya urban area in East Java, as defined in this study, are Indonesia's second- and third-largest urban areas, with populations of 6.9 million and 6.1 million, respectively. Bandung is far denser than Surabaya, but still not as dense as Jakarta. Bandung's two municipalities, Kota Bandung and Cimahi, were already nearly completely built up by 2000, and most of the urban growth has occurred in the surrounding regency of Bandung. Although it is less dense than the municipalities at the center, more than half of the urban land as well as more than half of the urban population are in Bandung regency.

Surabaya is also a "fragmented" city like Jakarta (map A.6). Most of its urban land and urban population are situated outside the boundaries of the city of Surabaya, and most of the growth in urban land and population occurred outside it as well, mostly in neighboring Gresik and Sidoarjo regencies.

Map A.6   Urban expansion in the Surabaya, Indonesia, urban area, 2000–10

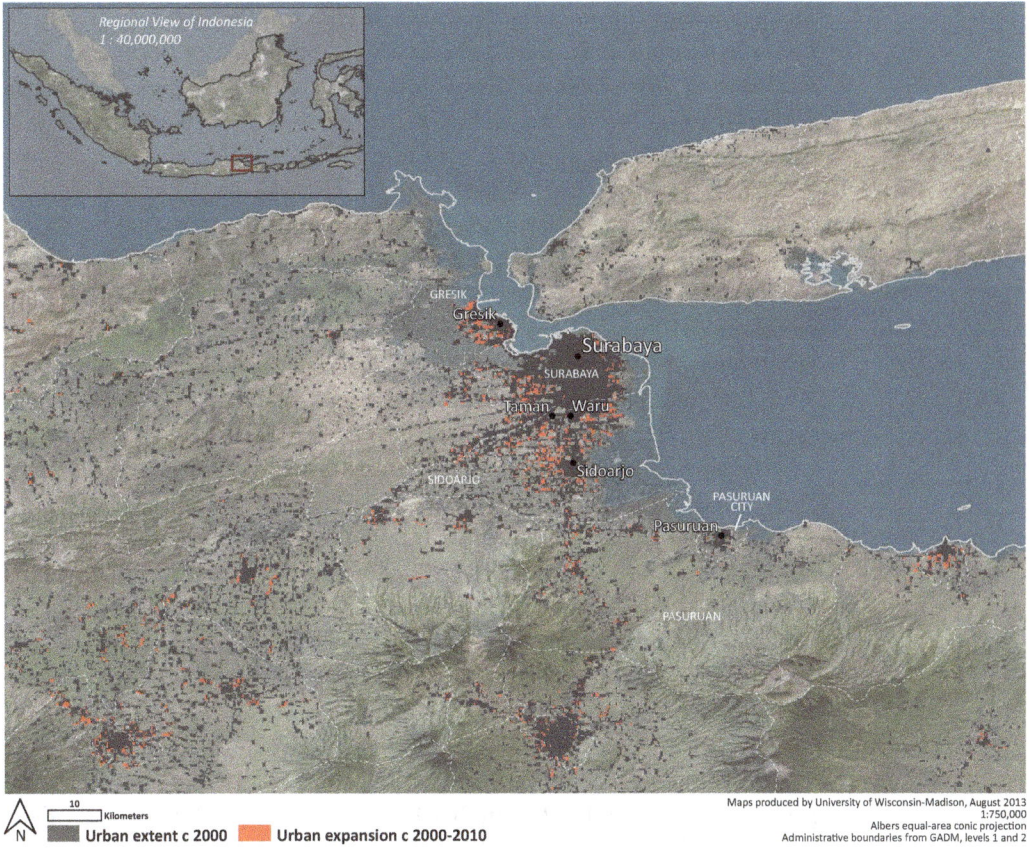

Regional View of Indonesia
1 : 40,000,000

GRESIK
Gresik
Surabaya
SURABAYA
Taman   Waru
SIDOARJO
Sidoarjo
PASURUAN
CITY
Pasuruan
PASURUAN

10
Kilometers

N

■ **Urban extent c 2000**   ■ **Urban expansion c 2000-2010**

Maps produced by University of Wisconsin-Madison, August 2013
1:750,000
Albers equal-area conic projection
Administrative boundaries from GADM, levels 1 and 2

Note: In this map, only labeled areas are counted as part of the Surabaya urban area.

Japan

Japan is among the most highly urbanized countries in East Asia. However, urban expansion and urban population growth between 2000 and 2010 were among the slowest in the region. Tokyo, although an enormous urban region covering 240 municipalities, lost its place as the largest urban area in the world during this period.

Despite being only the sixth-largest country in East Asia in total land area, Japan has the second-largest amount of urban land, after China: about 15,500 square kilometers in 2000, which increased to 16,200 square kilometers in 2010. In 2010, 4.3 percent of the area of the country was part of urban areas, the highest proportion of any in the region except Singapore (and Taiwan, China). However, built-up area in Japan is increasing very slowly. The rate of increase in built-up land, 0.4 percent a year, on average, was the slowest rate in the region. Almost every urban area in the country grew at less than 1 percent a year.

Japan had the third-largest urban population in the region (population in urban areas of more than 100,000 people), after China and Indonesia, 67 million in 2000, increasing to 77 million in 2010. It had the most highly urbanized population in the region with the exception of Singapore and Taiwan, China. However, it also had one of the lowest rates of urban population increase in the region, 1.4 percent a year.

With regard to urban population density, urban areas in Japan were less dense than those in the region as a whole, on average, about 4,700 people per square kilometer in 2010, up from about 4,300 in 2000. Even though wealthier countries are often thought to be associated with more urban sprawl, urban population increases in Japan did not appear to result in much urban expansion, with only about 60 square meters of new built-up land per additional urban resident, which was among the lowest in the region.

Japan has 2 megacities, the Tokyo urban area (32 million people in 2010) and the Osaka-Kobe urban area (12 million). Most of the urban land and urban population in the country was concentrated in these 2 urban areas (figures A.17 and A.18). Japan also had 1 urban area with between 5 million and 10 million residents, Nagoya; 4 between 1 million and 5 million; 14 between 500,000 and 1 million; and 38 between 100,000 and 500,000, for a total of 59 urban areas with more than 100,000 people. Figures A.19 and A.20 show changes in urban land and urban population in the 25 largest urban areas in Japan.

The Tokyo urban area is usually listed as the largest in the world. However, it was overtaken between 2000 and 2010, in both area and population, by the Pearl River Delta urban area in China (if the Pearl River Delta is considered a single entity, incorporating Dongguan, Foshan, Guangzhou, and Shenzhen).

Figure A.17   Japan: Urban land by population size category, 2000 and 2010

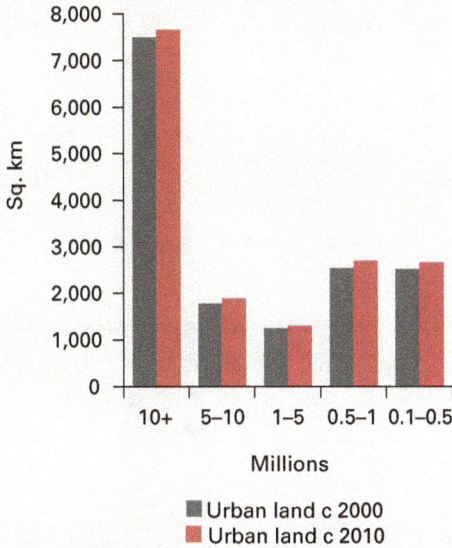

Urban land c 2000
Urban land c 2010

Source: Study team, incorporating WorldPop data, http://www.worldpop.org.uk/data/.

Figure A.18   Japan: Urban population by population size category, 2000 and 2010

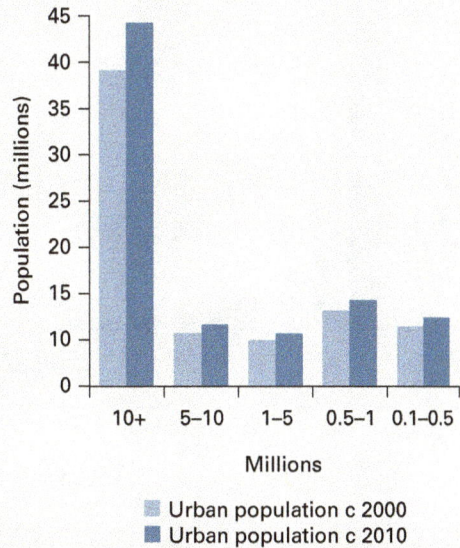

Urban population c 2000
Urban population c 2010

Source: Study team, incorporating WorldPop data, http://www.worldpop.org.uk/data/.

Figure A.19   Japan: The 25 largest urban areas by built-up area, 2000 and 2010

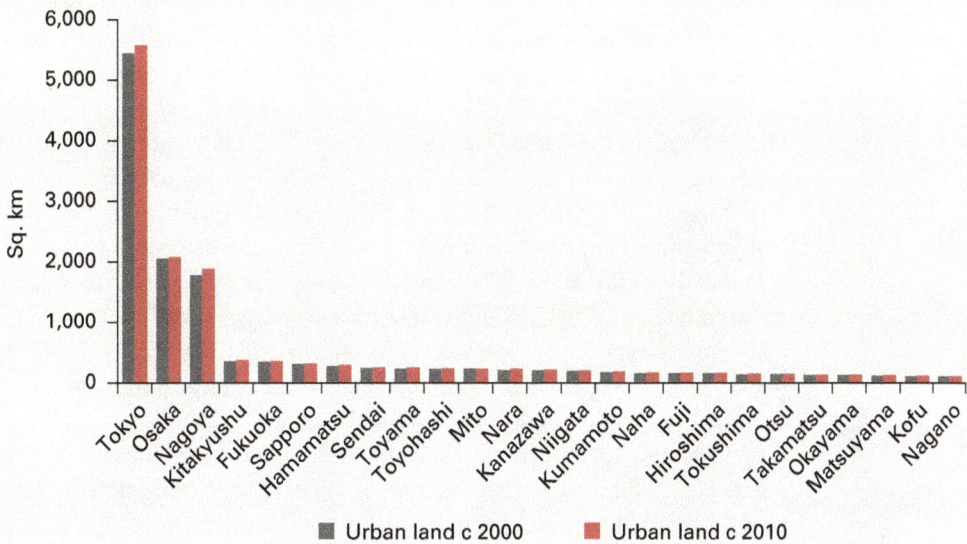

Urban land c 2000   Urban land c 2010

Source: Study team, incorporating WorldPop data, http://www.worldpop.org.uk/data/.

Figure A.20   **Japan: The 25 largest urban areas by population, 2000 and 2010**

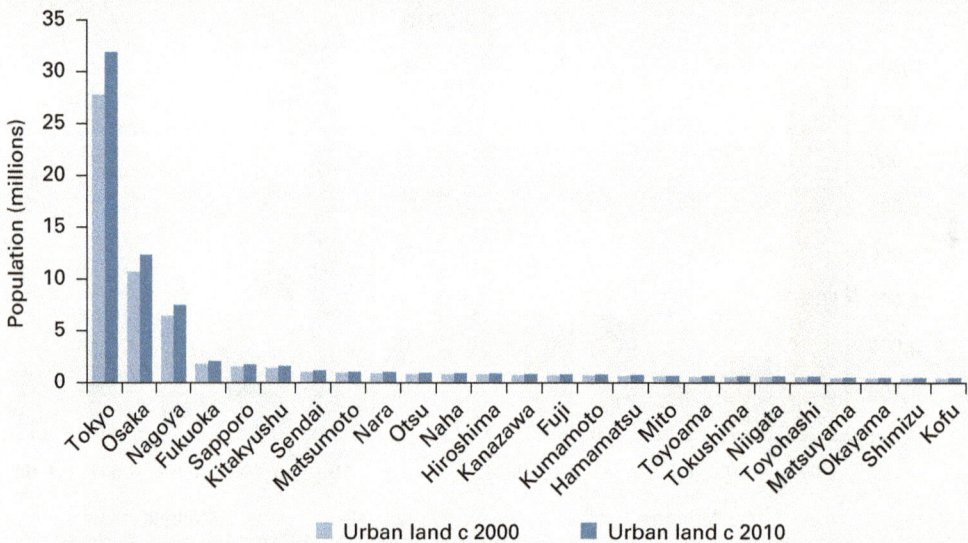

Source: Study team, incorporating WorldPop data, http://www.worldpop.org.uk/data/.

Tokyo is a famously large and administratively fragmented metropolis, covering 240 municipalities in Tokyo and six other prefectures. In total, it grew from approximately 5,400 square kilometers to 5,600 between 2000 and 2010, a very low growth rate of 0.2 percent a year. As of 2010, only about 20 percent of this area was within Tokyo itself, with 24 percent in Saitama Prefecture north of Tokyo, 19 percent in Kanagawa Prefecture to the south, and 16 percent in Chiba Prefecture to the east. Of the 240 municipalities, only 24 encompass more than just 1 percent of the total area. Yokohama, in Kanagawa Prefecture, is the municipality with the largest proportion, yet it too has less than 7 percent of the total built-up area of the urban area within it. Practically no urban growth occurred within Tokyo proper. The small amount of growth in the urban area as a whole was mostly to the north in Saitama Prefecture, as well as scattered further afield in Gunma, Tochigi, and Chiba Prefectures (map A.7).

Despite having arguably lost its global first-place position during this period, the Tokyo urban area still had an extremely large population by any standard: 28 million people in 2000, increasing to 32 million in 2010. This growth rate of 1.4 percent was slow compared with other East Asian urban areas, but it did result in an addition of more than 4 million people in 10 years. About 38 percent of the population of the urban area lived in Tokyo itself, while 21 percent lived in Kanagawa and 18 percent lived in Saitama. The greatest increase in population, about 1.6 million, took place within the jurisdiction of Tokyo. In the urban area as a whole, only 33 square meters were built per additional urban resident, among the lowest amounts

Map A.7   Urban expansion in the Tokyo, Japan, urban area, 2000–10

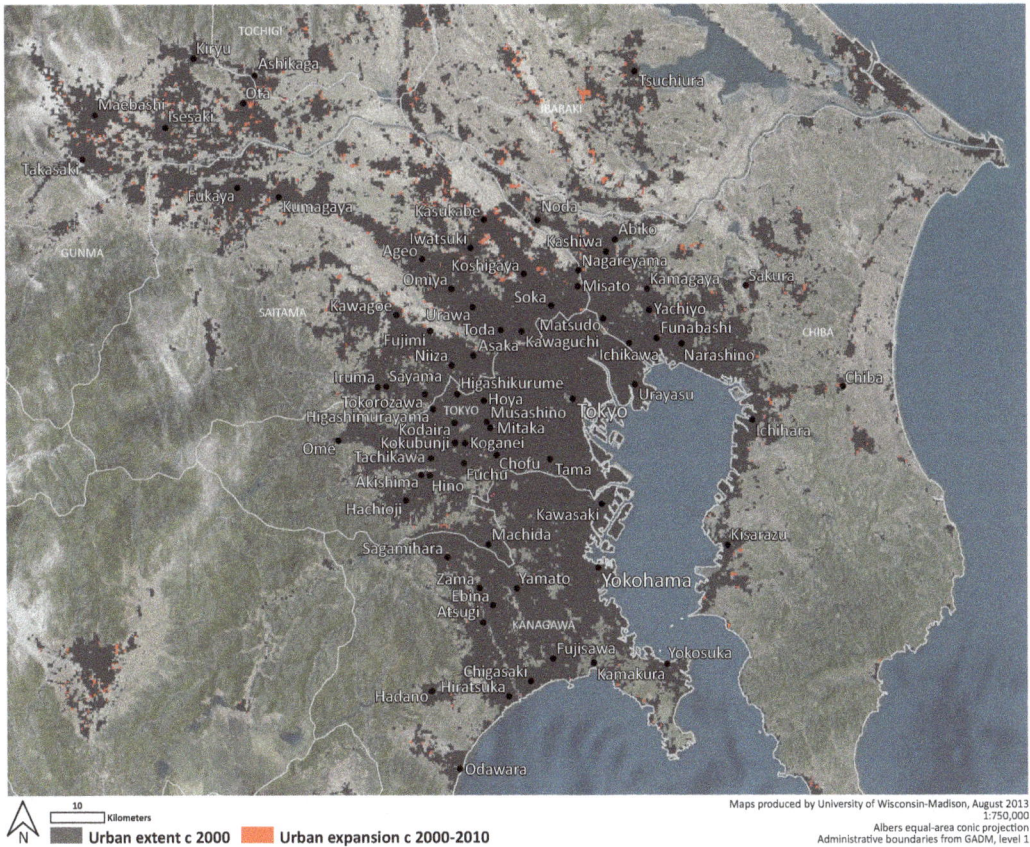

Maps produced by University of Wisconsin-Madison, August 2013
1:750,000
Albers equal-area conic projection
Administrative boundaries from GADM, level 1

■ Urban extent c 2000   ■ Urban expansion c 2000-2010

anywhere in East Asia. Tokyo had the lowest urban population density among any of the region's megacity urban areas, about 5,700 people per square kilometer in 2010.

The Osaka-Kobe urban area, which by this study's definition includes Kyoto, Kobe, and surrounding areas,[9] is Japan's second megacity. It comprised about 2,100 square kilometers in 2010, having almost ceased to expand spatially, with negligible growth (about 25 square kilometers) between 2000 and 2010 (map A.8). The average annual rate of growth, 0.1 percent, was the slowest of any urban area in East Asia of more than 5 million people. Both the Beijing and Shanghai urban areas became spatially larger than the Osaka-Kobe urban area during this period.

Despite still being larger in area than other megacity in the region, such as Jakarta, Manila, and Seoul, the Osaka-Kobe urban area has a smaller population due to its lower population density. Its urban population grew from 10.6 million people to 12.3 million between 2000 and 2010, an increase of 1.4 percent a year. Although among the slower rates of urban population growth of urban areas in the region, it significantly outpaced its spatial growth, resulting in an increase in density from 5,200 people per square kilometer to almost 6,000. However, this density was still lower

Map A.8   Urban expansion in the Osaka, Japan, urban area, 2000–10

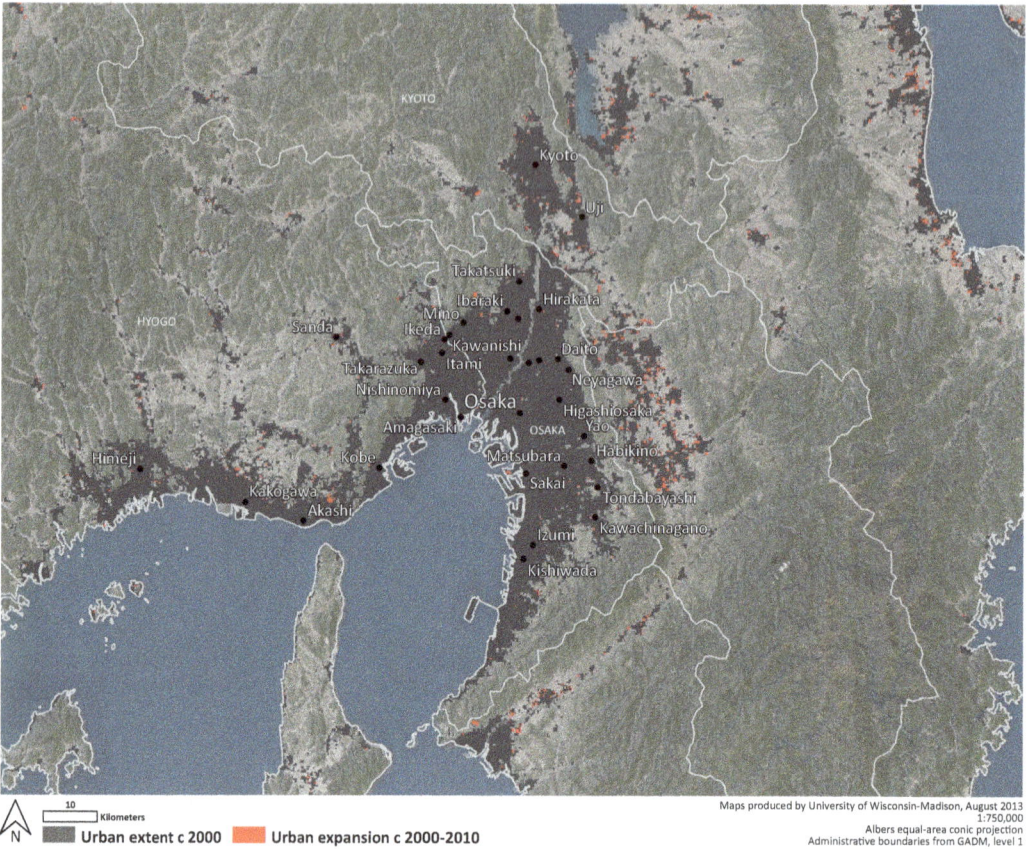

Maps produced by University of Wisconsin-Madison, August 2013
1:750,000
Albers equal-area conic projection
Administrative boundaries from GADM, level 1

Urban extent c 2000   Urban expansion c 2000-2010

than the average for the megacities in the region (7,300 people per square kilometer).

Of the built-up area, 49 percent was located within Osaka Prefecture, 40 percent was in Hyogo Prefecture, and the remainder in Kyoto Prefecture. The population was more concentrated within Osaka Prefecture, which had 59 percent of the population, or 7.3 million residents. The municipality of Osaka was home to more than 2 million people itself. Hyogo Prefecture had 29 percent of the population, or 3.5 million people, with Kobe municipality within it having more than a million people. The remaining 12 percent, or 1.5 million people, lived in Kyoto Prefecture, with Kyoto municipality having more than a million inhabitants as well.

The Republic of Korea

The Republic of Korea is at a relatively advanced stage of urbanization. Its urban areas are still growing, but densities have stabilized. The Seoul urban area, which is very densely populated, accounts for nearly half of the urban land and 60 percent of the urban population of the country.

In geographic size, the Republic of Korea is one of the smallest countries on the mainland of East Asia. It is also one of the most urbanized, with 2.5 percent of its total land area being built up in 2010, up from 2.2 percent in 2000 (compared with, for example, 0.9 percent of Vietnam and China or 0.5 percent of Indonesia in 2010). In absolute terms, the amount of urban land increased from 2,200 square kilometers to 2,500 during this period. At this relatively advanced stage of urbanization, this rate of urban growth (1.3 percent a year) is not rapid compared with most East Asian countries, slightly less than half the rate for the region as a whole.

Demographically, the Republic of Korea is one of the most urbanized countries in the region, with 24 million people in 2000 and 27 million in 2010 living in urban areas with more than 100,000 people. As of 2010, it had the fourth-largest urban population in the region, after China, Indonesia, and Japan. The Republic of Korea's urban population density remained the highest in the region, at 10,500 people per square kilometer in 2010. Its urban population is growing at a rate similar to that of its built-up area, 1.2 percent a year. This has resulted in stable overall urban density, making the Republic of Korea one of the few countries in East Asia in which urban density is not increasing.

The Seoul urban area, one of the region's megacity urban areas, is home to almost 16 million people. The country also has three urban areas of 1 million to 5 million people, four of 500,000 to 1 million, and eight of 100,000 to 500,000, as of 2010. Figures A.21 and A.22 show the growth in urban land and population in these urban areas between 2000 and 2010.

The Seoul urban area dominates the urban landscape of the Republic of Korea (map A.9). Half of the urban land and 60 percent of the urban population were located in Seoul in 2010 (figures A.23 and A.24). In spatial extent, it grew 1.1 percent a year between 2000 and 2010, from about 1,100 square kilometers to 1,200. This rate of growth was slightly slower than smaller urban areas in the country. During the same period, its population also grew at the same rate, 1.1 percent a year, from 14.3 million people to 15.9 million. The density of built-up areas of Seoul remained stable at about 13,300 people per square kilometer (more than twice as dense as the megacities of Japan). In 2000, Seoul was the densest megacity in the region, but it was overtaken by the Jakarta urban area by 2010.

The Seoul urban area, defined according to built-up area to include parts of Incheon and Gyeonggi-do, covers 59 districts, including 25 in the city of Seoul itself. Although the built-up areas of Seoul are dense, they are not all contiguous. Almost all the new growth (97 percent) occurred outside

Figure A.21   **The Republic of Korea: Urban areas by built-up area, 2000 and 2010**

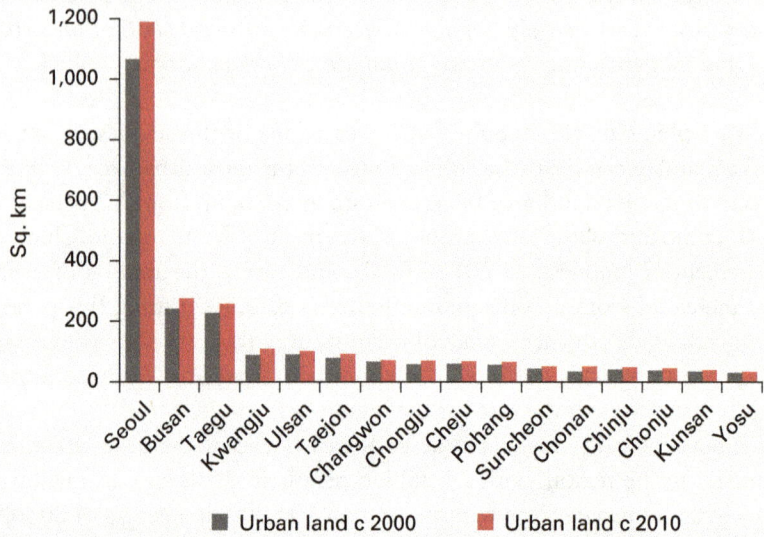

■ Urban land c 2000   ■ Urban land c 2010

Source: Study team, incorporating WorldPop data, http://www.worldpop.org.uk/data/.

Figure A.22   **The Republic of Korea: Urban areas by population, 2000 and 2010**

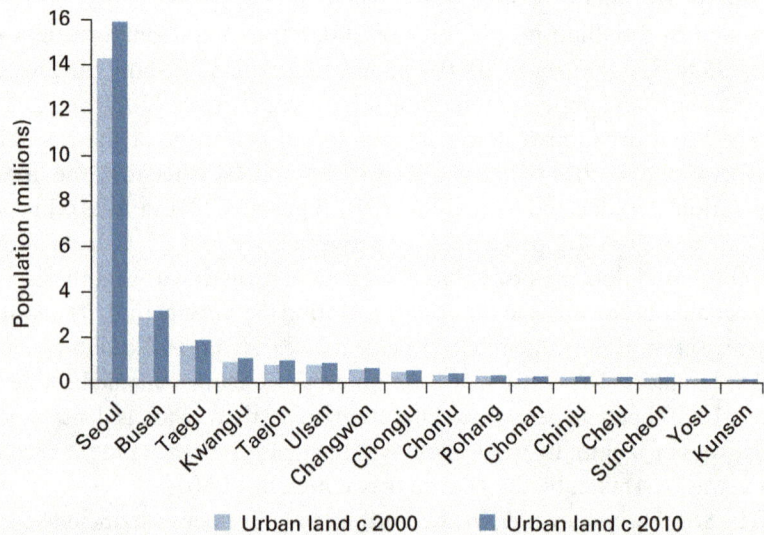

■ Urban land c 2000   ■ Urban land c 2010

Source: Study team, incorporating WorldPop data, http://www.worldpop.org.uk/data/.

Figure A.23 The Republic of Korea: Urban land by population size category, 2000 and 2010

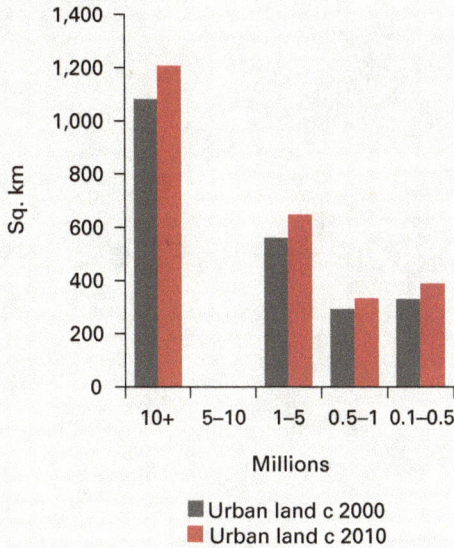

Sq. km

1,400
1,200
1,000
800
600
400
200
0

10+   5–10   1–5   0.5–1   0.1–0.5

Millions

■ Urban land c 2000
■ Urban land c 2010

Source: Study team, incorporating WorldPop data, http://www.worldpop.org.uk/data/.

Figure A.24 The Republic of Korea: Urban population by population size category, 2000 and 2010

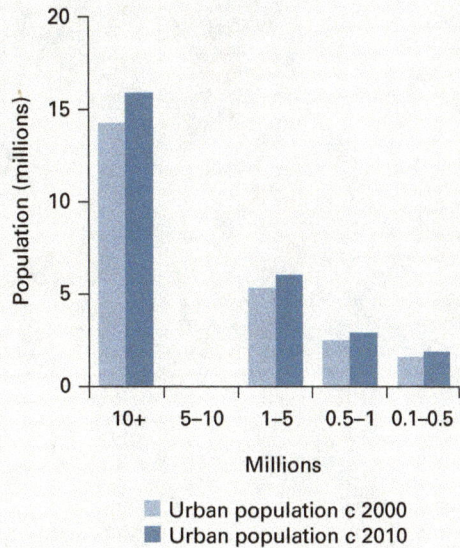

Population (millions)

20

15

10

5

0

10+   5–10   1–5   0.5–1   0.1–0.5

Millions

■ Urban population c 2000
■ Urban population c 2010

Source: Study team, incorporating WorldPop data, http://www.worldpop.org.uk/data/.

the administrative region of Seoul itself, with the majority in Gyeonggi-do, the surrounding province, mostly in the districts of Hwaseong to the south of the city, and Paju and Gimpo to the north. Approximately half of the population of the urban area (7.8 million in 2010) lived within the city of Seoul. The districts within Seoul with the highest residential density were Jungnang (with almost 64,000 people per square kilometer), Gandong, and Yangcheon. Outside the boundary of Seoul, historic towns such as Bucheon and Gwangmyeong form pockets of higher density within the broader urban area.

Map A.9   Urban expansion in the Seoul, Republic of Korea, urban area, 2000–10

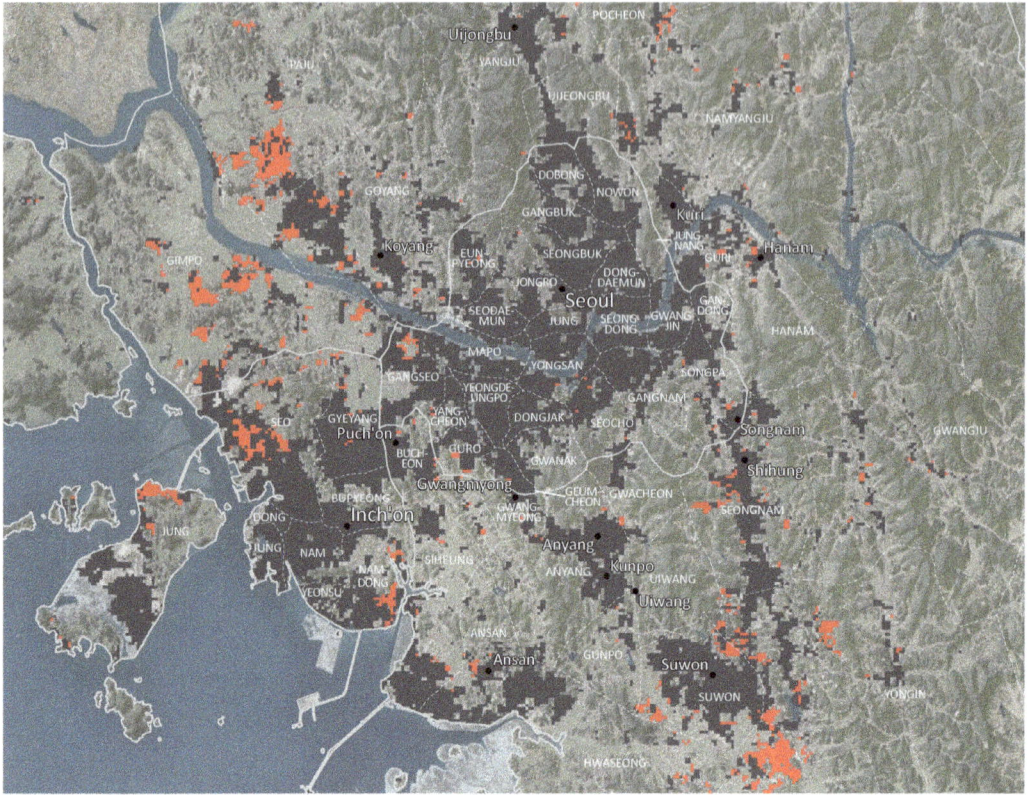

Maps produced by University of Wisconsin-Madison, August 2013
1:350,000
Albers equal-area conic projection
Administrative boundaries from GADM, levels 1 and 2

Urban extent c 2000   Urban expansion c 2000-2010

Lao People's Democratic Republic

Although it remains one of the least urban countries in the region, Lao PDR is starting to urbanize rapidly, with the highest rates of urban spatial expansion and urban population increase in East Asia. Its urban population more than doubled between 2000 and 2010. Vientiane, the capital, is very small by East Asian standards, but it doubled in size and population during this period. Urban population densities in Lao PDR were among the lowest in the region.

Lao PDR had the third-smallest amount of urban land among the countries studied, after Papua New Guinea and Timor-Leste. According to the figures in this study, the only urban area of more than 100,000 people was the capital, Vientiane, which covered less than 0.1 percent of the total land mass of the country. This was the second-lowest proportion of urban land in East Asia after Mongolia. However, the increase in urban land during this period, from 50 square kilometers in 2000 to 100 in 2010, was the fastest rate of increase of any country in the region, 7.3 percent a year.

The same applies to population: Lao PDR had the smallest urban population, but the highest rate of increase during this period. Estimates of urban population in Lao PDR vary greatly,[10] but when including only urban areas with more than 100,000 people, Lao PDR's urban population is situated entirely within the Vientiane urban area, which more than doubled from 134,000 (2.5 percent of the total population) in 2000 to 307,000 (5.0 percent) in 2010. This rate of urban population increase, 8.6 percent a year, was far higher than in any other country in the region; the second fastest was Cambodia at 4.4 percent. Lao PDR's urban population density was the second lowest in 2010 among the countries studied, after Brunei Darussalam, but increased slightly during this period, from 2,800 people per square kilometer to 3,200.

About a quarter of the urban area, as well as a quarter of the urban expansion, around Vientiane was in Chanthabuly district, while Hadxaifong, Sikhottabong, Sisattanak, Xaythany, and Xaysetha each had between 10 percent and 20 percent of the urban land as well as the urban expansion (map A.10).

Map A.10   Urban expansion in Vientiane, Lao PDR, 2000–10

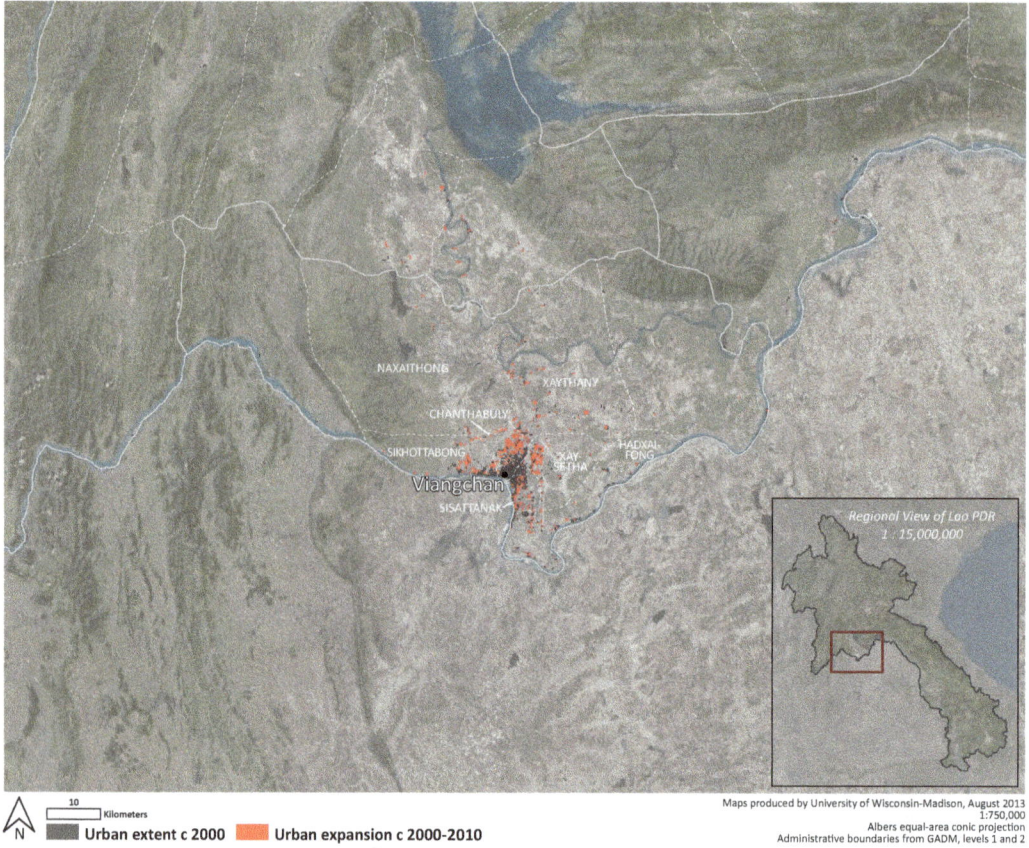

Maps produced by University of Wisconsin-Madison, August 2013
1:750,000
Albers equal-area conic projection
Administrative boundaries from GADM, levels 1 and 2

Urban extent c 2000   **Urban expansion c 2000-2010**

Malaysia

Malaysia is among the more urbanized countries of East Asia, and its urban population continues to increase rapidly. However, urban areas in Malaysia are among the least dense in East Asia. The Kuala Lumpur urban area is one of the largest in the region as measured by area, but not as measured by population.

Malaysia had the fourth-largest amount of built-up land in East Asia as of 2010. Its urban land grew from about 3,900 square kilometers to 4,600 between 2000 and 2010, an average annual growth rate of 1.5 percent, which was lower than the 2.4 percent average for the region. However the absolute amount of urban spatial expansion was among the highest in the region, lower than only China, Indonesia, and Vietnam. Urban areas covered approximately 1.4 percent of the total area of the country in 2010, which was among the highest in the region.

In comparison with the other countries, a lower proportion of increase in built-up land occurred on arable land (76 percent, as opposed to more than 85 percent for most countries). However, it also lost a larger proportion of its total arable land to built-up land during this period: 1.2 percent, as opposed to 0.7 percent for the region as a whole.[11]

The urban population of Malaysia (in urban areas of more than 100,000 people) increased during this period from 10.2 million (43 percent of the total population) to 15.0 million (53 percent), making it among the more urbanized countries and economies in the region in demographic terms, after Japan, the Republic of Korea, and Singapore (and Taiwan, China). However, because of its smaller total population, it had only the seventh-largest urban population in absolute terms. The rate of urban population growth, 4.0 percent a year, on average, was among the fastest in the region, surpassed only by Lao PDR, Cambodia (both of which have much smaller urban populations), and Vietnam.

Urban areas in Malaysia were, on average, among the least dense in East Asia, with an overall urban population density of 3,300 people per square kilometer in 2010, up from 2,600 in 2000, and lower than the regional average of almost 5,800 people per square kilometer.

As of 2010, Malaysia had 19 urban areas with more than 100,000 people: 1 urban area of more than 5 million people (Kuala Lumpur), 2 between 1 million and 5 million people (George Town and Johor Bahru), 5 of 500,000 to 1 million people, and 11 urban areas of between 100,000 and 500,000 people.

As of 2010, the Kuala Lumpur urban area was the eighth largest in the region, larger than some megacity urban areas like Jakarta, Manila, and Seoul despite its smaller population. It grew from about 1,500 square kilometers to 1,700 between 2000 and 2010 (figure A.25), an average annual growth rate of 1.2 percent, which was among the lower growth rates for urban areas of this size in the region.

Figure A.25   Malaysia: Urban areas by built-up area, 2000 and 2010

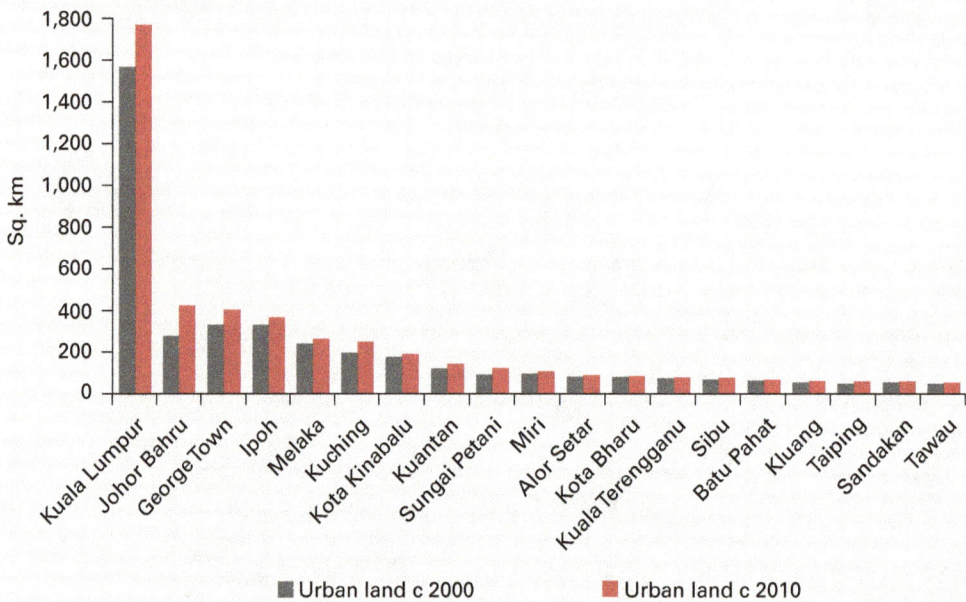

Source: Study team, incorporating WorldPop data, http://www.worldpop.org.uk/data/.

Despite being the eighth-largest urban area in size, because of its low density, the Kuala Lumpur urban area was only the twenty-second largest in population. The overall urban area grew from about 4.0 million inhabitants in 2000 to 5.8 million in 2010 (figure A.26), a relatively high average annual growth rate of 3.8 percent. It had a very low urban population density, just 3,300 people per square kilometer in 2010, up from 2,600 in 2000. This was the lowest of any urban area of 5 million inhabitants and above in East Asia, and the third lowest among the 131 urban areas with more than 1 million inhabitants in the region (with the second lowest being Johor Bahru, also in Malaysia).

For the purposes of this study, the Kuala Lumpur urban area includes the administrative areas of Kuala Lumpur and Putrajaya, as well as the eight surrounding districts of Selangor, and areas in and around Seremban. The pattern of growth of the Kuala Lumpur urban area is fairly fragmented and scattered, and during this period no major new corridors of growth appeared. Much of the new growth was infill development, closing some of the gaps between existing built-up areas (map A.11).

Johor Bahru saw rapid growth during this period, taking advantage of its location immediately across a narrow strait from Singapore (map A.12). Growing from 270 square kilometers to 420 between 2000 and 2010 (4.4 percent a year), it surpassed George Town and Ipoh to become the second-largest urban area in the country. However, despite rapid population

Figure A.26   Malaysia: Urban areas by population, 2000 and 2010

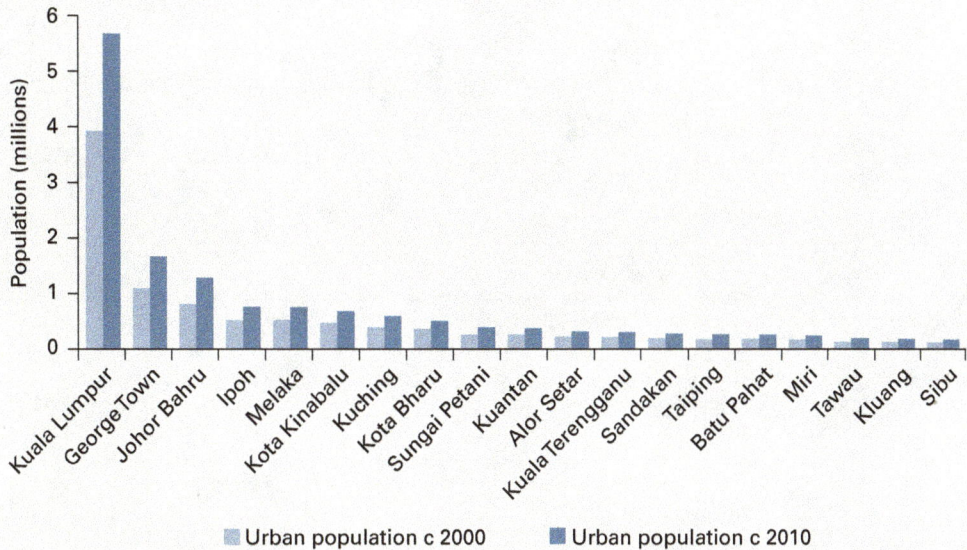

■ Urban population c 2000   ■ Urban population c 2010

Source: Study team, incorporating WorldPop data, http://www.worldpop.org.uk/data/.

Figure A.27   Malaysia: Urban land by population size category, 2000 and 2010

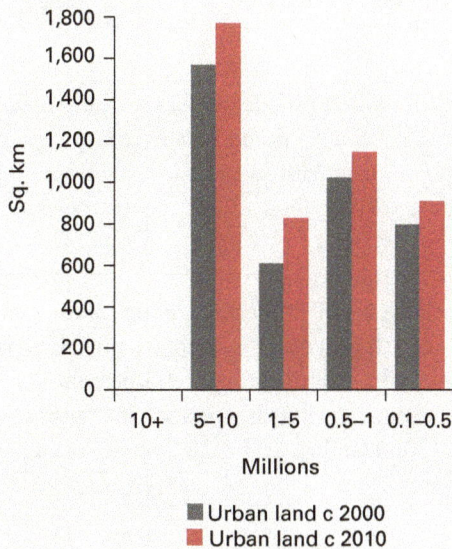

■ Urban land c 2000
■ Urban land c 2010

Source: Study team, incorporating WorldPop data, http://www.worldpop.org.uk/data/.

Figure A.28   Malaysia: Urban population by population size category, 2000 and 2010

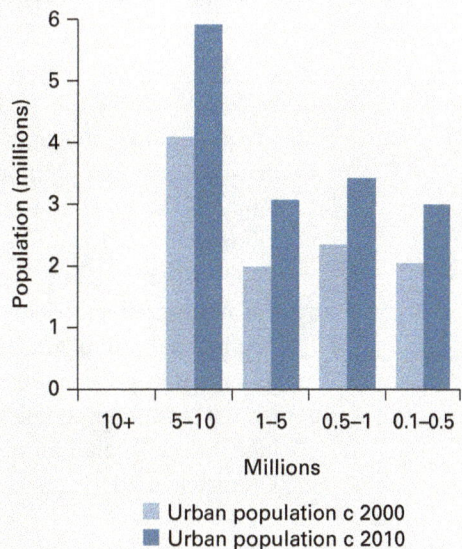

■ Urban population c 2000
■ Urban population c 2010

Source: Study team, incorporating WorldPop data, http://www.worldpop.org.uk/data/.

Map A.11   Urban expansion in the Kuala Lumpur, Malaysia, urban area, 2000–10

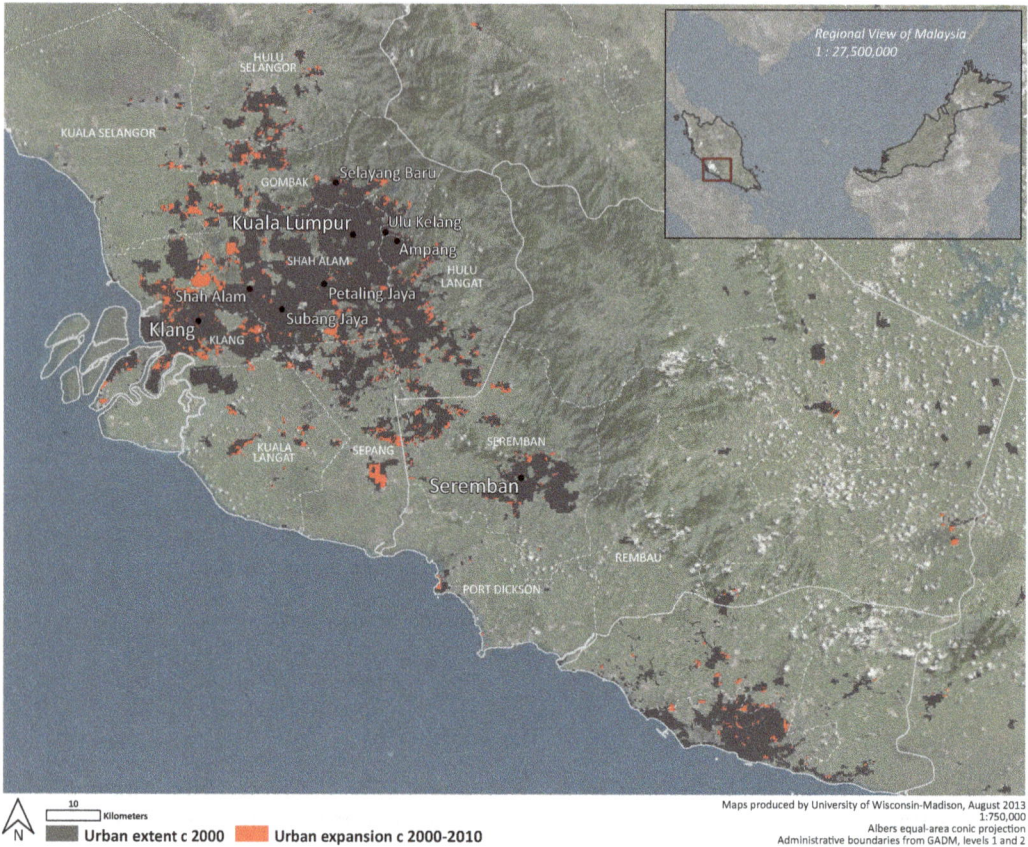

Maps produced by University of Wisconsin-Madison, August 2013
1:750,000
Albers equal-area conic projection
Administrative boundaries from GADM, levels 1 and 2

Kilometers

■ Urban extent c 2000   ■ Urban expansion c 2000-2010

Note: In this map, only labeled areas are counted as part of the Kuala Lumpur urban area.

growth from 820,000 people to 1.3 million (4.7 percent a year), it remained smaller than George Town in population. As noted earlier, it had very low density compared with other urban areas with more than 1 million inhabitants in the East Asia region as a whole, about 3,100 people per square kilometer in 2010.

The urban area of George Town (including Butterworth and surrounding areas) grew more slowly spatially, from about 330 square kilometers to 400 between 2000 and 2010, a growth rate of 2.0 percent a year. However, its rate of population increase was also relatively high, 4.3 percent a year, from 1.1 million people to 1.7 million during this period. Its density was higher than Kuala Lumpur's and Johor Bahru's, at 4,200 people per square kilometer in 2010.

Map A.12   Urban expansion in Johor Bahru, Malaysia, and Singapore, 2000–10

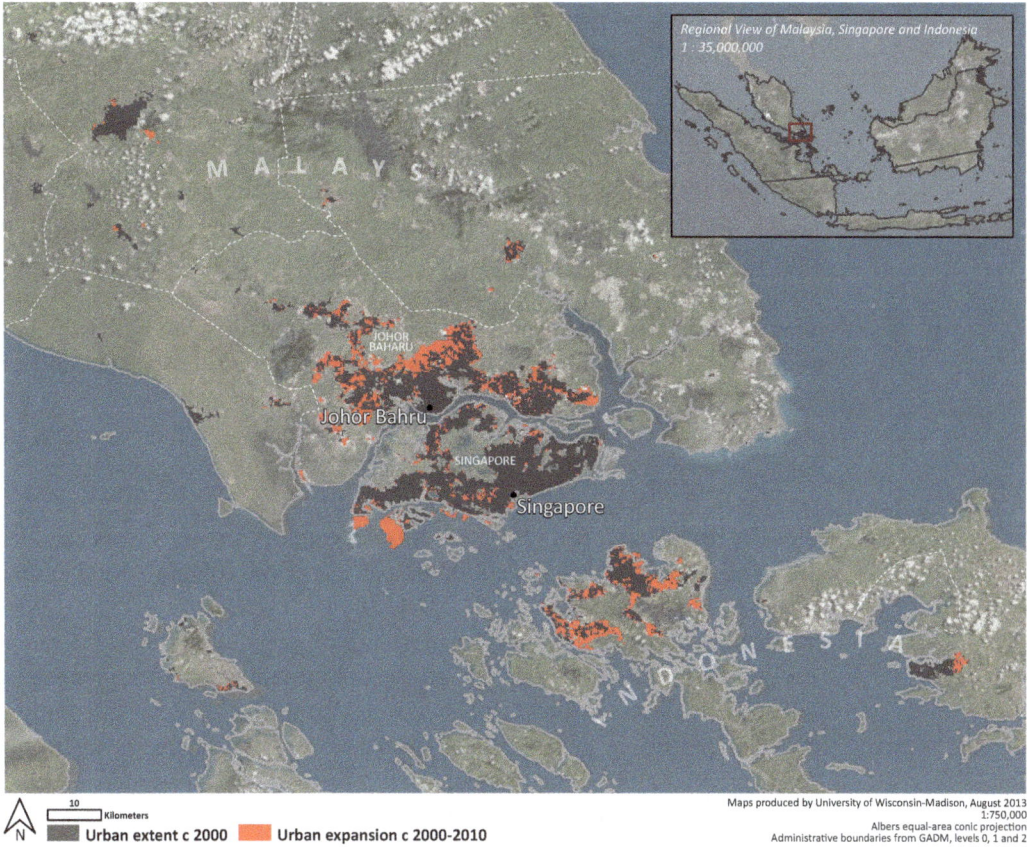

Regional View of Malaysia, Singapore and Indonesia
1 : 35,000,000

Urban extent c 2000   Urban expansion c 2000-2010

Maps produced by University of Wisconsin-Madison, August 2013
1:750,000
Albers equal-area conic projection
Administrative boundaries from GADM, levels 0, 1 and 2

Mongolia

Mongolia has a very small amount of built-up land, concentrated mostly in Ulaanbaatar. Ulaanbaatar has a low population density, and is expanding.

Despite being geographically one of the largest countries in East Asia (the third largest, after China and Indonesia), Mongolia has among the lowest amounts of urban area: 210 square kilometers in 2000, increasing to 270 square kilometers in 2010, all of which was in the capital, Ulaanbaatar, the only urban area with more than 100,000 people by the measure used in this study.[12] This represented an urban spatial expansion rate of 2.6 percent per year. Although Ulaanbaatar is not a very large or dense city by East Asian standards, 34 percent of the entire population of the country lives on less than 0.02 percent of the country's total land area here.

In most other countries in the region, the majority of the increase in built-up land occurred on arable land. However, in Mongolia, only 1.7 percent of the increase in built-up land occurred on land classified as arable. The arable land lost to urbanization during this period was negligible: 1.4 square kilometers, less than 0.001 percent of the country's total arable land.[13]

Mongolia has one of the smallest urban populations in the region. For the purposes of this regional study, only urban areas with more than 100,000 people are included, which means that the entire urban population of Mongolia lies in Ulaanbaatar, which had 927,000 people in 2010, up from 630,000 in 2000 (an annual growth rate of 4 percent) (map A.13).[14] Despite this small national urban population, the rate of change was relatively high, 3.9 percent per year. During this period, the proportion of the country's population living in Ulaanbaatar rose from 26 percent to 34 percent.

Urban expansion of Ulaanbaatar is characterized by the sprawl of low-density *ger* areas, which are residential neighborhoods consisting of traditional tent dwellings. Because of this pattern of urban development, the amount of new urban land per new urban resident between 2000 and 2010 was among the highest of the countries studied, 210 square meters per person. Urban areas in Mongolia remain less dense than in most other East Asian countries, but did increase from 3,000 people per square kilometer in 2000 to 3,400 in 2010.

Map A.13   **Urban expansion in Ulaanbaatar, Mongolia, 2000–10**

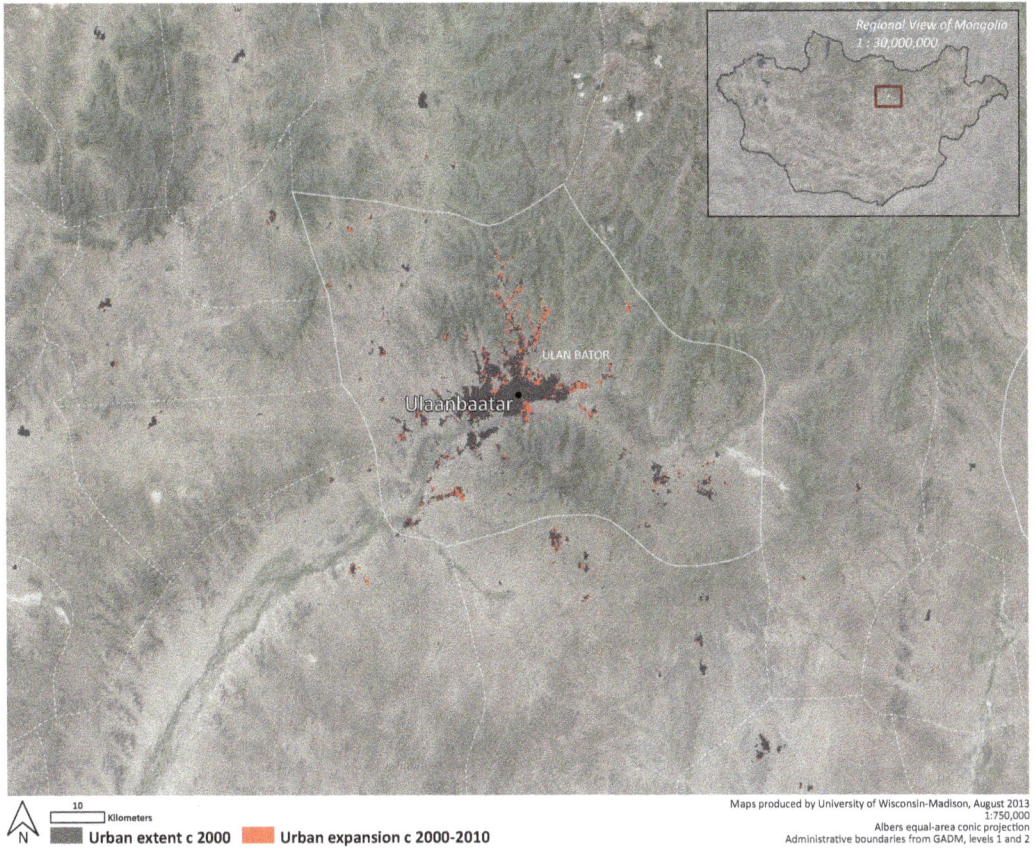

Regional View of Mongolia
1 : 30,000,000

ULAN BATOR

Ulaanbaatar

10 Kilometers

Urban extent c 2000   Urban expansion c 2000-2010

Maps produced by University of Wisconsin-Madison, August 2013
1:750,000
Albers equal-area conic projection
Administrative boundaries from GADM, levels 1 and 2

Myanmar

Myanmar is at a nascent stage of urbanization. Between 2000 and 2010, the country's urban population increased without the construction of large amounts of new urban area.

Urbanization in Myanmar during the first decade of the 2000s lagged behind that of its neighbors, likely as a result of Myanmar's economic isolation, which continued until about 2010. Despite being geographically one of the larger countries in the region, more than twice as large as Vietnam or Malaysia, it had less than a third of the urban area of Vietnam and a fifth of that of Malaysia. The amount of urban land in Myanmar increased during this period from 760 square kilometers to 830, an increase of just 0.8 percent per year, one of the lowest rates of increase in built-up land in the region. Urban areas covered just 0.1 percent of the area of Myanmar, the fifth lowest among the 18 countries studied.

Although the country's population remains largely rural, urban population growth was faster than spatial growth. The population in urban areas of Myanmar increased from 4.7 million in 2000 (10 percent of the population) to 6.2 million in 2010 (13 percent of the population). This increase of 1.5 million people represented an annual rate of growth of almost 2.8 percent, slightly lower than the average for the region (3.0 percent).

The density of urban areas was 6,200 people per square kilometer in 2000, increasing to 7,500 by 2010. This density was higher than the average for urban areas in the East Asia region as a whole, and the second-largest increase in density after Indonesia. However, new urban expansion has been very economical, with slightly more than 40 square meters of new urban land constructed per additional urban resident, the lowest ratio in the region with the exception of Indonesia.

As of 2010, Myanmar had no large urban areas by East Asian standards, but had two medium-sized ones in the 1 million to 5 million population range, Yangon and Mandalay (figure A.29). It has none between 500,000 and 1 million inhabitants, and eight urban areas between 100,000 and 500,000 (figures A.30 and A.31). (This study does not include Naypyidaw, a greenfield site to which the capital of Myanmar moved in the mid-2000s.)

Yangon, the capital until 2006, is Myanmar's largest urban area. However, spatially it barely grew during this period (map A.14), expanding at a rate of 0.5 percent a year between 2000 and 2010, from 370 square kilometers to 390. It has 19 percent of the total built-up land in Myanmar but only 10 percent of the new built-up land, suggesting that the gap between Yangon and other urban areas is diminishing. Yangon's population grew much faster than its area, at 2.6 percent a year from 2.6 million people to 3.4 million. The ratio between new land and new residents was just 24 square meters per additional resident, much lower than the average for urban areas in the country as a whole (69 square meters). This led to an increase in density in the urban area, from 7,100 people per square kilometer to 8,800.

Figure A.29   Myanmar: Urban areas by built-up area, 2000 and 2010

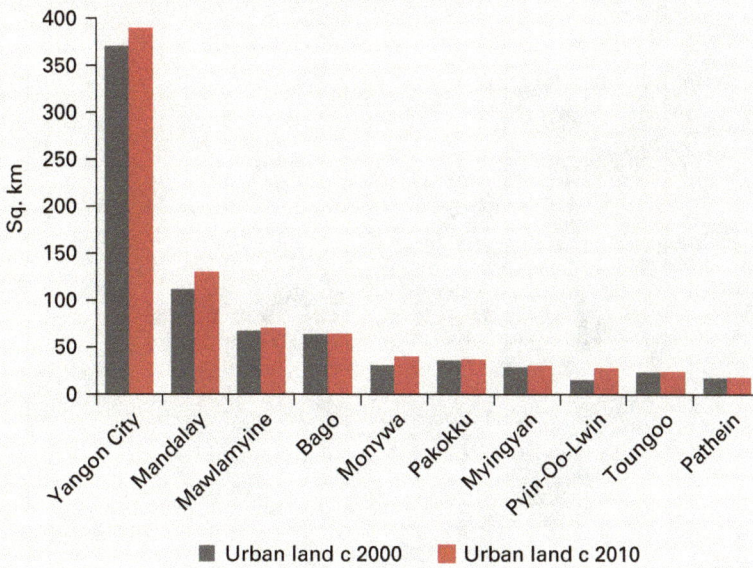

■ Urban land c 2000   ■ Urban land c 2010

Source: Study team, incorporating WorldPop data, http://www.worldpop.org.uk/data/.

Figure A.30   Myanmar: Urban land by population size category, 2000 and 2010

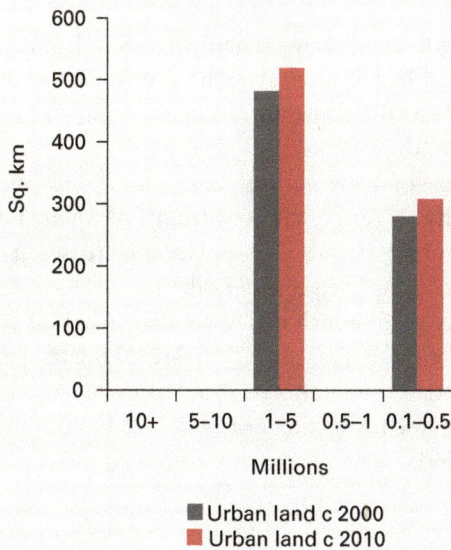

■ Urban land c 2000
■ Urban land c 2010

Source: Study team, incorporating WorldPop data, http://www.worldpop.org.uk/data/.

Figure A.31   Myanmar: Urban population by population size category, 2000 and 2010

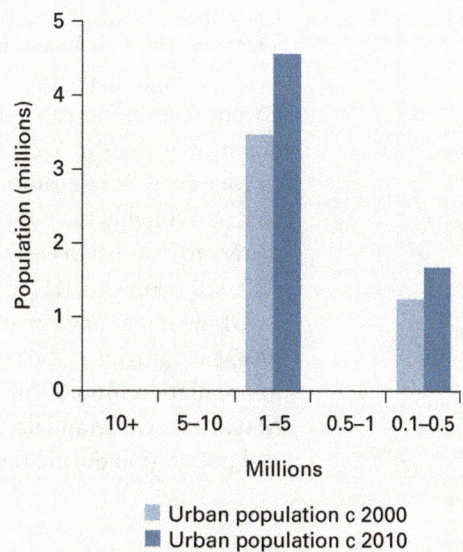

■ Urban population c 2000
■ Urban population c 2010

Source: Study team, incorporating WorldPop data, http://www.worldpop.org.uk/data/.

Map A.14   Urban expansion in the Yangon, Myanmar, urban area, 2000–10

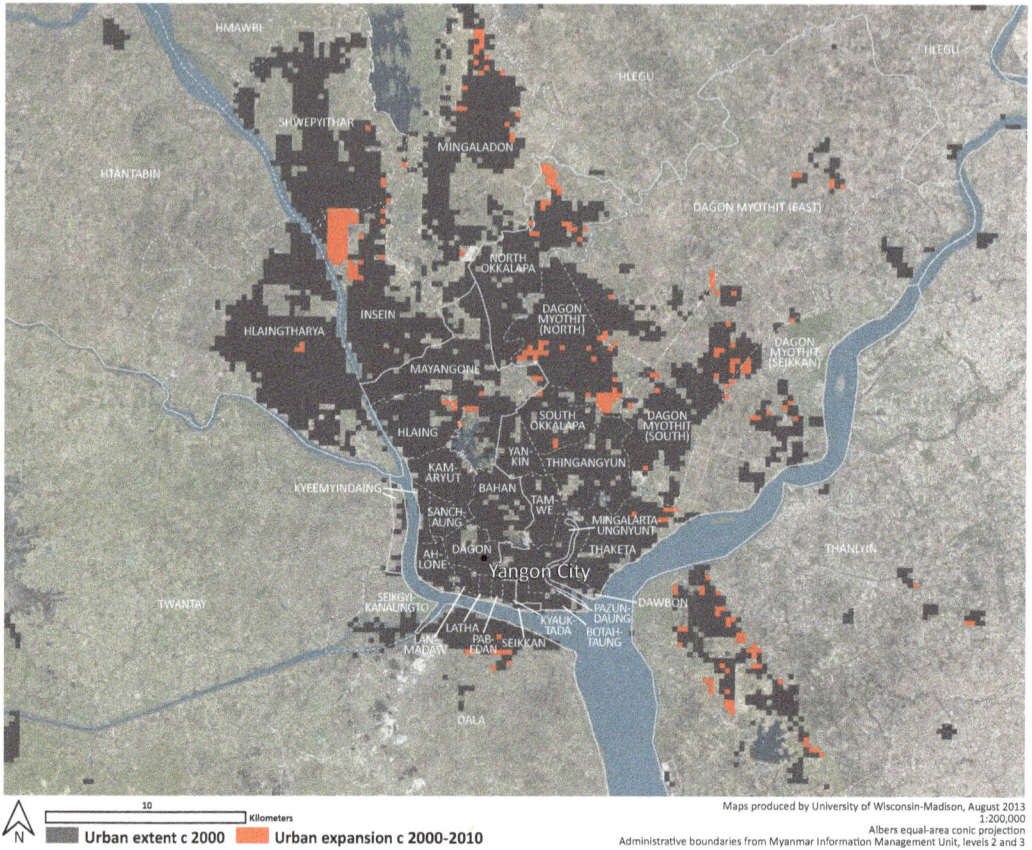

Maps produced by University of Wisconsin-Madison, August 2013
1:200,000
Albers equal-area conic projection
Administrative boundaries from Myanmar Information Management Unit, levels 2 and 3

■ Urban extent c 2000   ■ Urban expansion c 2000-2010

The townships of Insein in North Yangon and Thanlyin in South Yangon saw the highest proportion of urban spatial growth as well as the fastest population increases. However, the densest townships remained in the downtown areas in West and South Yangon.

Mandalay is one-third the size of Yangon, both in size and population, so it had roughly the same density as Yangon. It grew from 110 square kilometers to 130 between 2000 and 2010, and its population increased from 820,000 people to 1.13 million during the same period.

Of the remaining urban areas, all of which had fewer than 500,000 people, Mawlamyine is the largest of these spatially (70 square kilometers) and in population (460,000). The small urban area of Pyin Oo Lwin (formerly Maymyo) near Mandalay is notable for having nearly doubled in both size and population during this period.

The Philippines

The urban landscape of the Philippines is polarized, with one megacity urban area, Manila, and a number of much smaller urban areas. There is a "missing middle," an absence of medium-sized competitors to the capital. The Manila urban area is notable not just for its size and density but also for its extreme administrative fragmentation: 85 municipalities and cities are involved in its governance. Urban areas in the Philippines are among the densest in the region, and are becoming denser.

In 2010, the Philippines had the eighth-largest amount of built-up area in the East Asia region. In absolute terms, the increase in built-up land in the Philippines between 2000 and 2010, from 1,800 square kilometers to 2,300 (2.4 percent per year), was the sixth highest in the region in both absolute and proportional terms. The Philippines has the fifth-largest urban population in the region, increasing during this period from 17 million people to 23 million (3.3 percent a year). The population of the country that was "urban" by this report's definition (living in urban areas of more than 100,000 people) was 25 percent in 2010, which was lower than the proportion for the region as a whole (36 percent).

The average population density of urban areas in the Philippines, 10,300 people per square kilometer in 2010, was the second highest in the region, slightly less than the Republic of Korea's. Unlike the Republic of Korea's urban population density, which has stabilized, that of the Philippines increased from 9,500 people per square kilometer in 2000.

The Philippines is home to one of the region's megacities of 10 million or more inhabitants: the Manila urban area, home to 16.5 million people in 2010. The next largest urban area in the country as measured by population, Cebu, is much smaller, at 1.5 million. Three urban areas are in the 500,000 to 1 million population range, and another 16 are in the 100,000 to 500,000 range, as of 2010.

The Manila urban area is the Philippines' undisputed primate city, with no close competitors. In 2010, it had 56 percent of the urban land in the country and more than 70 percent of the country's urban population, though these proportions decreased slightly between 2000 and 2010. It is spatially seven times larger than the second-largest urban area, Angeles City (figures A.32 and A.33), and 10 times more populous than the second most populous urban area, Cebu. Manila grew spatially from about 1,000 square kilometers to 1,300 between 2000 and 2010 (2.2 percent a year). During this period, the population of this urban area increased from 12.2 million people to 16.5 million (3.1 percent a year).

The Manila urban area is also one of the densest in the Philippines—only two urban areas, both under 500,000 in population, have higher urban population densities. Also, like almost all urban areas in the country, Manila is becoming even denser. Its population density increased from 11,900 people per square kilometer to almost 13,000 between 2000 and 2010.

Figure A.32   The Philippines: The 20 largest urban areas by built-up area, 2000 and 2010

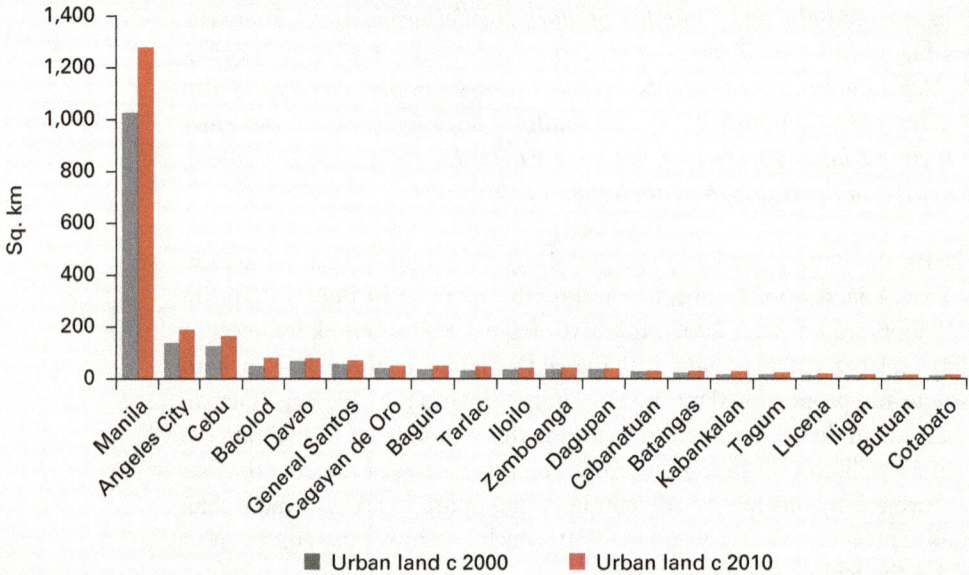

■ Urban land c 2000   ■ Urban land c 2010

Source: Study team, incorporating WorldPop data, http://www.worldpop.org.uk/data/.

Figure A.33   The Philippines: Urban land by population size category, 2000 and 2010

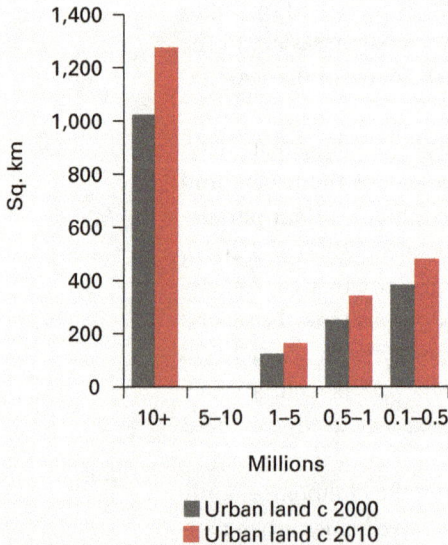

Millions

■ Urban land c 2000
■ Urban land c 2010

Source: Study team, incorporating WorldPop data, http://www.worldpop.org.uk/data/.

Figure A.34   The Philippines: Urban population by population size category, 2000 and 2010

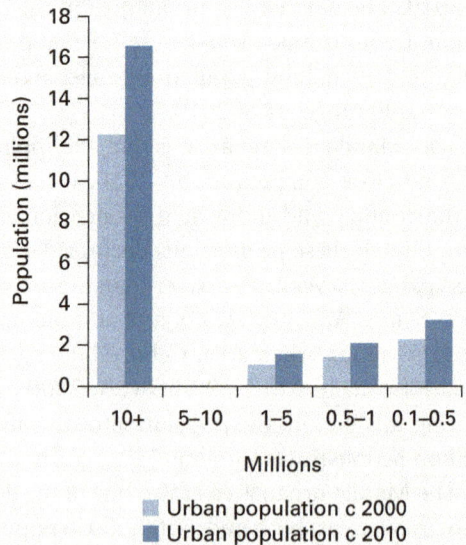

Millions

■ Urban population c 2000
■ Urban population c 2010

Source: Study team, incorporating WorldPop data, http://www.worldpop.org.uk/data/.

The fact that Metropolitan Manila is composed of 17 separate local government units makes it an oft-cited case of metropolitan fragmentation. In
fact, the built-up area of the urban area shows that this vastly understates
the issue. The urban area, as defined here, based on built-up extents, covers an incredible 85 municipalities and cities in seven provinces including
Metro Manila.

Less than 40 percent of the overall built-up land in the Manila urban
area is within Metro Manila's administrative boundaries, as of 2010. However, Metro Manila is home to nearly 70 percent of the overall population.
Less than 3 percent of the urban land is in the City of Manila itself (which
is within Metro Manila), but more than 10 percent of the population lives
there. The individual municipality or city with both the largest amount of
urban land and the largest population is Quezon City in Metro Manila. It
has 10 percent of the overall urban land and 16 percent of the overall population. The surrounding provinces of Bulacan, Cavite, Laguna, and Rizal
each administer between 10 percent and 20 percent of the overall area, but
smaller proportions of the total population.

Most of Metro Manila was already built up by 2000, so almost all the
new spatial growth (94 percent) occurred in the neighboring provinces, as
is evident from map A.15. Nearly 30 percent of the new spatial growth
since 2000 was in Cavite to the south of Metro Manila, and about 25 percent each in Bulacan to the north and Laguna to the southeast. About half
the population growth occurred in Metro Manila, mostly in Quezon City
(an increase of more than 500,000 people), Kalookan City (an increase of
300,000 people), and the City of Manila (300,000 also). Metro Manila is
much denser than the rest of the urban area, with the City of Manila the
densest local unit (almost 48,000 people per square kilometer). In total, the
administrative area of Metro Manila added nearly 2.3 million additional
residents with a negligible increase in urban built-up area (just 14 square
kilometers).

Of the four other urban areas in the Philippines with populations of
more than 500,000, Cebu has the largest population. It grew rapidly from
1 million people to 1.5 million (4.1 percent a year) between 2000 and 2010.
However, the Angeles City urban area, though it has fewer than 700,000
people, has a larger area (190 square kilometers) than Cebu (160 square
kilometers) due to its much lower density. Davao, despite having a larger
population than Angeles City, more than 800,000 people, was less than
half as large as measured by spatial extents. Bacolod was one of only two
urban areas in which population density declined.

These midlevel urban areas provide an interesting contrast in administrative arrangements. The Angeles City urban area (which includes San Fer-
nando) is a "fragmented" urban area—no single municipality or city within
it has more than 50 percent of its urban area. The Bacolod urban area is a
"spillover" urban area—Bacolod City has 80 percent of the built-up area,
but urbanization has spilled over into surrounding jurisdictions. Davao is
a "contained" urban area—the entire urban area falls within Davao City
itself.

Map A.15   Urban expansion in the Manila, the Philippines, urban area, 2000–10

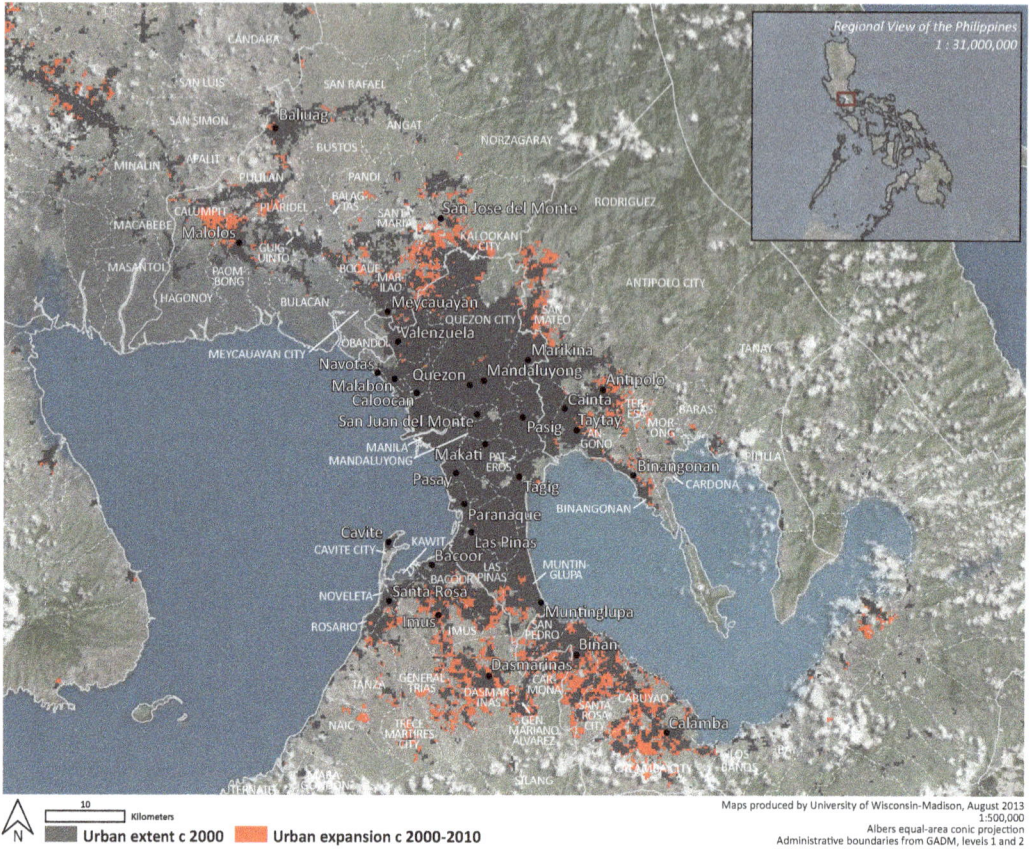

Maps produced by University of Wisconsin-Madison, August 2013
1:500,000
Albers equal-area conic projection
Administrative boundaries from GADM, levels 1 and 2

Urban extent c 2000   Urban expansion c 2000-2010

Note: In this map, only labeled areas are counted as part of the Manila urban area.

Thailand

Urban growth in Thailand during 2000–10 was not particularly rapid by East Asian standards. Urbanization was dominated by the Bangkok urban area. Bangkok is the fifth-largest urban area in East Asia in area, and the ninth largest in population. Like most large urban areas in the region, Bangkok is administratively fragmented, with more than 60 percent of the urban area located outside the boundaries of the Bangkok Metropolitan Administration.

Thailand has the sixth-largest amount of urban land (tied with Malaysia) in the East Asia region as of 2010. Its urban area grew from about 2,400 square kilometers to 2,700 between 2000 and 2010, an average annual growth rate of 1.4 percent. This growth rate was slower than the average for the region (2.4 percent). Built-up land covered approximately 0.5 percent of the total area of the country in 2010, which was also lower than the region as a whole. Most of the increase in built-up land occurred on arable land, but accounted for the loss of just 0.2 percent of the total arable land in the country.[15]

The urban population of Thailand (the population living in urban areas of more than 100,000 people) increased during this period from 9.3 million (15 percent of the total population) to slightly less than 11.8 million (17 percent). The average annual rate of urban population growth, 2.3 percent, was slightly slower than that for the region as a whole (3.0 percent).

On average, urban areas in Thailand were also less densely populated than in other countries in the region. The overall urban population density in Thailand was about 4,000 people per square kilometer in 2000, increasing slightly to 4,300 in 2010, whereas the average for the region was about 5,800 people per square kilometer in 2010. On average, the amount of new urban land per additional urban resident was 140 square meters, equivalent to the average for the region as a whole.

Urbanization in Thailand is dominated by the Bangkok urban area (figures A.35–A.38), which at 9.6 million people in 2010 almost joined the ranks of the megacities of the region. No other urban area in Thailand has more than even 500,000 people, leaving Bangkok with no close domestic competitors.

The Bangkok urban area grew from 1,900 square kilometers to 2,100 between 2000 and 2010, making it the fifth-largest urban area in East Asia in 2010, larger than megacities such as Jakarta, Manila, and Seoul. However, its average annual rate of growth, 1.1 percent, was among the slowest for urban areas in the region with more than 5 million inhabitants, faster only than Hong Kong SAR, China, and the larger Japanese urban areas. In 2010, the Bangkok urban area accounted for nearly 80 percent of the total urban area in Thailand, but just 62 percent of the new urban growth between 2000 and 2010, suggesting that the gap between it and other urban areas is narrowing slowly.

Figure A.35   Thailand: Urban areas by built-up area, 2000 and 2010

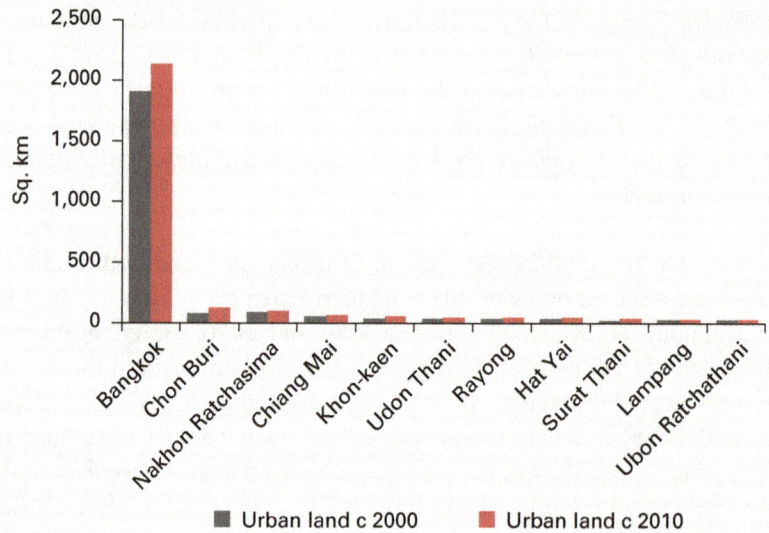

■ Urban land c 2000   ■ Urban land c 2010

Source: Study team, incorporating WorldPop data, http://www.worldpop.org.uk/data/.

Figure A.36   Thailand: Urban areas by population, 2000 and 2010

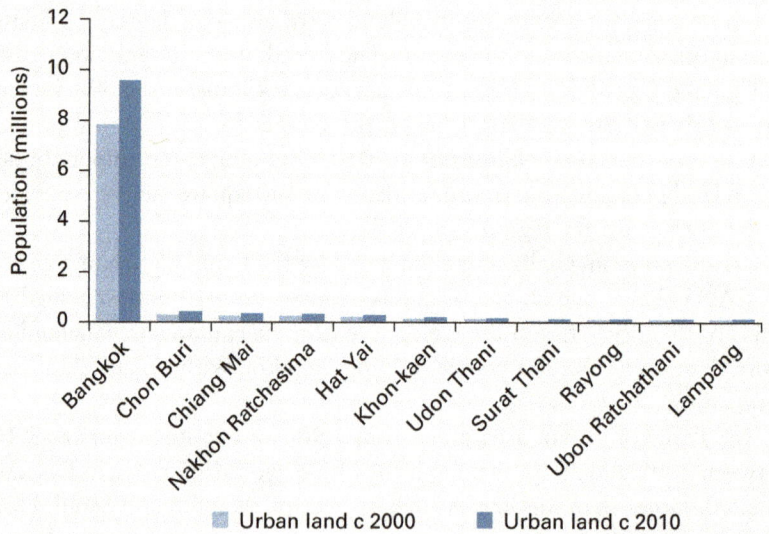

■ Urban land c 2000   ■ Urban land c 2010

Source: Study team, incorporating WorldPop data, http://www.worldpop.org.uk/data/.

The urban population of the Bangkok urban area grew from 7.8 million people to 9.6 million between 2000 and 2010 (figure A.36), a relatively modest annual growth rate of 2.0 percent. As of 2010, 81 percent of the urban population of Thailand lived there (down from 84 percent in 2000).

Figure A.37 Thailand: Urban land by population size category, 2000 and 2010

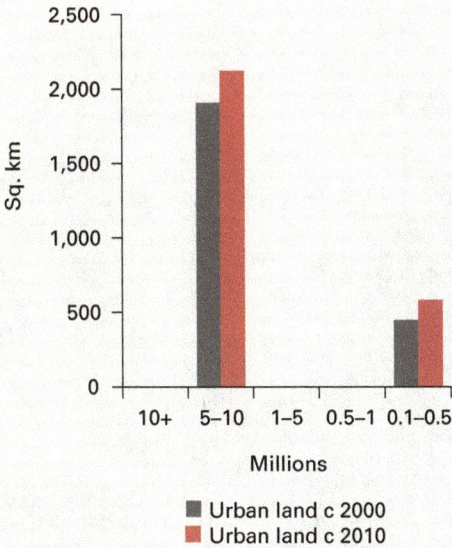

Source: Study team, incorporating WorldPop data, http://www.worldpop.org.uk/data/.

Figure A.38 Thailand: Urban population by population size category, 2000 and 2010

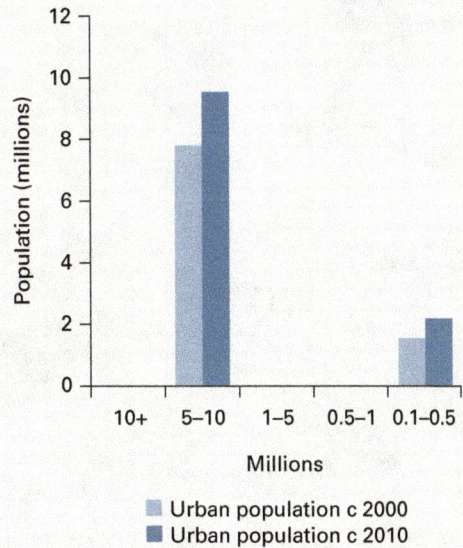

Source: Study team, incorporating WorldPop data, http://www.worldpop.org.uk/data/.

The population density for the urban area was 4,100 people per square kilometer in 2000, increasing to 4,500 in 2010, lower than the average for urban areas in East Asia in the 5 million to 10 million population category (6,600 people per square kilometer).

The urban extents of the Bangkok urban area spread beyond the administrative area of Bangkok into several surrounding provinces (map A.16). In total the urban area included 117 districts, of which 50 are under the Bangkok Metropolitan Administration. As of 2010, only 38 percent of the total urban area was within the jurisdiction of the Bangkok Metropolitan Administration itself, 23 percent was in Samut Prakan province to the south, 10 percent in Pathum Thani to the north, and between 5 percent and 10 percent each in Nakhon Pathom and Nonthaburi to the northwest and Phra Nakhon Si Ayutthaya in the far north. Of the urban expansion between 2000 and 2010, only 22 percent occurred within the Bangkok administrative area, while 26 percent occurred in Samut Prakan, 15 percent in Nakhon Pathom, and 11 percent in Phra Nakhon Si Ayutthaya. No major new corridors of urban expansion emerged during this decade, just scattered, fragmented peripheral growth.

As in many cities, population is concentrated in the center, so while Bangkok itself comprises only 38 percent of the urban land, it is home to 57 percent of the urban population (about 5.4 million people), with 15 percent in Samut Prakan. A little more than half the increase in urban population, about 900,000 people, occurred within Bangkok proper, with another 15

Map A.16   Urban expansion in the Bangkok, Thailand, urban area, 2000–10

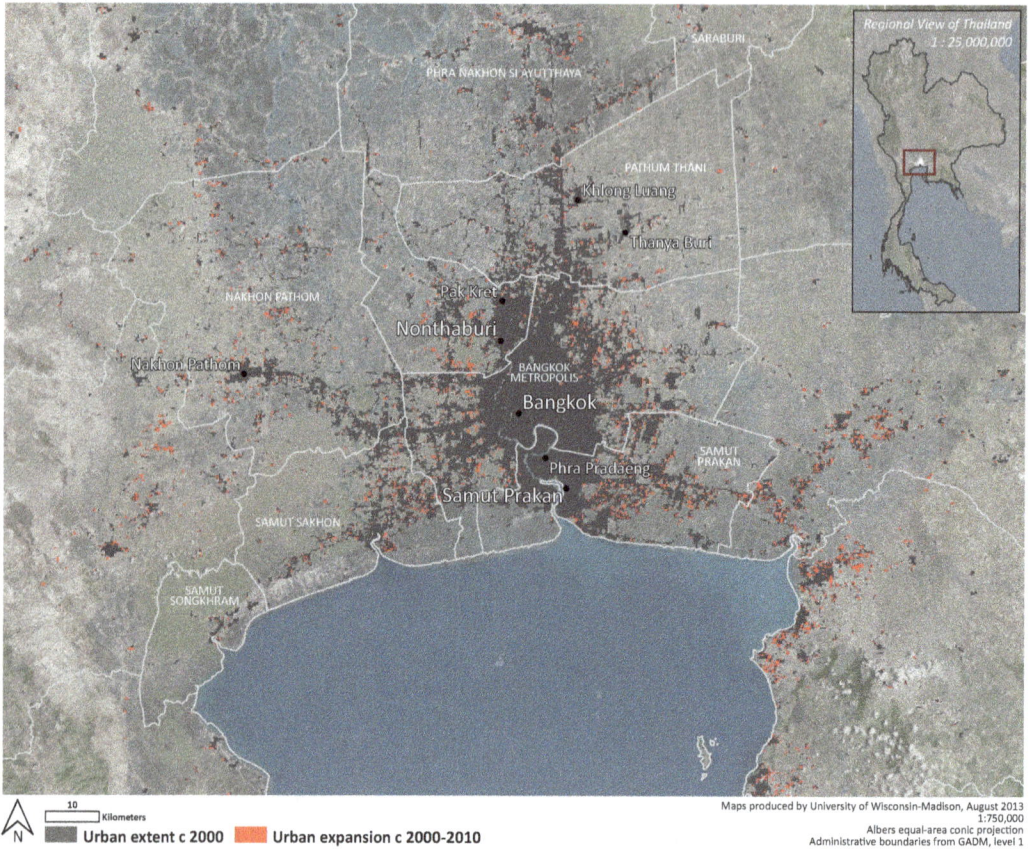

Kilometers 10

N

■ Urban extent c 2000   ■ Urban expansion c 2000-2010

Maps produced by University of Wisconsin-Madison, August 2013
1:750,000
Albers equal-area conic projection
Administrative boundaries from GADM, level 1

percent of growth (260,000 people) occurring in Samut Prakan. Each of the 50 districts within the Bangkok Metropolitan Administration had a higher urban population density than those in surrounding provinces, about 7,000 people per square kilometer, on average. Each of them also increased in density during this period.

Of the remaining nine urban areas with more than 100,000 people, Chon Buri was the largest in built area (130 square kilometers), and also had the greatest amount of new urban area (40 square kilometers), likely because of its large industrial developments. Chon Buri was also the largest in population (430,000 people) and population increase (150,000 people). It is close enough to Bangkok that it might eventually merge with the Bangkok urban area.

Surat Thani was the fastest-growing urban area spatially, growing from 20 square kilometers in 2000 to 36 in 2010, at 5.8 percent a year, as well as in population, more than doubling from 62,000 people to 131,000 during this period. The densest urban areas were Hat Yai (5,900 people per square kilometer in 2010) and Chiang Mai (5,000 people per square kilometer).

Vietnam

Vietnam is rapidly urbanizing, both spatially and demographically. Despite a large amount of urban expansion, its cities are becoming denser. The urban landscape is dominated by the two large urban areas, Hanoi and Ho Chi Minh City, which grew much faster than all others, adding vast amounts of new land while remaining very dense.

Vietnam's position in the urban hierarchy jumped during the 2000–10 decade from having the seventh-largest amount of urban land in 2000 (2,200 square kilometers) to the fifth-largest amount in 2010 (2,900 square kilometers), overtaking Thailand and the Republic of Korea. This increase of 700 square kilometers was among the largest in the region; only China's and Indonesia's urban land increased more in absolute terms. Urban areas in Vietnam grew spatially at 2.8 percent per year, among the fastest rates in the region. Of the total land area of Vietnam, 0.9 percent is part of urban areas, a similar proportion to China, but higher than Indonesia and the Philippines. Most of the increase in built-up land (94 percent) took place on arable land, but urban growth accounted for the loss of only 0.6 percent of the total arable land in the country.[16]

Vietnam has the sixth-largest urban population in East Asia, 23 million people. Between 2000 and 2010, its urban population increased by 7.5 million people. This rate of urban population increase, 4.1 percent per year, was one of the highest rates in the region, slower than only Lao PDR and Cambodia, which are much smaller. During this period, the Vietnamese urban population changed from 19 percent urban (living in urban areas of 100,000 people or more) to 26 percent.

At 7,700 people per square kilometer in 2010, urban areas in Vietnam were denser, on average, than in the region as a whole, though not as dense as Indonesia, the Republic of Korea, or the Philippines. However, the overall average urban density increased, up from 6,800 people per square kilometer in 2000.

Vietnam does not have any megacities of 10 million or more people, but the urban areas of Ho Chi Minh City (7.8 million people) in southern Vietnam and Hanoi (5.6 million people) in the north are among the region's largest. These two urban areas dominate the country's urban landscape as measured by both urban land and population (figures A.39 and A.40). In addition, Vietnam has 1 urban area in the 1 million to 5 million range (Hai Phong), 6 between 500,000 and 1 million, and 21 between 100,000 and 500,000 people.

The most notable thing about urban expansion in Vietnam is the rapid growth of the Hanoi and Ho Chi Minh City urban areas. Their rates of expansion (3.8 percent and 4.0 percent per year, respectively) are much faster than those of urban areas in other East Asian countries, except China. If they continue to grow at the current rate, by 2020 they will both be twice as large as they were in 2000. They are also growing much faster than

Figure A.39 **Vietnam: Urban land by population size category, 2000 and 2010**

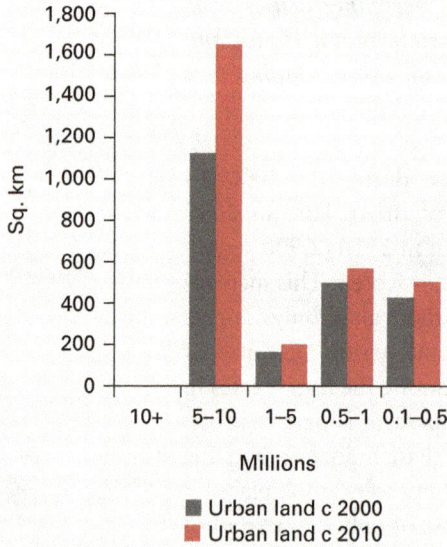

Figure A.40 **Vietnam: Urban population by population size category, 2000 and 2010**

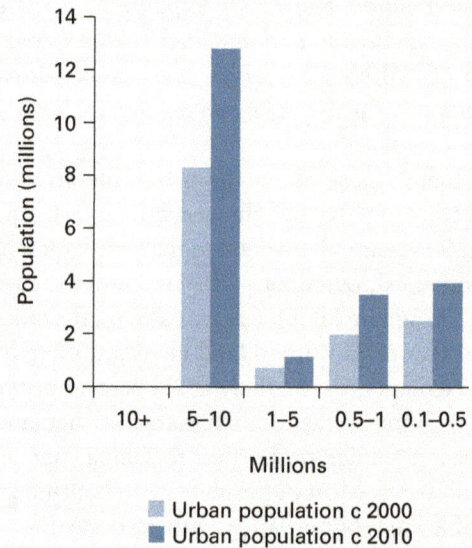

Source: Study team, incorporating WorldPop data, http://www.worldpop.org.uk/data/.

Source: Study team, incorporating WorldPop data, http://www.worldpop.org.uk/data/.

other Vietnamese urban areas. Of Vietnamese urban areas with populations greater than 500,000, only Da Nang's rate of growth (3.5 percent) comes close.

Spatially, both the Hanoi urban area (850 square kilometers in 2010) and the Ho Chi Minh City urban area (810 square kilometers in 2010) expanded almost equally between 2000 and 2010 in absolute terms—just less than 270 square kilometers (figure A.41). This expansion was greater than in any other urban area in the region outside China, including much larger urban areas such as Jakarta, Manila, Seoul, and Tokyo. More than 50 percent of the urban land in the country is in these two urban areas, and the gap between them and other urban areas in Vietnam is widening, with 75 percent of the new urban spatial growth in the country occurring in these two urban areas. However, the proportion of urban population in these urban areas has remained essentially the same during this period, at slightly less than 60 percent in both 2000 and 2010.

Almost all urban areas in the country are becoming denser, with the notable exception of the most populous one, Ho Chi Minh City, which saw a slight reduction in density from 2000 to 2010 despite a growth in population of 2.5 million people (3.9 percent a year). Hanoi, which remains less densely populated than Ho Chi Minh City, added 2.1 million people during this period (4.8 percent a year).

Even though the administrative area of Ho Chi Minh City province is very large and remains half unbuilt, expansion of the urban area is already

Figure A.41   Vietnam: The 25 largest urban areas by built-up area, 2000 and 2010

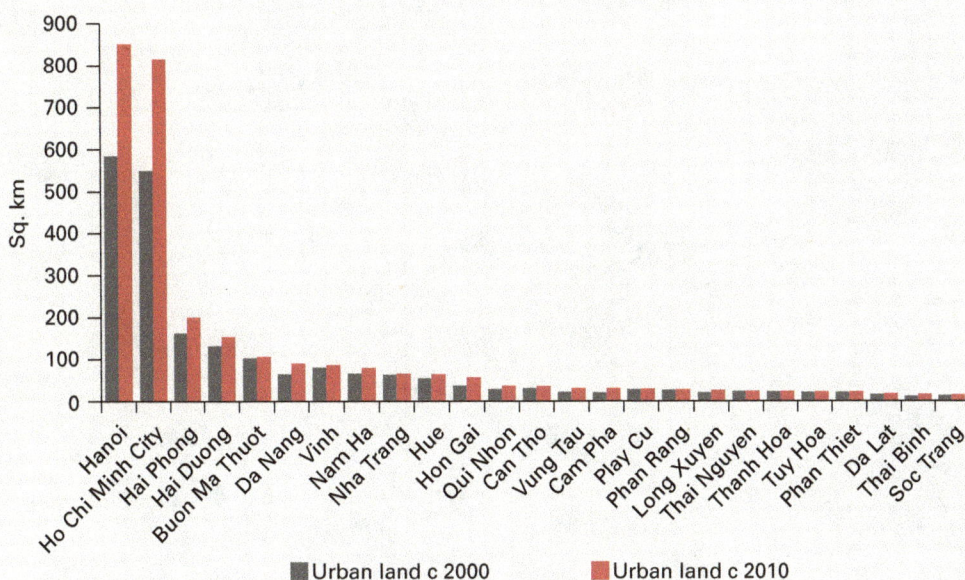

Source: Study team, incorporating WorldPop data, http://www.worldpop.org.uk/data/.

pushing into adjacent provinces (map A.17). In total, the urban area is spread across 35 districts in five provinces. Of the approximately 820 square kilometers of Ho Chi Minh City's overall urban area as of 2010, only about half (53 percent) is within the administrative boundaries of Ho Chi Minh City itself; 23 percent is in Binh Duong to the north and 18 percent is in Dong Nai to the east. More important, 70 percent of the new expansion since 2000 occurred outside Ho Chi Minh City, mostly in Binh Duong (42 percent), as is apparent from map A.18.

In fact, the slight drop in population density for the overall urban area is due entirely to the growth in these peripheral areas, where there have been large new industrial developments. Almost 80 percent of the growth in population occurred within the province of Ho Chi Minh City itself, and all districts within Ho Chi Minh City actually became much denser in population.

The Hanoi urban area is spatially larger than the Ho Chi Minh City urban area, but less populated. The pattern of development in Hanoi is fairly different from that in Ho Chi Minh City. Hanoi is situated in the Red River Delta, which is characterized by hundreds of dispersed pockets of settlement, including small towns, in contrast to the mostly unified cluster of Ho Chi Minh City. As map A.19 suggests, new growth around Hanoi has been similarly dispersed, although since 2000 the dispersed settlements appear to be connecting into more continuous corridors of development along highways, such as the spur heading northeast from the center of Hanoi through Bac Ninh, and another heading east toward Hai Duong.

Map A.17   Urban expansion in the Ho Chi Minh City, Vietnam, urban area, 2000–10

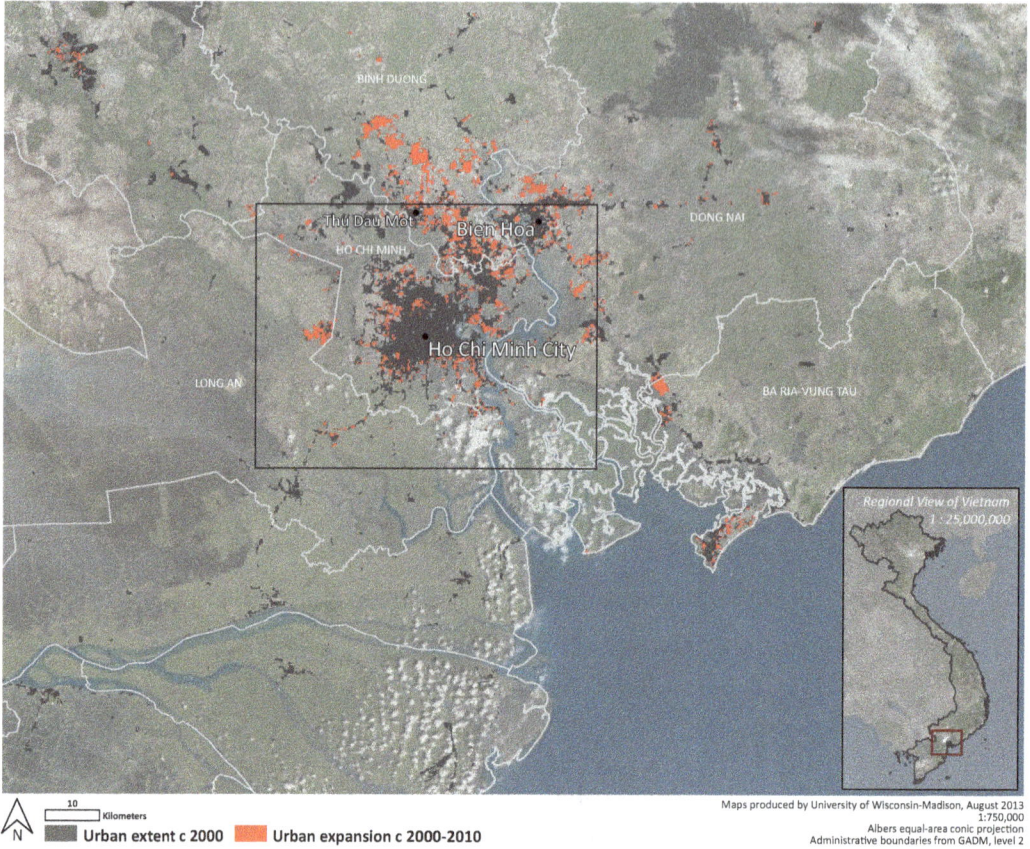

Maps produced by University of Wisconsin-Madison, August 2013
1:750,000
Albers equal-area conic projection
Administrative boundaries from GADM, level 2

N

Kilometers   10

■ Urban extent c 2000   ■ Urban expansion c 2000-2010

In total, the Hanoi urban area, as defined in this study, covers 850 square kilometers over 40 districts in five provinces. By this definition, 37 percent of the built-up land and only 31 percent of the increase in built-up land since 2000 falls within Hanoi province. The places with the largest increases in urban population density were the already dense districts in the traditional city center, such as Dong Da, Hai Ba Trung, and Hoan Kiem, where in 2010 population density exceeded 40,000 people per square kilometer. Dong Da and Hai Ba Trung also added more than 100,000 people each, with practically no increase in built-up land. So although Hanoi may be expanding rapidly, the very dense city center continues to get denser. As in Ho Chi Minh City, this increase in density in the city center is possibly attributable to the industrial expansion of the city, which creates jobs, in turn attracting people to the city, who find accommodation in existing residential neighborhoods.

Map A.18 **Urban expansion in the Ho Chi Minh City, Vietnam, urban area, 2000–10 (zoomed in)**

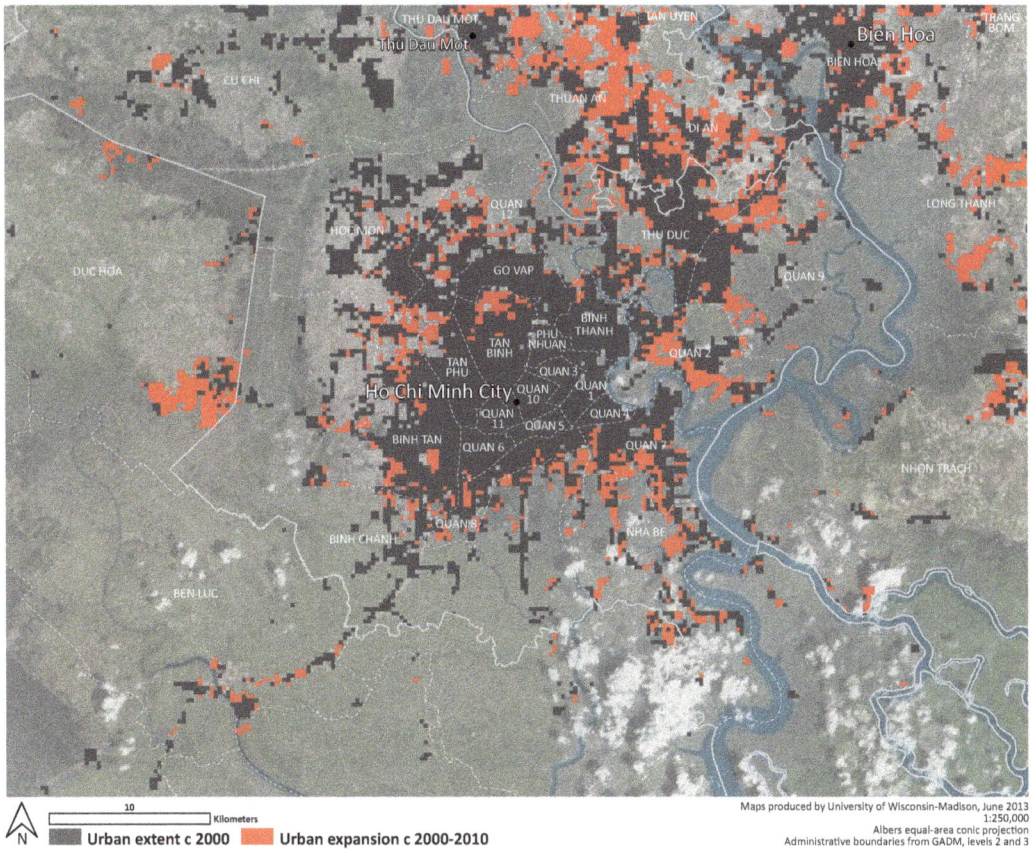

Urban extent c 2000 ■ Urban expansion c 2000-2010 ■

Maps produced by University of Wisconsin-Madison, June 2013
1:250,000
Albers equal-area conic projection
Administrative boundaries from GADM, levels 2 and 3

At 200 square kilometers, Hai Phong is less than a quarter the size of the two large urban areas, and at 1.2 million inhabitants is also much smaller in population. Although it is less dense than the Hanoi or Ho Chi Minh City urban areas, its density increased between 2000 and 2010 as its rate of population growth (4.1 percent) exceeded its rate of spatial growth (2.1 percent).

As noted, Hanoi is located in the Red River Delta, which is thickly settled with many small towns and cities, unlike the southeast region of Vietnam, which includes Ho Chi Minh City. As a result, the Red River Delta in total has twice the built-up land that the southeast region has, even though it does not have much more population (figures A.42 and A.43).

Map A.19   Urban expansion in the Red River Delta, Vietnam, 2000–10

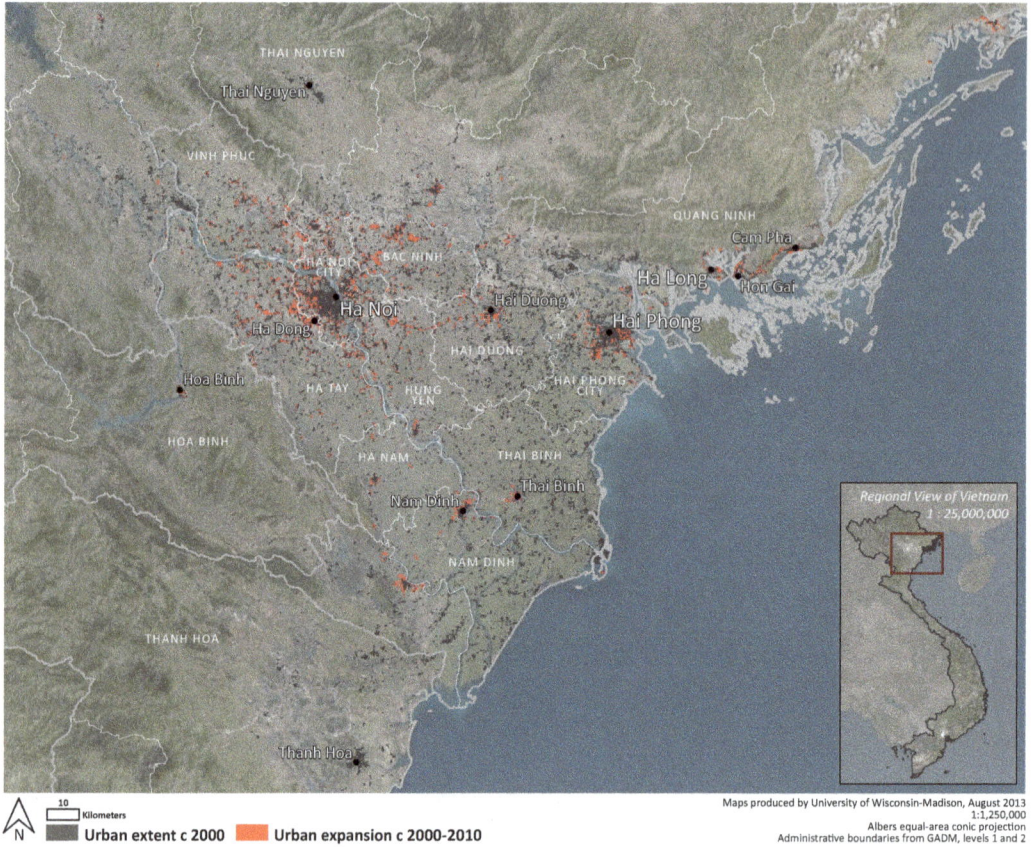

Maps produced by University of Wisconsin-Madison, August 2013
1:1,250,000
Albers equal-area conic projection
Administrative boundaries from GADM, levels 1 and 2

■ Urban extent c 2000   ■ Urban expansion c 2000-2010

Figure A.42   Vietnam: Urban land by region, 2000 and 2010

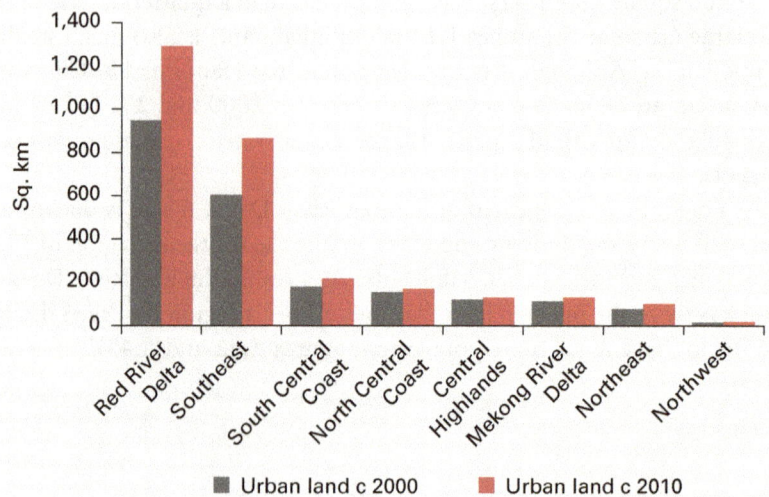

■ Urban land c 2000   ■ Urban land c 2010

Source: Study team, incorporating WorldPop data, http://www.worldpop.org.uk/data/.

Figure A.43   Vietnam: Urban population by region, 2000 and 2010

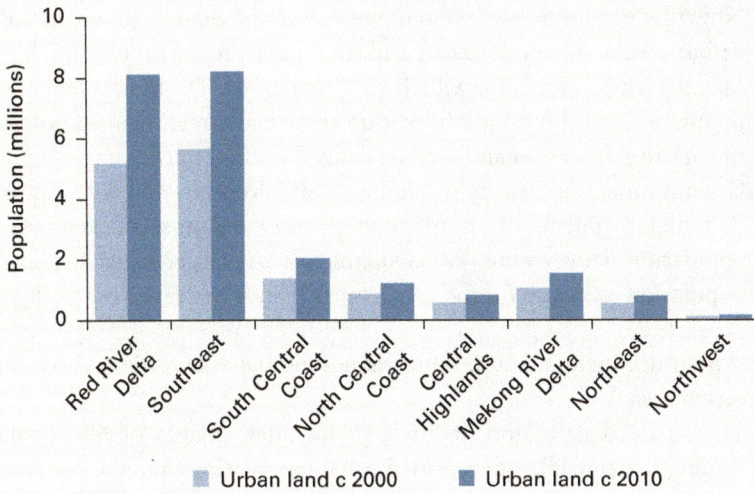

Source: Study team, incorporating WorldPop data, http://www.worldpop.org.uk/data/.

Notes

1. The total amount of land picked up as built up beyond this urban area was 290 square kilometers in 2010.
2. Arable land was estimated using 2000–03 maps of agricultural land using a 500 meter grid (MODIS-based estimates [Friedl and others 2010]), where pixels with more than 40 percent of land under cultivation are considered arable. Note that this measure does not indicate the relative productivity of the arable land consumed by urbanization, nor its relative accessibility to population centers, issues that should be considered when examining changes in land use from agricultural to urban.
3. An urban area may include more than one "city" by administrative definitions. See chapter 1.
4. This regional grouping of provinces follows that of the National Bureau of Statistics of China, where east coast China consists of Beijing, Fujian, Guangdong, Hainan, Hebei, Jiangsu, Shandong, Shanghai, Tianjin, and Zhejiang; central China consists of, Anhui, Henan, Hubei, Hunan, Jiangxi and Shanxi; northeast China consists of Heilongjiang, Jilin and Liaoning; and western China consists of Chongqing, Gansu, Guangxi, Guizhou, Inner Mongolia, Ningxia, Qinghai, Shaanxi, Sichuan, Tibet, Xinjiang, and Yunnan.
5. As with any measure of density, these figures should be viewed with caution because of the "modifiable areal unit problem," that is, the arbitrary size of the district boundaries affects the average density reported. For example, parts of Pudong may be far denser than the

Puxi district, but the density in Pudong is lower because it is averaged over a larger area.

6. Note that economic regions in figure A.9 are based on Chinese national definitions, and include urban and rural areas in several provinces, not only the urban areas after which they are named. The figures include all population and built-up land within these economic regions, not only the urban population and land as defined in this study.

7. Urban population density in Indonesia should be viewed with caution. As noted in appendix C, in many small and medium-sized urban areas, population figures were only available for the larger regencies, so the population estimates for the urban areas themselves relied on modeling.

8. See note 2.

9. It does not include Nara, which is nearby but is considered a distinct urban area.

10. The national definition of "urban" includes villages of 600 people, leading to a much larger reported urban population than the one stated here.

11. See note 2.

12. Mongolia was one of the countries with the largest difference between "built-up" land and "urban" land. A larger amount of area, 760 square kilometers in 2010, was captured by the satellite imagery as built up, but it was scattered around the country in other settlements. Tov province, which surrounds Ulaanbaatar, and Dornod in the east of the country each have about 90 square kilometers of built-up land. Orhon and Darhan-Uul, home to Erdenet and Darkhan, respectively, sometimes considered the other Mongolian cities, have less than 20 square kilometers of built-up land each, and fewer than 100,000 people.

13. See note 2.

14. Official estimates of the population of Ulaanbaatar are higher, more than 1 million people in 2010.

15. See note 2.

16. See note 2.

References

Angel, S., M. Valdivia, and R. M. Lutzy. 2011. "Urban Expansion, Land Conversion, and Affordable Housing: The Case of Zhengzhou." In *China's Housing Reform and Outcomes*, edited by J. Yanyun Man. Cambridge, MA: Lincoln Institute of Land Policy.

Day, P. 2012. "Ordos: The Biggest Ghost Town in China." *BBC News*, March 17.

Friedl, M. A., D. Sulla-Menashe, B. Tan, A. Schneider, N. Ramankutty, A. Sibley, and X. Huang. 2010. "MODIS Collection 5 Global Land Cover: Algorithm Refinements and Characterization of New Datasets." *Remote Sensing of Environment* 114 (1): 168–82.

World Bank and Development Research Center of the State Council, P.R. China. 2014. *Urban China: Toward Efficient, Inclusive, and Sustainable Urbanization.* World Bank: Washington, DC.

Young, I. W. 2013. "Can China Breathe Life into 'Ghost Towns'?" *CNN*, May 28.

Urban Expansion in East Asia, Excluding China, 2000–10

Because of China's large size and population, regional averages for East Asia as a whole are often distorted by trends in China. Because Chinese urbanization is unique in many ways, as discussed earlier in this report, this appendix examines a few trends in urbanization in East Asia excluding China.

The East Asia region excluding China had 41,000 square kilometers of urban land in 2000, growing to 45,000 square kilometers in 2010, an average annual growth rate of 1.1 percent. Despite China's large total area, a higher proportion of its land was urbanized than in the rest of the region; excluding China, 0.57 percent of total land was in urban areas in 2000, increasing to 0.64 percent in 2010.

The total urban population of the region excluding China increased from 233 million in 2000 to 300 million in 2010, an average annual growth rate of 2.5 percent. Thus, when China is excluded, the rate of urban population growth is more than twice as high as the rate of urban spatial expansion. The proportion of the region's total population that is urbanized is roughly similar when excluding China—31 percent in 2000 and 37 percent in 2010—as it is when including China.

Trends by Country Income Group

The same proportion of China's land is in urban areas as the average for other upper-middle-income countries (0.7 percent in 2000 and 0.9 percent in 2010). However, China's population was slightly more urbanized than the populations of the other upper-middle-income countries (Malaysia and Thailand), which means that when China is excluded, a lower proportion of the populations of upper-middle-income countries is urbanized (27

Figure B.1 Proportion of urban population by income group, excluding China, 2000 and 2010

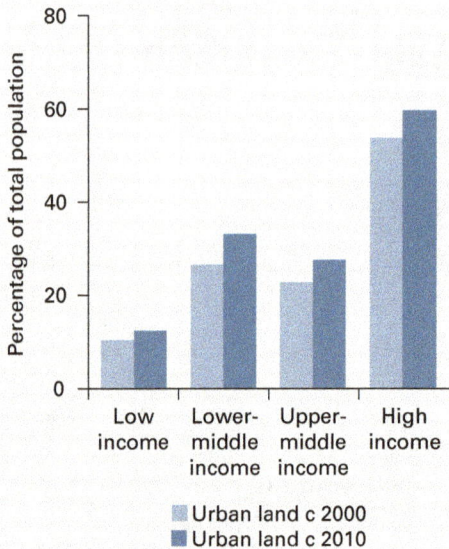

Urban land c 2000
Urban land c 2010

Source: Study team, incorporating WorldPop data, http://www.worldpop.org.uk/data/.

Figure B.2 Rate of urban spatial expansion by income group, excluding China, 2000–10

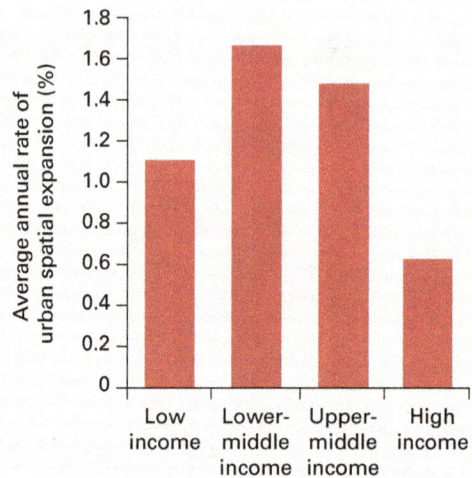

Source: Study team, incorporating WorldPop data, http://www.worldpop.org.uk/data/.

percent in 2010) than of the populations of lower-middle-income countries (33 percent; figure B.1).

China's rate of urban population growth was similar to that of other upper-middle-income countries, but the rate of urban spatial expansion was much lower in Malaysia and Thailand, meaning that when China is excluded, the annual rate of spatial expansion is actually higher in lower-middle-income countries (1.7 percent) than in upper-middle-income countries (1.5 percent; figure B.2).

Trends by Urban Area

China has 15 of the 25 largest urban areas in East Asia by land area. When China is excluded, Indonesia has 6 of the largest 25, followed by 5 in Japan and 4 in Malaysia (figure B.3). China has 12 of the top 25 largest urban areas by population. When China is excluded, Indonesia has 8 of the largest 25, while Japan has 4, and the Republic of Korea and Taiwan, China, have 3 each (figure B.4).

Trends by Size Categories

When China is excluded, the relative importance of different size categories changes significantly. In the rest of East Asia, the five megacities then have

Figure B.3 East Asia, excluding China: The 25 largest urban agglomerations by Area, 2000 and 2010

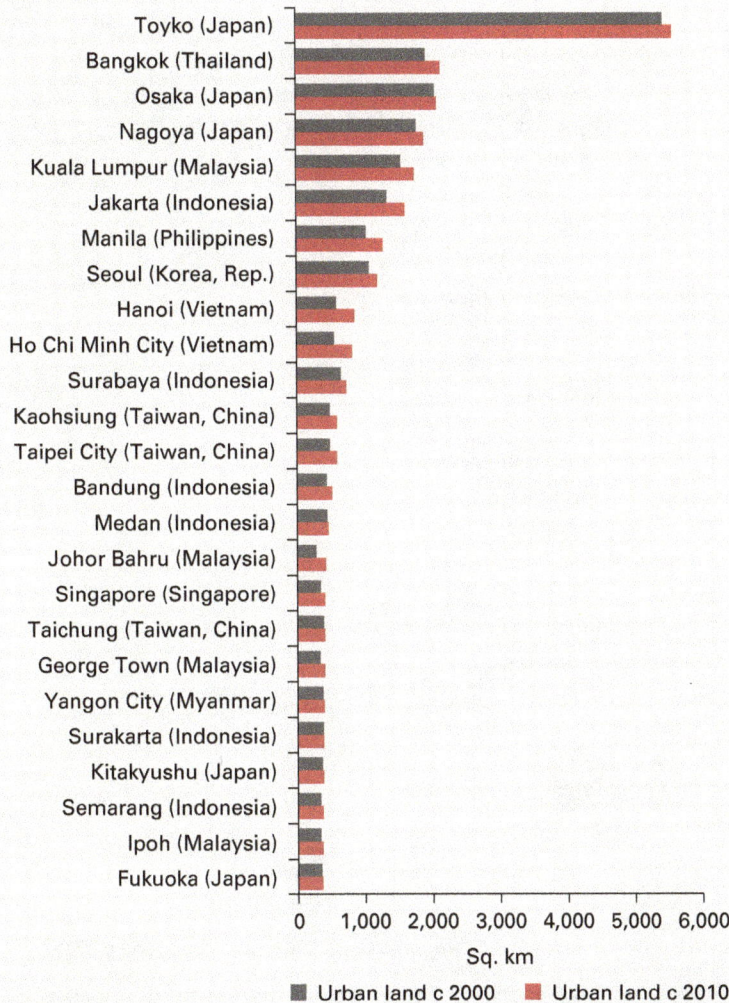

Source: Study team, incorporating WorldPop data, http://www.worldpop.org.uk/data/.

the largest amount of urban land (11,700 square kilometers), far more than the 157 urban areas in the smallest size category (7,600 square kilometers; table B.1 and figure B.5). However, the rate of growth of the megacities is less than half that of urban areas in the next category, with urban areas of 5 million to 10 million people. Thus, although the overall proportion of land in the different size categories remained almost stable between 2000 and 2010, there was a small shift in proportion away from the megacities toward this second category.

Outside China the megacities also dominate population, even though the megacities are growing more slowly than urban areas in other categories (figure B.6 and table B.2).

Figure B.4   East Asia, excluding China: The 25 largest urban agglomerations by population, 2000 and 2010

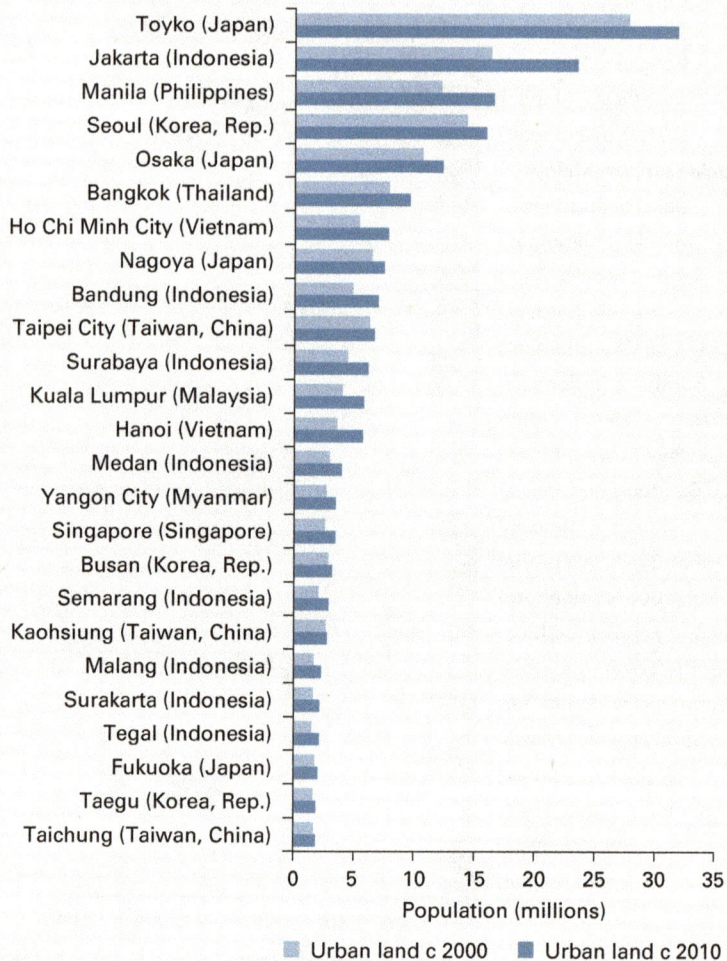

Toyko (Japan)
Jakarta (Indonesia)
Manila (Philippines)
Seoul (Korea, Rep.)
Osaka (Japan)
Bangkok (Thailand)
Ho Chi Minh City (Vietnam)
Nagoya (Japan)
Bandung (Indonesia)
Taipei City (Taiwan, China)
Surabaya (Indonesia)
Kuala Lumpur (Malaysia)
Hanoi (Vietnam)
Medan (Indonesia)
Yangon City (Myanmar)
Singapore (Singapore)
Busan (Korea, Rep.)
Semarang (Indonesia)
Kaohsiung (Taiwan, China)
Malang (Indonesia)
Surakarta (Indonesia)
Tegal (Indonesia)
Fukuoka (Japan)
Taegu (Korea, Rep.)
Taichung (Taiwan, China)

Population (millions)
0   5   10   15   20   25   30   35

Urban land c 2000   Urban land c 2010

Source: Study team, incorporating WorldPop data, http://www.worldpop.org.uk/data/.

Density

Urban population densities in the rest of East Asia were higher than in China. On average, the total urban population density in the rest of the region was about 5,800 people per square kilometer in 2000 and 6,600 people per square kilometer in 2010. When Chinese urban areas are excluded, megacities remain the densest, but urban areas in the middle category, with 1 million to 5 million people, are more dense, on average, than urban areas with 5 million to 10 million residents (figure B.7). Because China's urban areas were denser than those in the other upper-middle-income countries (Malaysia and Thailand), the average density of urban areas in upper-middle-income countries decreases from 5,200 people per square kilometer to 3,700 when China is excluded.

Table B.1   Urban land by population size category, excluding China

Population size category (millions)	Total number of urban areas	Urban land (sq. km)		Increase in urban land, 2000–10 (sq. km)	Proportion of total urban land (%)		Average annual rate of urban expansion (%)
		2000	2010		2000	2010	
10 or more	5	10,911	11,709	798	26.7	25.6	0.7
5–10	8	7,911	9,237	1,327	19.3	20.2	1.6
1–5	37	8,209	9,259	1,051	20.1	20.2	1.2
0.5–1	62	7,146	8,010	863	17.5	17.5	1.1
0.1–0.5	157	6,740	7,595	854	16.5	16.6	1.2
Total	**269**	**40,917**	**45,810**	**4,893**	**100**	**100**	**1.1**

Source: Study team, incorporating WorldPop data, http://www.worldpop.org.uk/data/.
Note: Numbers may not add to totals because of rounding.

Figure B.5   Urban land by population size category, excluding China, 2000 and 2010

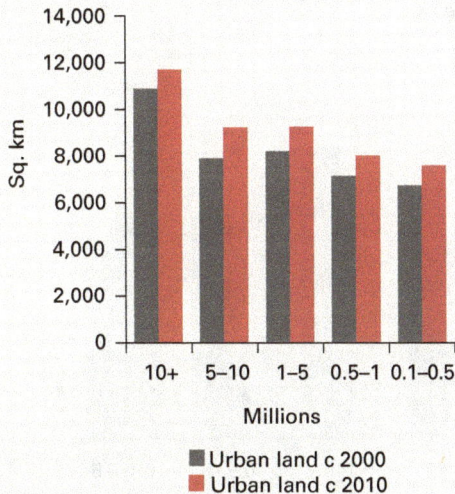

Source: Study team, incorporating WorldPop data, http://www.worldpop.org.uk/data/.

Figure B.6   Urban population by population size category, excluding China, 2000 and 2010

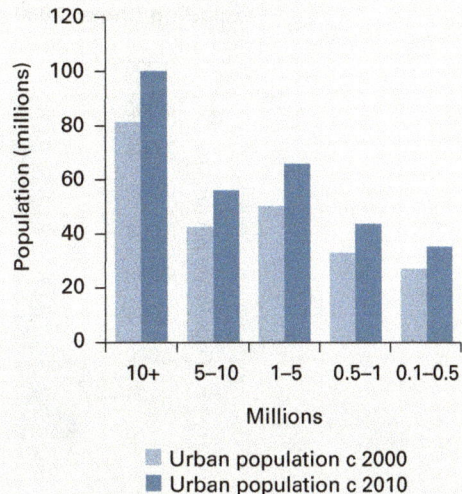

Source: Study team, incorporating WorldPop data, http://www.worldpop.org.uk/data/.

Metropolitan Fragmentation

Urban areas outside China display more metropolitan fragmentation and spillover beyond local administrative boundaries. When China is included, 60 percent of the urban areas in the region are "contained," and 24 percent are "spillover" urban areas. However, when China is excluded, there are more spillover urban areas (41 percent) than contained urban areas (38 percent). When China is excluded, the proportion of "fragmented" urban areas increases from 15 percent to 21 percent.

Table B.2   Urban population by population size category, excluding China

Population size category (millions)	Urban population (millions)		Increase in urban population, 2000–10 (millions)	Proportion of total urban population (%)		Average annual rate of increase in urban population (%)
	2000	2010		2000	2010	
10 or more	81.10	99.91	18.81	34.7	33.3	2.1
5–10	42.41	55.83	13.42	18.2	18.6	2.8
1–5	50.15	65.68	15.53	21.5	21.9	2.7
0.5–1	32.97	43.65	10.68	14.1	14.5	2.8
0.1–0.5	26.85	35.21	8.36	11.5	11.7	2.7
Total	**233.48**	**300.28**	**66.80**	**100**	**100**	**2.5**

Source: Study team, incorporating WorldPop data, http://www.worldpop.org.uk/data/.
Note: Numbers may not add to totals because of rounding.

Figure B.7   Urban population density by population size category, excluding China, 2000 and 2010

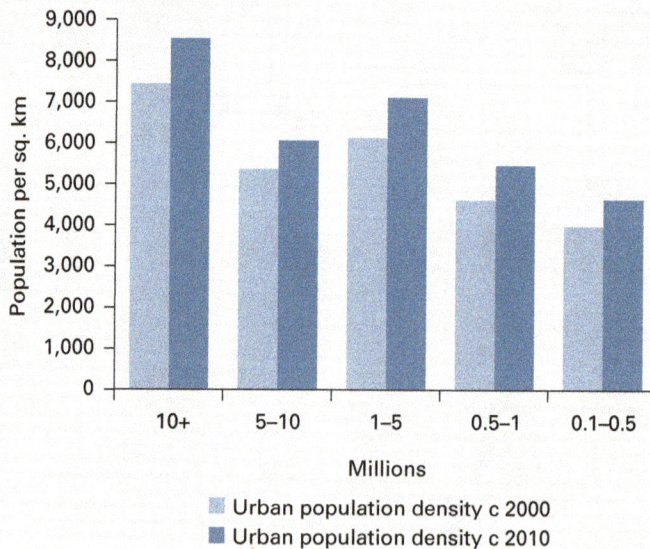

Source: Study team, incorporating WorldPop data, http://www.worldpop.org.uk/data/.

Methodologies and Accessing the Data

Methodologies

Mapping Built-Up Areas

To create maps of built-up extents throughout the region, change-detection methods were applied to analyze Moderate Resolution Imaging Spectroradiometer (MODIS) satellite data (Mertes and others, forthcoming). These maps rely on a geophysical definition of built-up areas: built-up land refers to places dominated by the "built environment," which includes all nonvegetative, human-constructed elements (roads, buildings, and the like) with greater than 50 percent coverage of a landscape unit (here, a 250 meter pixel, that is, a square area of land with sides measuring 250 meters). The maps of urban expansion were produced using multiple classifications of MODIS time series imagery. To establish potential locations of urban land, the study region was first established by merging all city point data (table C.1) and the 2000 MODIS map of urban extent (Schneider, Friedl, and Potere 2010), and buffering these areas by 100 kilometers. The 2010 urban extent was classified within these areas using a three-year window of imagery, an optimization algorithm that prioritized cloud-free data at the city level, advanced data-mining algorithms (boosted decision trees [Quinlan 1993]) supplied with exemplars from interpretation of very high resolution Google Earth imagery, and a data fusion approach that combined 250-meter enhanced vegetation index (EVI) data and 500-meter multispectral satellite data. It was assumed that all urban expansion was unidirectional (that is, that land could only change from not built up to built up, and not vice versa), so a multidate composite change-detection technique was applied to areas within the 2010 urban extent. Ten years of EVI data (2001–10) were used as input to a boosted decision tree to map (1) stable urban areas and (2) areas that developed between 2000 and 2010.[1]

Table C.1   City point location information

Location	Data set	Producer	Citation	Notes
Global	GRUMP city points	CIESIN, IFPRI, CIAT	Center for International Earth Science Information Network (CIESIN), Columbia University; International Food Policy Research Institute (IFPRI); World Bank; and Centro Internacional de Agricultura Tropical (CIAT) (2004) Global Rural-Urban Mapping Project (GRUMP): Settlement points, 2000. http://sedac.ciesin.columbia.edu.	Point data set of 67,935 cities, towns, and settlements
Global	Urban areas with >750,000 inhabitants, 2011	UN Department of Economic and Social Affairs Population Division	United Nations (UN) Department of Economic and Social Affairs Population Division (2013) Urban areas with >750,000 inhabitants in 2011. http://esa.un.org/unup/GIS-Files/gis_1.htm.	Point data set of 633 cities of more than 750,000 persons
Global	Universe of cities	Angel, Lincoln Institute of Land Policy	Angel (2012)	Point data set of 3,943 cities of more than 100,000 persons
China	Chinese city point data	Chinese Academy of Sciences	Chinese Academy of Sciences (2011) Beijing, China.	Point data set of 664 cities
Global	Google Earth populated places	Google	Google Earth Pro v7.1.2 (2013) Layers: populated places. http://www.google.com/earth.	City point location used to verify, geolocate, and update city points
Global	MODIS 500-meter map of global urban extent	University of Wisconsin-Madison	Schneider, Friedl, and Potere (2010)	Map of 88,578 urban patches greater than 1 square kilometer used to verify, geolocate, and update city points

Source: Study team.
Note: MODIS = Moderate Resolution Imaging Spectroradiometer. All data sets were synthesized and cross-checked to produce a point data set of 1,448 cities in East Asia. This information was later used to develop the urban area boundaries used for assessment of urban trajectories.

Assessing Accuracy

The final maps were assessed using a stratified random sample of more than 8,600 sites labeled by multiple analysts in a double-blind procedure. Overall accuracy measures for the maps at the country level range between

79 percent and 93 percent for urban extent and between 70 percent and 91 percent for urban expansion, confirming their suitability for this analysis (Mertes and others, forthcoming).

Map accuracy was examined using a two-tiered approach. The procedure allows each land cover class to be evaluated in a manner consistent with the data and methodology used given that the classification was also performed in two stages. The quality of the 2010 urban extent was assessed (tier one), then the urban expansion map accuracy was evaluated (tier two). In tier one, only urban and nonurban classes were evaluated. In tier two, only areas within the 2010 urban extent were considered, to assess the urban and urban expansion classes.

The tier one test sites were assessed in Google Earth using high-resolution data (≤ 4 meters) in a double-blind assessment procedure by a team of photo-interpretation analysts. A final review of all sites was conducted for quality control and to assign labels (designating built up vs. not built up) in instances in which analysts disagreed. The overall accuracy of the 2010 map of urban extent (tier one) was 84 percent (kappa = 0.62), and was fairly consistent across countries (ranging from 79 percent to 93 percent) (table C.2). Producer's accuracy (the probability that an urban pixel known to be urban is labeled urban in the map) for the urban class was high for the region (85 percent), indicating that urban areas were well captured, with few errors of omission (table C.2). At 64 percent, the user's accuracy (the probability that an urban pixel in the map will be urban if visited on the ground) for the region was reasonable, but suggests that map errors were predominantly the result of commission errors in which nonurban areas were mislabeled as urban land. As a result, the total urban land area may have been overestimated in some locations, particularly the Lao People's Democratic Republic, Malaysia, and Thailand, where user's accuracies were less than 61 percent.

The tier two assessment was designed to evaluate the accuracy of the urban expansion maps. Because the spectral and temporal signatures of urban areas and urban expansion vary considerably across tropical, temperate, and arid regions, as well as across political boundaries (Small and Lu 2006), country boundaries and a biome stratification were used to distribute samples across the region. Once the sample distribution was established, sites were selected at random from the buffered city point data using the MODIS raster grid. Each site then corresponds to a 250-meter MODIS pixel, corresponding to the data used for the change detection. Following the same procedure as the tier one assessment, each site was assessed in Google Earth and assigned one of three labels: urban land, urban expansion, or nonurban land. The overall accuracy for the tier two urban expansion maps is 75 percent (kappa = 0.36), slightly lower than the overall 2010 (tier one) accuracy (table C.3).[2] More-developed locations (for instance, Japan; the Republic of Korea; and Taiwan, China) generally have higher accuracies (more than 80 percent) than other locations likely because of low growth rates in these highly urbanized places. These locations also largely

Table C.2   Tier one accuracy assessment results for the urban class

Country/economy	Tier one accuracy (%)			Test sites (number)	
	Overall[a]	Producer's[b]	User's[c]	Total[d]	Urban[e]
Myanmar	93	100	68	95	15
Korea, Dem. People's Rep.	93	88	64	67	8
Korea, Rep.	91	71	81	215	41
Lao PDR	90	100	60	21	4
Cambodia	89	89	89	18	9
Thailand	87	73	58	324	51
Japan	86	91	74	563	185
Philippines	86	94	62	227	48
Indonesia	85	84	66	529	132
Singapore	85	89	80	20	9
Vietnam	85	77	68	209	53
China	83	85	62	4,034	1,042
Taiwan, China	80		0	5	0
Malaysia	79	97	60	201	63
Region	**84**	**85**	**64**	**6,528**	**1,660**

Source: Study team.
Note: Cells left blank indicate there were no expansion sites drawn in the sample.
a. The average accuracy for the urban class.
b. Reference-based accuracy. This measure assesses the probability that an urban pixel known to be urban is labeled urban in the map. Lower accuracy in this category indicates that the errors are due to omitting urban pixels from the map (for example, labeling an urban pixel as nonurban).
c. Map-based accuracy. This measure assesses the probability that an urban pixel in the map will be urban if visited on the ground. Lower accuracy in this category indicates that the error is from labeling a nonurban pixel as urban.
d. Number of test sites in sample (urban and nonurban).
e. Number of test sites in sample that are urban. This number can help interpret very low or high producer's or user's accuracy (smaller sample indicates errors are more likely due to chance).

fall into temperate and forest biomes, which tend to have higher accuracy than drier arid and semi-arid areas. This result is related to the spectral and temporal signatures of the EVI data used for change detection, given that peak EVI in arid regions may be quite similar before and after change (that is, land outside the city that is spectrally bright and sparsely vegetated is converted to spectrally bright urban land).

Mapping Population Distribution

The population maps were produced as part of the AsiaPop project (subsequently a part of WorldPop; see acknowledgments), with which this study worked closely. For each study country, census-derived population counts reported at as fine an administrative level as available were assembled for the 2000 and 2010 rounds of censuses, when possible. In some cases, if a census was not undertaken for a representative period, or the data were not available, population estimates from government sources were used. For each case in which the 2000 and 2010 censuses for countries were

Table C.3   Tier two accuracy assessment, by country

Country/economy	Tier two accuracy (%)			Test sites (number)	
	Overall	Producer's[a]	User's[b]	Total[c]	Expansion[d]
Japan	91	100	17	243	5
Korea, Dem. People's Rep.	90	0		20	0
Taiwan, China	86	71	50	28	3
Mongolia	85	0		20	0
Korea, Rep.	82	71	59	40	10
Lao PDR	80	75	86	20	7
Singapore	80	75	86	20	2
Indonesia	79	36	36	148	11
Malaysia	79	8	100	67	1
Philippines	78	100	33	36	5
Cambodia	75	71	71	20	7
Myanmar	75	33	50	20	2
Thailand	74	33	20	39	5
China	71	64	51	1,324	166
Vietnam	70	53	80	43	15
Region	**75**	**61**	**50**	**2,086**	**419**

Source: Study team.
Note: Cells left blank indicate there were no expansion sites drawn in the sample.
a. Reference-based accuracy. This measure assesses the probability that an urban expansion pixel known to be new urban land is labeled correctly on the map. Lower accuracy in this category indicates that the errors are due to the omission of urban expansion pixels from the map (for example, labeling an urban expansion pixel as urban).
b. Map-based accuracy. This measure assesses the probability that an urban expansion pixel in the map will be urban expansion (for example, new urban land 2000–10) if visited on the ground. Lower accuracy in this category indicates that the error is from labeling an urban pixel as urban expansion.
c. Number of test sites in sample (urban and urban expansion).
d. Number of test sites in sample that are new urban land (urban expansion 2000–10). This number can help interpret very low or high producer's or user's accuracy (smaller sample indicates errors are more likely due to chance).

undertaken not exactly in 2000 or 2010, UN growth rates were used to adjust population totals to match 2000 or 2010 estimates (United Nations, Department of Economic and Social Affairs, Population Division, 2012). Geographic information system (GIS) administrative boundary files for each country for 2000 and 2010 were also assembled. The census (and other) population counts for each administrative boundary were matched to the corresponding units to create spatial representations of the 2000 and 2010 population count data at as high an administrative-unit level for each country as possible.

These administrative-unit-level population data were then disaggregated to approximately 100 meter by 100 meter grid cell estimates using the modeling procedures outlined in Tatem and others (2007), Linard and others (2012), and Gaughan and others (2013), and full details on the mapping approach can be found in these papers. In brief, the 2000 and 2010

MODIS-derived built-up extents described above were integrated with detailed land cover data derived from the "Landsat" remote sensing project run by the U.S. Geological Survey and NASA. These refined land cover data sets were then combined with land cover–based population density weightings derived from exceptionally fine resolution census data, and used to disaggregate the administrative-unit-level population counts to the 100 meter by 100 meter grid.

The population distribution maps used publicly available census data. They are more reliable for places where the available census data were highly disaggregated relative to the size of a settlement, that is, where census units are small, as in Vietnam, and for larger urban areas. Where the available census figures were for administrative units that are much larger than urban areas, for example, in Mongolia and parts of Indonesia, estimates of urban populations relied more heavily on modeling.[3]

Defining Urban Areas

As noted earlier, in this study an urban area was not defined according to the local administrative boundary alone. So where is an urban area considered to end? Strict contiguity cannot be the deciding factor because urban

Map C.1   Urban expansion in Hanoi, Hai Phong, and Ha Long, Vietnam, 2000–10

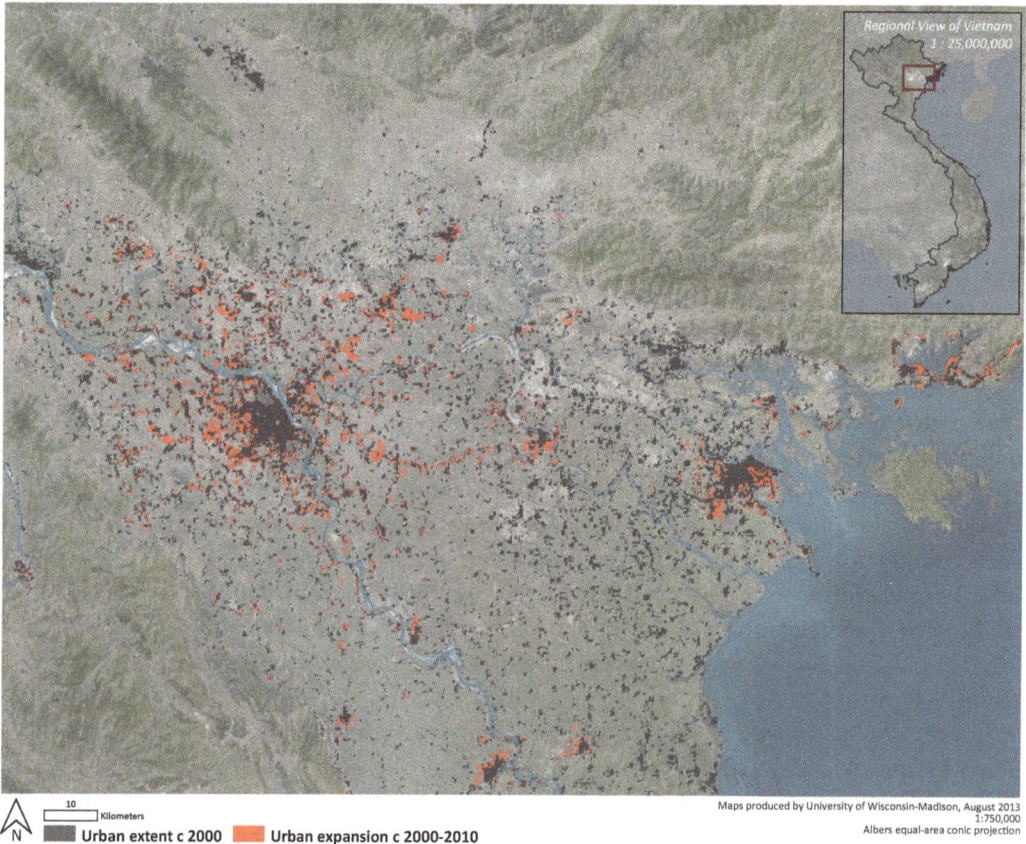

Urban extent c 2000   Urban expansion c 2000-2010

Maps produced by University of Wisconsin-Madison, August 2013
1:750,000
Albers equal-area conic projection

Map C.2   Urban expansion in Hanoi, Hai Phong, and Ha Long, Vietnam, 2000–10 (with provincial boundaries)

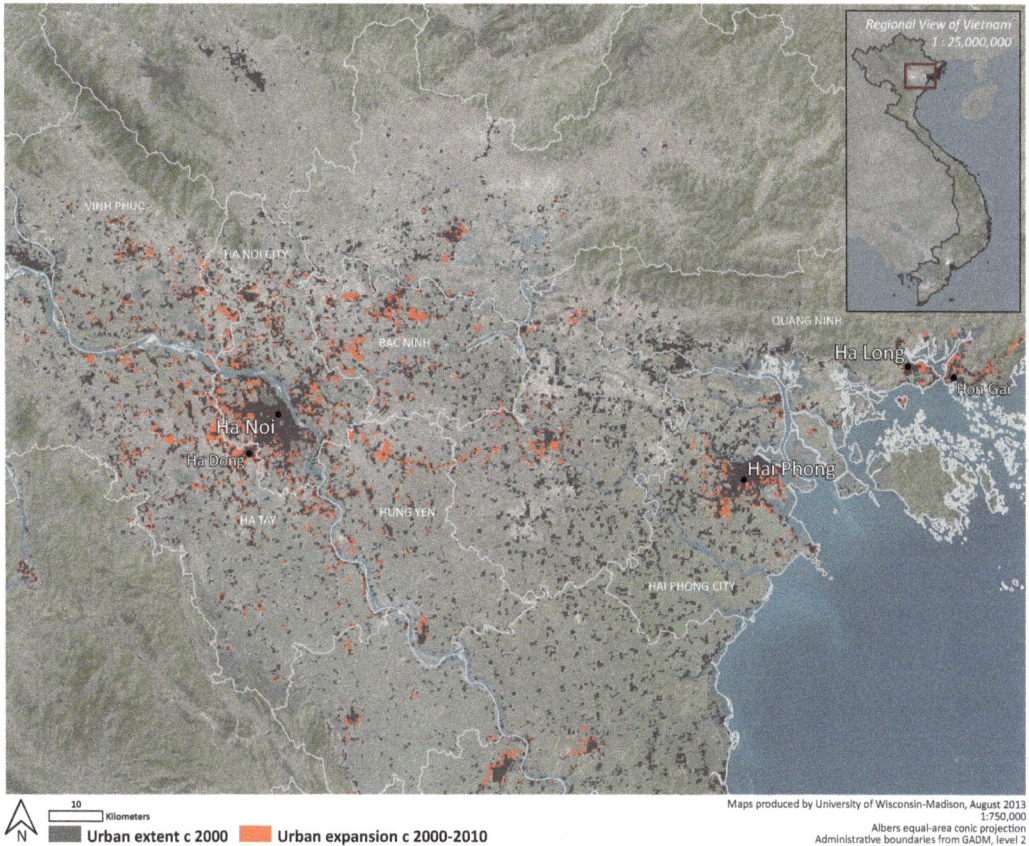

Maps produced by University of Wisconsin-Madison, August 2013
1:750,000
Albers equal-area conic projection
Administrative boundaries from GADM, level 2

■ Urban extent c 2000   ■ Urban expansion c 2000-2010

areas are often physically broken up by natural or other obstructions but still function as unified economic, social, or political entities. A number of standardized methods for defining urban areas were considered, for example, including areas within some predefined radius from the city center, or thresholds for proportion of built-up area or density. However, given the variety in size, form, and rate of expansion among the hundreds of urban areas examined, and the absence of supplementary information at this scale (such as commuting patterns, job locations, industrial location, and the like), none of these standardized formulas would have resulted in satisfactory definitions across countries and settlement sizes, given the input data. Instead, each urban area was considered individually, and administrative units were "hand-selected"; within these administrative units, all built-up area would be considered part of the urban area.

Maps C.1 through C.3, of the Red River Delta in Vietnam, illustrate how this study defines the physical extents of urban areas. As with all the maps included in this report, gray represents built-up areas in 2000, and red represents areas that were built up between 2000 and 2010. Map C.1 shows

Map C.3   Urban expansion in Hanoi, Hai Phong, and Ha Long, Vietnam, 2000–10 (with district boundaries)

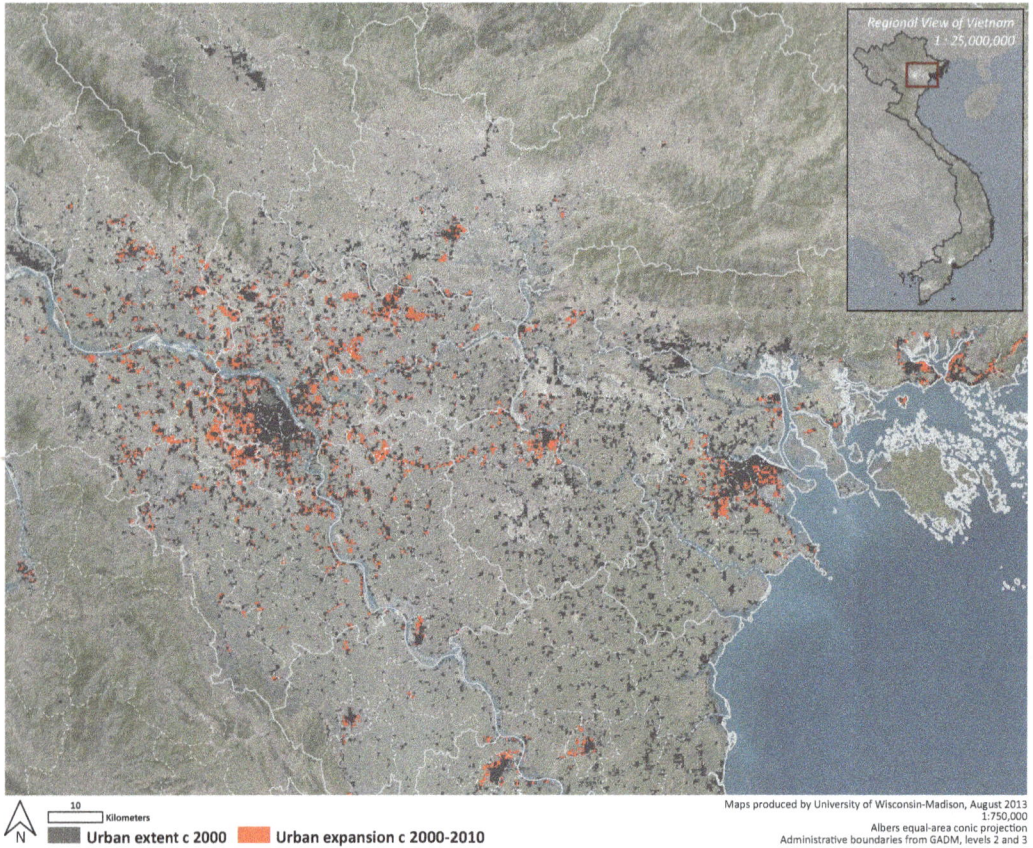

Urban extent c 2000   Urban expansion c 2000-2010

Maps produced by University of Wisconsin-Madison, August 2013
1:750,000
Albers equal-area conic projection
Administrative boundaries from GADM, levels 2 and 3

the pattern of built-up areas in this part of the country, which includes the cities of Hanoi, Hai Phong, and Ha Long. There are also hundreds of small pockets of settlement, some of which, arguably, may be considered part of the greater urban areas around these cities.

How are these built-up areas grouped into distinct urban areas? Overlaying this map with provincial boundaries, as in map C.2, does not yield satisfactory definitions. Hanoi and Hai Phong are provincial-level cities, but their urban extents appear to spill over into neighboring provinces.

For the purposes of this analysis, we further overlaid district-level boundaries (map C.3), which provided units of analysis that could then be grouped together. Those districts that appeared to belong to an urban area around Hanoi were selected. These districts included a group of districts to the west, belonging to four provinces besides Hanoi itself. All the pixels identified as built-up within these districts (the grey ones for 2000 and both the red and the grey for 2010) were included in this study's definition of the Hanoi urban area.

Similarly, the extents of the urban area of Shanghai are difficult to isolate from the broader network of urbanization surrounding it. On one hand,

Map C.4   **Urban expansion in the Shanghai, China, urban area, 2000–10**

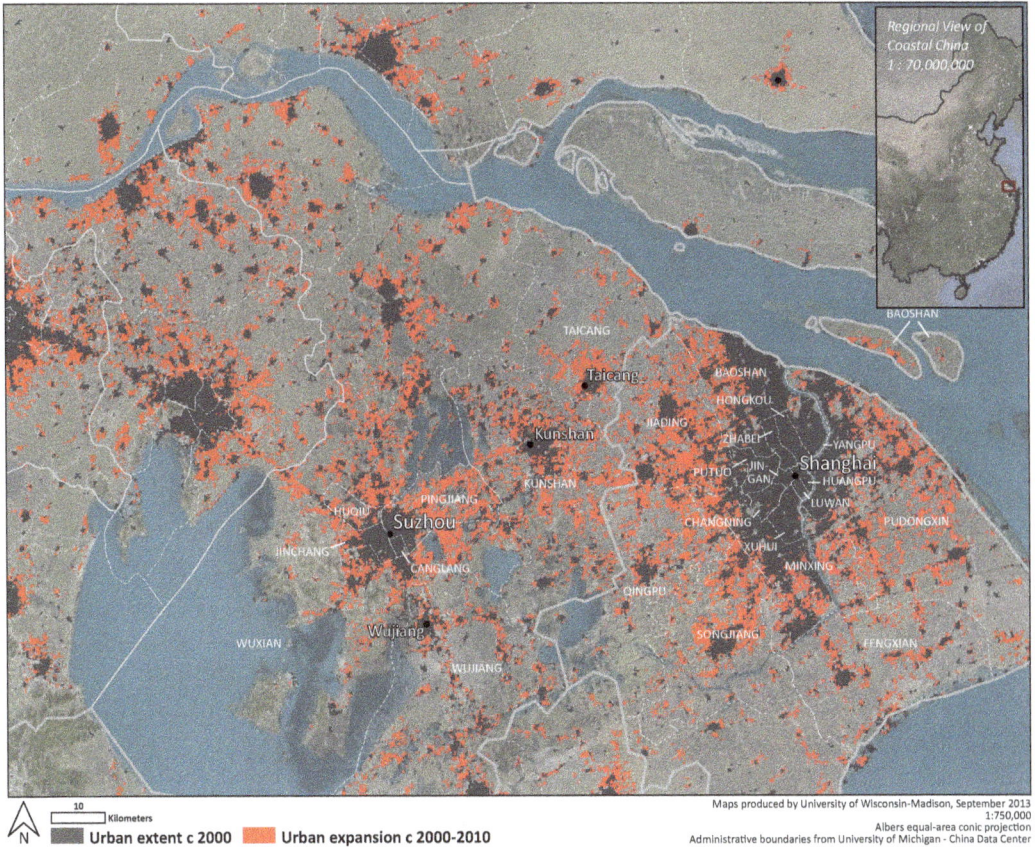

Maps produced by University of Wisconsin-Madison, September 2013
1:750,000
Albers equal-area conic projection
Administrative boundaries from University of Michigan - China Data Center

Urban extent c 2000   Urban expansion c 2000-2010

it is clear from map C.4 that looking only at the administrative area of Shanghai (within the thicker grey boundary to the east of the map) does not take into account urban areas immediately adjacent, which are useful to think of as belonging to the same urban area. On the other hand, it is not helpful to consider this entire part of coastal China as one urban entity. For the purposes of this analysis, several districts of Shanghai, along with Suzhou district and the counties of Kunshan, Taicang, and Wujiang in Suzhou Prefecture, were included as part of the Shanghai urban area.

Most urban areas are easier to define than these. Given that these definitions may not suit everyone, the data used for the analysis in this report are being released publicly, so that others may experiment with definitions and analysis that fit their purposes.

Accessing the Data

This report summarizes the findings of this study, but an equally important output of this effort is the underlying spatial data, which we hope will allow other teams of researchers to combine information on urban extents

Figure C.1   Screenshot of the World Bank's PUMA tool for exploring urban spatial data

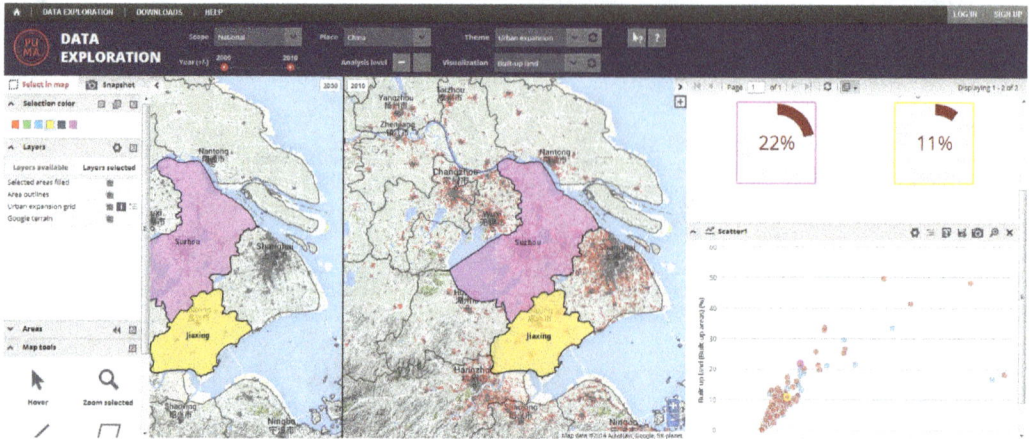

Note: PUMA = Platform for Urban Management and Analysis.

and populations with other data sources. For example, the maps of urban expansion can be combined with layers showing disaster risk vulnerability, locations of government investments and policies, transport networks, and a practically unlimited number of other types of information that might not be foreseen today.

To facilitate such efforts, all the data produced for this study are being publicly released at puma.worldbank.org, both through an interactive online mapping tool called Platform for Urban Management and Analysis (PUMA), which allows users with no GIS training to view the data, as well as in the form of downloadable GIS files and spreadsheets.

Notes

1. Because missing observations frequently occur within or near cities due to cloud cover, three full years of monthly satellite data were selected for each time point (2000–2002 for circa 2000 data, and 2008–2010 for circa 2010 maps). While the input data covered multiple years, feature selection, testing, and analysis were all conducted using year 2000 and 2010 data (Mertes and others, forthcoming).

2. This is as expected because change events are rare, particularly at continental scales, and are thus consistently mapped with lower accuracy than stable areas in land cover mapping efforts (Strahler and others 2006). In addition, some of the errors counted in the tier one accuracy assessment are also reflected in the tier two results. After removing sites mislabeled as nonurban land from the tier two sample, accuracies increase 5 percent to 15 percent depending on location.

3. For example, for urban areas in Indonesia that do not have their own municipal boundaries, the smallest available census unit is the large surrounding regency. As a result, the proportion of the population that is

urban can only be modeled, that is, estimated using a formula. Population data for such urban areas, for example, Garut and Tasikmalaya, should be used with caution.

References

Angel, S. 2012. *Planet of Cities.* Cambridge, MA: Lincoln Institute of Land Policy.

Gaughan, A. E., F. R. Stevens, C. Linard, P. Jia, and A. J. Tatem. 2013. "High Resolution Population Distribution Maps for Southeast Asia in 2010 and 2015." *PLoS ONE* 8 (2): e5588.

Linard, C., M. Gilbert, R. Snow, A. Noor, and A. Tatem. 2012. "Population Distribution, Settlement Patterns and Accessibility across Africa in 2010." *PLoS ONE* 7 (2): e31743.

Mertes, C., A. Schneider, D. Sulla-Menashe, A. Tatem, and B. Tan. Forthcoming. "Detecting Change in Urban Areas at Continental Scales with MODIS Data." *Remote Sensing of Environment.*

Quinlan, J. 1993. *C4 5: Programs for Machine Learning.* New York: Morgan Kaufmann.

Schneider, A., M. Friedl, and D. Potere. 2010. "Mapping Urban Areas Globally Using MODIS 500m Data." *Remote Sensing of Environment* 114 (8): 1733–46.

Small, C., and J. Lu. 2006. "Estimation and Vicarious Validation of Urban Vegetation Abundance." *Remote Sensing of Environment* 100 (4): 441–56.

Strahler, A. H., L. Boschetti, G. M. Foody, M. A. Friedl, M. C. Hansen, and M. Herold. 2006. "Global Land Cover Validation: Recommendations for Evaluation and Accuracy." European Commission—DG Joint Research Centre, Institute for Environment and Sustainability, Luxembourg.

Tatem, A. J., A. M. Noor, C. von Hagen, A. Di Gregorio, and S. I. Hay. 2007. "High Resolution Population Maps for Low Income Nations: Combining Land Cover and Census in East Africa." *PLoS ONE* 2 (12): e1298.

United Nations, Department of Economic and Social Affairs, Population Division. 2012. *World Urbanization Prospects: The 2011 Revision.* New York: United Nations. CD-ROM edition.

Changes in Urban Land, Population, and Density by Country

Table D.1   Changes in urban land, population, and density by country

Country	Area within administrative boundary[a] (sq. km)	Urban land,[b] 2000 (sq. km)	Urban land,[b] 2010 (sq. km)	Increase in urban land, 2000–10 (sq. km)	Total urban land, as a share of total land area, 2000 (%)	Total urban land, as a share of total land area, 2010 (%)	Average annual rate of increase in urban land, 2000–10 (%)
Brunei Darussalam	5,765	144	180	36	2.5	3.1	2.2
Cambodia	181,354	107	164	56	0.1	0.1	4.3
China	9,453,309	65,741	89,389	23,647	0.7	0.9	3.1
Indonesia	1,890,973	8,939	10,013	1,075	0.5	0.5	1.1
Japan	372,468	15,539	16,165	626	4.2	4.3	0.4
Korea, Dem. People's Rep.	122,755	306	321	15	0.2	0.3	0.5
Korea, Rep.	100,229	2,233	2,539	306	2.2	2.5	1.3
Lao PDR	229,878	48	97	49	0.0	0.0	7.3
Malaysia	329,424	3,924	4,572	648	1.2	1.4	1.5
Mongolia	1,566,250	210	271	61	0.0	0.0	2.6
Myanmar	670,747	762	828	66	0.1	0.1	0.8
Papua New Guinea	462,840	43	44	1	0.0	0.0	0.3
Philippines	295,988	1,779	2,257	479	0.6	0.8	2.4
Singapore	755	337	404	66	44.6	53.4	1.8
Taiwan, China	36,224	1,690	1,938	247	4.7	5.3	1.4
Thailand	514,093	2,359	2,705	346	0.5	0.5	1.4
Timor-Leste	15,007	28	28	0	0.2	0.2	0.0
Vietnam	328,385	2,208	2,924	716	0.7	0.9	2.8
Total	16,576,445	106,397	134,838	28,441	0.6	0.8	2.4

Source: Study team, incorporating WorldPop data, http://www.worldpop.org.uk/data/.

Note: Numbers may not add to totals because of rounding.

a. Administrative boundary data provided by GADM (2013); Myanmar Information Management Unit (2013); and the University of Michigan China Data Center (2013).

b. Maps of urban expansion produced by A. Schneider and team, University of Wisconsin–Madison, 2013, at a 250-meter resolution. In the underlying maps, pixels containing at least 50 percent constructed surfaces are considered built up. Urban land refers to built-up land in urban areas of 100,000 people and more.

c. Population data were taken from AsiaPop population distribution maps for built-up areas within the urban expansion map. Urban population refers to population mapped to urban land as defined in note b.

Urban population,[c] 2000	Urban population,[c] 2010	Change in urban population, 2000–10	Average annual rate of change of urban population (%)	Average urban population density, 2000 (persons/ sq. km)	Average urban population density, 2010 (persons/ sq. km)	Urban expansion per additional urban inhabitant (sq. m/ person)
155,900	230,300	74,400	4.0	1,079	1,278	481
917,645	1,405,381	487,736	4.4	8,546	8,596	115
345,844,670	477,232,691	131,388,021	3.3	5,261	5,339	180
66,555,373	94,329,271	27,773,898	3.5	7,446	9,421	39
66,510,957	76,527,309	10,016,352	1.4	4,280	4,734	63
2,623,722	2,918,281	294,559	1.1	8,566	9,081	51
23,629,279	26,682,593	3,053,314	1.2	10,584	10,511	100
134,290	307,044	172,754	8.6	2,809	3,167	284
10,154,126	14,959,677	4,805,551	4.0	2,588	3,272	135
631,407	926,999	295,592	3.9	3,008	3,419	207
4,696,086	6,214,646	1,518,560	2.8	6,163	7,510	43
190,406	233,051	42,645	2.0	4,428	5,274	28
16,829,863	23,280,178	6,450,315	3.3	9,463	10,314	74
2,539,073	3,412,239	873,166	3.0	7,529	8,457	76
13,368,812	14,319,702	950,890	0.7	7,909	7,391	260
9,336,866	11,750,518	2,413,652	2.3	3,958	4,344	143
115,901	180,734	64,833	4.5	4,085	6,369	0
15,088,917	22,597,771	7,508,854	4.1	6,835	7,729	95
579,323,293	*777,508,385*	*198,185,092*	*3.0*	*5,445*	*5,766*	*144*

Figure D.1   Changes in urban land and population by country, 2000–10

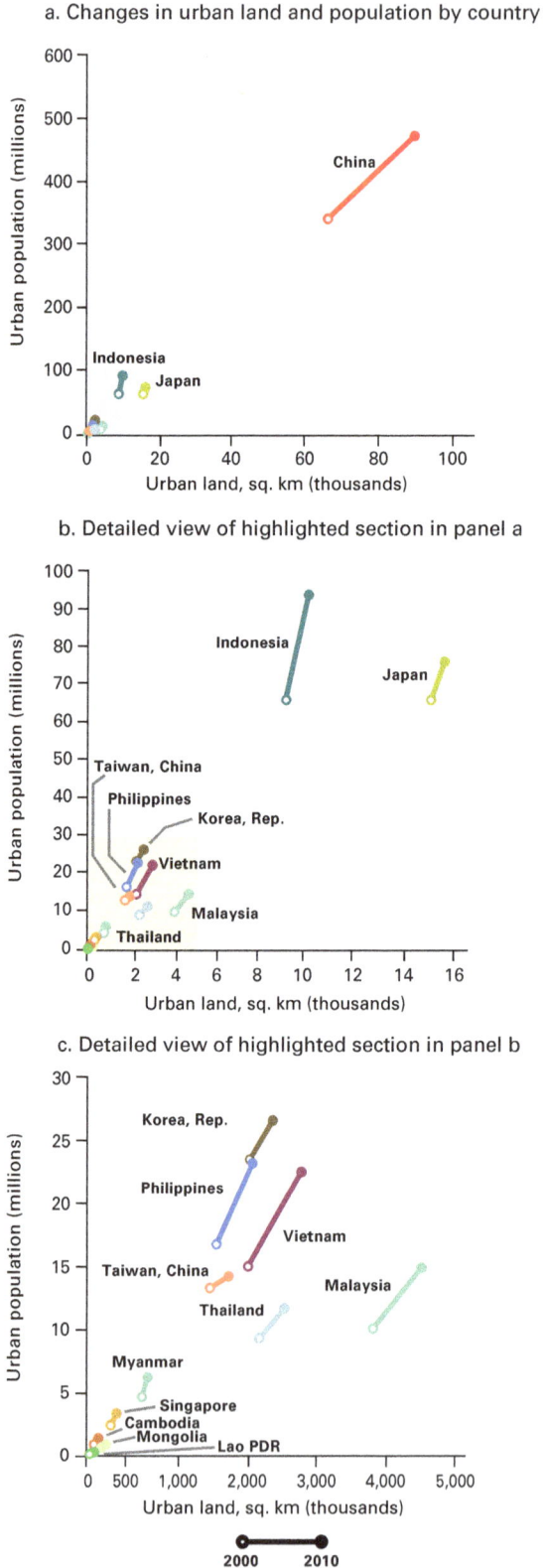

a. Changes in urban land and population by country

b. Detailed view of highlighted section in panel a

c. Detailed view of highlighted section in panel b

2000   2010

Source: Study team, incorporating WorldPop data, http://www.worldpop.org.uk/data/.

Changes in Urban Land, Population, and Density in Urban Areas with More Than 1 Million People

Table E.1   Changes in urban land, population, and density in urban areas with more than 1 million people

Rank by 2010 urban population	Urban area name	Country/economy	Urban land,[a] 2000 (sq. km)	Urban land,[a] 2010 (sq. km)	Increase in urban land, 2000–10 (sq. km)	Average annual rate of increase in urban land, 2000–10 (%)
Urban areas with more than 10 million people in 2010						
1	Pearl River Delta urban area	China	4,478	6,969	2,491	4.5
2	Tokyo urban area	Japan	5,434	5,570	136	0.2
3	Shanghai urban area	China	1,605	3,482	1,877	8.1
4	Jakarta urban area	Indonesia	1,338	1,600	262	1.8
5	Beijing urban area	China	1,827	2,716	889	4.0
6	Manila urban area	Philippines	1,024	1,275	251	2.2
7	Seoul urban area	Korea, Rep.	1,067	1,192	124	1.1
8	Osaka urban area	Japan	2,047	2,073	25	0.1
	Subtotal		*18,820*	*24,876*	*6,056*	*2.8*
Urban areas with 5 million to 10 million people in 2010						
9	Bangkok urban area	Thailand	1,910	2,126	216	1.1
10	Tianjin urban area	China	1,127	1,655	528	3.9
11	Shantou urban area	China	980	1,207	227	2.1
12	Chengdu urban area	China	605	1,069	464	5.9
13	Ho Chi Minh City urban area	Vietnam	549	815	266	4.0
14	Nagoya urban area	Japan	1,772	1,882	110	0.6
15	Wuhan urban area	China	713	945	232	2.9
16	Hong Kong SAR urban area	China	201	219	18	0.9
17	Bandung urban area	Indonesia	433	512	78	1.7
18	Shenyang urban area	China	816	1,035	219	2.4
19	Taipei City urban area	Taiwan, China	477	587	110	2.1
20	Hangzhou urban area	China	518	1,318	800	9.8
21	Surabaya urban area	Indonesia	644	726	82	1.2
22	Kuala Lumpur urban area	Malaysia	1,541	1,739	199	1.2
23	Xi'an urban area	China	476	735	260	4.5
24	Hanoi urban area	Vietnam	584	851	266	3.8
25	Chongqing urban area	China	328	593	265	6.1
	Subtotal		*13,673*	*18,013*	*4,340*	*2.8*
Urban areas with 1 million to 5 million people in 2010						
26	Quanzhou urban area	China	643	924	281	3.7
27	Nanjing urban area	China	241	448	208	6.4
28	Xiamen urban area	China	493	777	284	4.6
29	Taiyuan urban area	China	561	728	167	2.6

Urban population,[b] 2000	Urban population,[b] 2010	Change in urban population, 2000–10	Average annual rate of change of urban population (%)	Average urban population density, 2000 (persons/ sq. km)	Average urban population density, 2010 (persons/ sq. km)	Urban expansion per additional urban inhabitant (sq. m/ person)	Administrative boundary arrangement[c]
26,835,836	41,757,816	14,921,980	4.5	5,993	5,992	167	Fragmented
27,695,526	31,788,261	4,092,735	1.4	5,097	5,707	33	Fragmented
14,020,969	24,196,318	10,175,349	5.6	8,735	6,949	184	Fragmented
16,291,976	23,431,674	7,139,698	3.7	12,174	14,643	37	Fragmented
10,754,014	16,707,094	5,953,080	4.5	5,887	6,151	149	Fragmented
12,202,314	16,521,948	4,319,634	3.1	11,916	12,958	58	Fragmented
14,277,211	15,898,238	1,621,027	1.1	13,378	13,342	77	Fragmented
10,637,811	12,273,967	1,636,156	1.4	5,196	5,922	16	Fragmented
132,715,657	*182,575,316*	*49,859,659*	*3.2*	*7,052*	*7,339*	*121*	
7,825,880	9,555,372	1,729,492	2.0	4,098	4,495	125	Fragmented
6,266,363	8,788,168	2,521,805	3.4	5,561	5,311	209	Fragmented
6,692,103	8,458,895	1,766,792	2.4	6,826	7,006	128	Fragmented
4,636,284	8,323,450	3,687,166	6.0	7,662	7,787	126	Fragmented
5,309,190	7,761,835	2,452,645	3.9	9,671	9,528	108	Fragmented
6,368,802	7,426,344	1,057,542	1.5	3,594	3,946	104	Fragmented
5,474,500	7,342,134	1,867,634	3.0	7,677	7,768	124	Fragmented
6,665,000	7,024,200	359,200	0.5	33,232	32,129	50	Contained
4,797,409	6,946,592	2,149,183	3.8	11,068	13,571	36	Spillover
5,842,383	6,904,495	1,062,112	1.7	7,162	6,673	206	Fragmented
6,203,242	6,640,562	437,320	0.7	13,001	11,309	252	Fragmented
3,464,101	6,386,447	2,922,346	6.3	6,687	4,844	274	Spillover
4,395,779	6,104,808	1,709,029	3.3	6,822	8,410	48	Fragmented
3,972,896	5,750,078	1,777,182	3.8	2,579	3,306	112	Fragmented
4,187,660	5,736,306	1,548,646	3.2	8,806	7,801	168	Fragmented
3,534,648	5,642,882	2,108,234	4.8	6,049	6,634	126	Fragmented
3,347,836	5,035,794	1,687,958	4.2	10,218	8,497	157	Fragmented
88,984,076	*119,828,362*	*30,844,286*	*3.0*	*6,508*	*6,652*	*141*	
3,451,403	4,789,766	1,338,363	3.3	5,368	5,184	210	Fragmented
2,837,423	4,505,328	1,667,905	4.7	11,798	10,051	125	Fragmented
2,342,286	4,267,814	1,925,528	6.2	4,747	5,491	147	Fragmented
3,162,224	4,243,100	1,080,876	3.0	5,637	5,830	154	Fragmented

(Table continues next page)

Table E.1   Changes in urban land, population, and density in urban areas with more than 1 million people *(continued)*

Rank by 2010 urban population	Urban area name	Country/economy	Urban land,[a] 2000 (sq. km)	Urban land,[a] 2010 (sq. km)	Increase in urban land, 2000–10 (sq. km)	Average annual rate of increase in urban land, 2000–10 (%)
30	Qingdao urban area	China	690	804	114	1.5
31	Medan urban area	Indonesia	438	456	18	0.4
32	Harbin urban area	China	446	533	87	1.8
33	Zhengzhou urban area	China	244	404	161	5.2
34	Changsha urban area	China	249	444	195	5.9
35	Hefei urban area	China	217	406	188	6.4
36	Anshan urban area	China	718	848	130	1.7
37	Dalian urban area	China	493	550	57	1.1
38	Changchun urban area	China	614	767	153	2.3
39	Yangon City urban area	Myanmar	371	390	19	0.5
40	Singapore urban area	Singapore	337	404	66	1.8
41	Shijiazhuang urban area	China	447	496	49	1.1
42	Fuzhou urban area	China	368	525	156	3.6
43	Kunming urban area	China	307	445	138	3.8
44	Busan urban area	Korea, Rep.	240	275	35	1.4
45	Jinan urban area	China	257	305	48	1.7
46	Wenzhou urban area	China	205	299	94	3.8
47	Semarang urban area	Indonesia	329	365	36	1.0
48	Wuxi urban area	China	228	489	261	7.9
49	Ningbo urban area	China	310	630	320	7.4
50	Kaohsiung urban area	Taiwan, China	384	400	16	0.4
51	Changzhou urban area	China	205	477	272	8.8
52	Nanchang urban area	China	232	337	106	3.8
53	Urumqi urban area	China	326	466	140	3.6
54	Zibo urban area	China	453	508	55	1.1
55	Taizhou urban area	China	175	370	195	7.8
56	Malang urban area	Indonesia	250	265	15	0.6
57	Lanzhou urban area	China	163	194	30	1.7
58	Xinxiang urban area	China	335	396	62	1.7
59	Surakarta urban area	Indonesia	376	379	2	0.1
60	Tegal urban area	Indonesia	216	248	33	1.4
61	Guiyang urban area	China	106	150	44	3.5
62	Tangshan urban area	China	421	525	104	2.2
63	Fukuoka urban area	Japan	343	356	13	0.4
64	Xuzhou urban area	China	249	325	76	2.7
65	Baotou urban area	China	273	337	64	2.1
66	Taegu urban area	Korea, Rep.	226	255	29	1.2
67	Luoyang urban area	China	144	193	49	3.0

Urban population,[b] 2000	Urban population,[b] 2010	Change in urban population, 2000–10	Average annual rate of change of urban population (%)	Average urban population density, 2000 (persons/ sq. km)	Average urban population density, 2010 (persons/ sq. km)	Urban expansion per additional urban inhabitant (sq. m/ person)	Administrative boundary arrangement[c]
3,253,798	4,163,504	909,706	2.5	4,717	5,178	125	Fragmented
2,909,037	3,929,132	1,020,095	3.1	6,649	8,624	18	Fragmented
2,842,427	3,809,061	966,634	3.0	6,374	7,153	90	Fragmented
1,993,042	3,805,762	1,812,720	6.7	8,179	9,414	89	Fragmented
2,233,013	3,680,654	1,447,641	5.1	8,954	8,290	134	Fragmented
1,677,081	3,623,909	1,946,828	8.0	7,717	8,937	97	Spillover
3,242,167	3,494,160	251,993	0.8	4,515	4,122	515	Fragmented
2,737,479	3,488,541	751,062	2.5	5,550	6,339	76	Fragmented
2,489,821	3,477,619	987,798	3.4	4,058	4,534	155	Spillover
2,637,028	3,416,962	779,934	2.6	7,113	8,771	24	Fragmented
2,539,073	3,412,239	873,166	3.0	7,529	8,457	76	Contained
2,606,693	3,384,804	778,111	2.6	5,836	6,826	63	Fragmented
2,421,588	3,380,510	958,922	3.4	6,576	6,445	163	Fragmented
2,295,856	3,158,163	862,307	3.2	7,469	7,097	160	Spillover
2,832,947	3,132,865	299,918	1.0	11,798	11,384	117	Fragmented
2,255,667	2,952,471	696,804	2.7	8,792	9,694	69	Fragmented
1,693,733	2,920,413	1,226,680	5.6	8,247	9,767	76	Fragmented
2,025,802	2,857,742	831,940	3.5	6,155	7,832	43	Fragmented
1,713,658	2,808,589	1,094,931	5.1	7,520	5,744	238	Contained
1,552,379	2,752,235	1,199,856	5.9	5,010	4,370	267	Fragmented
2,623,091	2,719,206	96,115	0.4	6,834	6,797	169	Spillover
1,578,729	2,698,018	1,119,289	5.5	7,706	5,654	243	Spillover
1,726,117	2,496,129	770,012	3.8	7,456	7,400	137	Spillover
1,634,389	2,460,166	825,777	4.2	5,015	5,279	170	Spillover
1,985,469	2,320,662	335,193	1.6	4,380	4,569	163	Fragmented
1,378,319	2,285,429	907,110	5.2	7,882	6,179	215	Fragmented
1,635,664	2,242,804	607,140	3.2	6,544	8,463	25	Spillover
1,618,504	2,179,529	561,025	3.0	9,910	11,264	54	Fragmented
1,775,110	2,137,221	362,111	1.9	5,304	5,393	170	Fragmented
1,589,226	2,125,451	536,225	3.0	4,225	5,615	4	Fragmented
1,433,025	2,106,735	673,710	3.9	6,640	8,480	48	Fragmented
1,482,035	2,104,868	622,833	3.6	13,924	13,997	71	Fragmented
1,836,665	2,103,384	266,719	1.4	4,359	4,004	390	Fragmented
1,735,889	1,992,756	256,867	1.4	5,058	5,592	51	Fragmented
1,483,869	1,910,886	427,017	2.6	5,949	5,873	178	Spillover
1,380,563	1,895,406	514,843	3.2	5,058	5,623	125	Spillover
1,589,839	1,845,485	255,646	1.5	7,035	7,227	115	Fragmented
1,237,071	1,841,029	603,958	4.1	8,587	9,539	81	Fragmented

(Table continues next page)

Table E.1 Changes in urban land, population, and density in urban areas with more than 1 million people *(continued)*

Rank by 2010 urban population	Urban area name	Country/economy	Urban land,[a] 2000 (sq. km)	Urban land,[a] 2010 (sq. km)	Increase in urban land, 2000–10 (sq. km)	Average annual rate of increase in urban land, 2000–10 (%)
68	Baoding urban area	China	445	494	49	1.1
69	Huhehaote urban area	China	241	291	50	1.9
70	Taichung urban area	Taiwan, China	199	244	44	2.0
71	Nanning urban area	China	176	236	59	2.9
72	Yogyakarta urban area	Indonesia	233	234	0	0.0
73	Cixi urban area	China	187	437	250	8.9
74	Sapporo urban area	Japan	307	315	8	0.2
75	GeorgeTown urban area	Malaysia	326	396	70	2.0
76	Datong urban area	China	325	351	26	0.8
77	Cirebon urban area	Indonesia	149	171	22	1.4
78	Linyi urban area	China	245	348	103	3.6
79	Palembang urban area	Indonesia	199	205	6	0.3
80	Tasikmalaya urban area	Indonesia	78	93	15	1.8
81	Makassar urban area	Indonesia	113	139	26	2.1
82	Handan urban area	China	237	253	16	0.6
83	Huaiyin urban area	China	308	327	19	0.6
84	Weifang urban area	China	290	319	29	1.0
85	Kitakyushu urban area	Japan	353	372	19	0.5
86	Cebu urban area	Philippines	123	161	38	2.8
87	Changzhi urban area	China	262	304	41	1.5
88	Denpasar urban area	Indonesia	210	227	17	0.8
89	Anyang urban area	China	217	242	25	1.1
90	Jiaozuo urban area	China	259	328	69	2.4
91	Xining urban area	China	131	215	83	5.0
92	Phnom Penh urban area	Cambodia	107	164	56	4.3
93	Tongzhou urban area	China	84	186	102	8.3
94	Haikou urban area	China	167	195	27	1.5
95	P'yongyang urban area	Korea, Dem. People's Rep.	125	133	8	0.7
96	Jiexiu urban area	China	344	413	68	1.8
97	Yantai urban area	China	200	246	46	2.1
98	Jember urban area	Indonesia	227	231	3	0.1
99	Sukabumi urban area	Indonesia	76	96	19	2.3
100	Liuzhou urban area	China	119	154	36	2.6
101	Johor Bahru urban area	Malaysia	271	416	145	4.4
102	Putian urban area	China	291	355	64	2.0
103	Jilin urban area	China	271	292	21	0.8
104	Kediri urban area	Indonesia	248	274	26	1.0

Urban population,[b] 2000	Urban population,[b] 2010	Change in urban population, 2000–10	Average annual rate of change of urban population (%)	Average urban population density, 2000 (persons/ sq. km)	Average urban population density, 2010 (persons/ sq. km)	Urban expansion per additional urban inhabitant (sq. m/ person)	Administrative boundary arrangement[c]
1,537,185	1,835,688	298,503	1.8	3,454	3,713	165	Fragmented
1,249,880	1,825,047	575,167	3.9	5,196	6,278	87	Fragmented
1,641,289	1,815,569	174,280	1.0	8,230	7,445	255	Spillover
1,175,617	1,799,783	624,166	4.4	6,663	7,642	95	Contained
1,352,200	1,799,090	446,890	2.9	5,799	7,701	1	Fragmented
1,014,606	1,747,370	732,764	5.6	5,424	4,000	341	Spillover
1,464,374	1,705,112	240,738	1.5	4,763	5,414	31	Spillover
1,107,706	1,682,629	574,923	4.3	3,399	4,253	121	Fragmented
1,392,065	1,661,874	269,809	1.8	4,288	4,737	97	Fragmented
1,132,600	1,656,403	523,803	3.9	7,611	9,683	42	Spillover
1,198,264	1,655,936	457,672	3.3	4,886	4,753	225	Fragmented
1,192,519	1,602,228	409,709	3.0	5,998	7,806	16	Spillover
1,060,054	1,594,737	534,683	4.2	13,515	17,090	28	Spillover
1,094,912	1,591,997	497,085	3.8	9,684	11,464	52	Spillover
1,379,549	1,590,079	210,530	1.4	5,824	6,296	75	Fragmented
1,367,428	1,562,746	195,318	1.3	4,442	4,781	97	Fragmented
983,235	1,550,370	567,135	4.7	3,391	4,864	51	Fragmented
1,355,953	1,539,317	183,364	1.3	3,846	4,141	104	Fragmented
1,017,447	1,527,407	509,960	4.1	8,268	9,461	75	Fragmented
1,237,616	1,482,858	245,242	1.8	4,716	4,881	169	Fragmented
1,070,835	1,473,252	402,417	3.2	5,098	6,488	42	Fragmented
1,227,106	1,465,481	238,375	1.8	5,648	6,056	104	Spillover
1,194,575	1,430,027	235,452	1.8	4,608	4,362	291	Fragmented
953,312	1,425,406	472,094	4.1	7,267	6,643	177	Fragmented
917,645	1,405,381	487,736	4.4	8,546	8,596	115	Fragmented
788,922	1,401,105	612,183	5.9	9,413	7,551	166	Fragmented
954,719	1,395,896	441,177	3.9	5,706	7,175	62	Contained
1,236,843	1,393,413	156,570	1.2	9,934	10,482	54	Spillover
1,190,879	1,383,251	192,372	1.5	3,457	3,352	354	Fragmented
909,546	1,364,297	454,751	4.1	4,556	5,553	101	Fragmented
1,021,160	1,358,347	337,187	2.9	4,494	5,890	10	Spillover
895,799	1,357,948	462,149	4.2	11,758	14,201	42	Spillover
1,035,513	1,329,755	294,242	2.5	8,716	8,617	121	Spillover
820,597	1,297,170	476,573	4.7	3,026	3,116	305	Contained
1,106,458	1,278,041	171,583	1.5	3,806	3,603	373	Contained
1,199,748	1,261,145	61,397	0.5	4,433	4,318	349	Fragmented
903,834	1,256,399	352,565	3.3	3,646	4,586	74	Spillover

(Table continues next page)

Table E.1   Changes in urban land, population, and density in urban areas with more than 1 million people *(continued)*

Rank by 2010 urban population	Urban area name	Country/economy	Urban land,[a] 2000 (sq. km)	Urban land,[a] 2010 (sq. km)	Increase in urban land, 2000–10 (sq. km)	Average annual rate of increase in urban land, 2000–10 (%)
105	Maoming urban area	China	135	152	17	1.2
106	Qinhuangda urban area	China	256	306	50	1.8
107	Yingkou urban area	China	405	442	37	0.9
108	Xingtai urban area	China	186	203	17	0.9
109	Hai Phong urban area	Vietnam	161	199	37	2.1
110	Yinchuan urban area	China	72	157	85	8.2
111	Lingxi urban area	China	73	143	70	6.9
112	Xiangtan urban area	China	74	156	82	7.8
113	Jiangyin urban area	China	104	280	176	10.4
114	Daqing urban area	China	236	253	17	0.7
115	Jinzhou urban area	China	237	262	25	1.0
116	Zhangjiakou urban area	China	226	245	19	0.8
117	Garut urban area	Indonesia	34	46	12	3.1
118	Mandalay urban area	Myanmar	111	130	18	1.5
119	Sendai urban area	Japan	237	252	15	0.6
120	Cikampek urban area	Indonesia	92	106	14	1.4
121	Kaifeng urban area	China	193	202	10	0.5
122	Dandong urban area	China	158	210	52	2.9
123	Huaibei urban area	China	174	192	18	1.0
124	Chifeng urban area	China	189	247	58	2.7
125	Cianjur urban area	Indonesia	60	69	9	1.4
126	Kwangju urban area	Korea, Rep.	87	108	21	2.2
127	Huainan urban area	China	117	122	5	0.4
128	Changshu urban area	China	87	244	157	10.8
129	Yungkang urban area	Taiwan, China	216	226	11	0.5
130	Cilacap urban area	Indonesia	94	101	7	0.7
131	Zhanjiang urban area	China	103	130	27	2.3
	Subtotal		*26,584*	*33,927*	*7,343*	*2.5*

Source: Study team, incorporating WorldPop data, http://www.worldpop.org.uk/data/.

Note: Numbers may not add to totals because of rounding.

a. Maps of urban expansion were produced by A. Schneider and team, University of Wisconsin-Madison, 2013, at a 250-meter resolution. In these maps, pixels containing at least 50 percent constructed surfaces are considered built up. Urban land refers to built-up land in urban areas of 100,000 people and more.

b. Population data were taken from AsiaPop population distribution maps for built-up areas within the urban expansion map. Urban population refers to population mapped to urban land as defined in note a.

c. "Contained" refers to urban areas whose built-up land is contained within a single administrative boundary; "spillover" refers to those in which some built-up area (less than half) is outside the primary administrative boundary; "fragmented" refers to those in which no single administrative boundary has even half the total urban area. Administrative boundary data provided by GADM (2013); Myanmar Information Management Unit (2013); and the University of Michigan China Data Center (2013).

Urban population,[b] 2000	Urban population,[b] 2010	Change in urban population, 2000–10	Average annual rate of change of urban population (%)	Average urban population density, 2000 (persons/ sq. km)	Average urban population density, 2010 (persons/ sq. km)	Urban expansion per additional urban inhabitant (sq. m/ person)	Administrative boundary arrangement[c]
982,408	1,250,113	267,705	2.4	7,294	8,241	64	Spillover
967,441	1,235,994	268,553	2.5	3,784	4,043	186	Fragmented
1,117,204	1,228,493	111,289	1.0	2,757	2,778	332	Fragmented
1,046,755	1,221,274	174,519	1.6	5,620	6,003	98	Fragmented
817,540	1,221,115	403,575	4.1	5,066	6,144	93	Fragmented
640,602	1,214,059	573,457	6.6	8,944	7,736	149	Fragmented
837,401	1,201,395	363,994	3.7	11,413	8,383	192	Spillover
675,776	1,192,105	516,329	5.8	9,155	7,633	160	Fragmented
710,260	1,190,623	480,363	5.3	6,846	4,254	367	Contained
941,134	1,188,452	247,318	2.4	3,995	4,704	69	Fragmented
992,998	1,153,086	160,088	1.5	4,198	4,403	158	Spillover
995,515	1,151,806	156,291	1.5	4,405	4,706	120	Fragmented
666,347	1,136,920	470,573	5.5	19,671	24,749	26	Contained
821,889	1,130,511	308,622	3.2	7,375	8,709	60	Fragmented
967,641	1,118,370	150,729	1.5	4,077	4,439	97	Spillover
762,106	1,116,340	354,234	3.9	8,295	10,556	39	Contained
992,299	1,096,110	103,811	1.0	5,148	5,415	93	Spillover
885,944	1,090,500	204,556	2.1	5,596	5,196	252	Fragmented
794,811	1,086,694	291,883	3.2	4,570	5,653	63	Spillover
901,473	1,076,946	175,473	1.8	4,776	4,365	331	Fragmented
715,682	1,066,550	350,868	4.1	11,854	15,415	25	Contained
875,400	1,037,511	162,111	1.7	10,098	9,634	130	Fragmented
760,337	1,028,920	268,583	3.1	6,492	8,421	19	Fragmented
514,981	1,013,254	498,273	7.0	5,902	4,151	315	Contained
966,804	1,010,274	43,470	0.4	4,481	4,464	243	Spillover
720,831	1,007,170	286,339	3.4	7,679	9,978	25	Contained
728,541	1,001,648	273,107	3.2	7,052	7,712	97	Fragmented
154,651,309	211,889,294	57,237,985	3.2	5,817	6,245	128	

www.ingramcontent.com/pod-product-compliance
Lightning Source LLC
Chambersburg PA
CBHW082356270326
41935CB00013B/1638